KT-466-608

THE
SHOP GIRLS

Withdrawn from ...

3011780133989 2

THE
SHOP GIRLS

*A True Story of Hard Work, Friendship and
Fashion in an Exclusive 1950s Department Store*

ELLEE SEYMOUR

sphere

SPHERE

First published in Great Britain in 2014 by Sphere

Copyright © 2014 by Ellee Seymour

The moral right of the author has been asserted.

All rights reserved.
No part of this publication may be reproduced, stored in a
retrieval system, or transmitted, in any form or by any means, without
the prior permission in writing of the publisher, nor be otherwise circulated
in any form of binding or cover other than that in which it is published
and without a similar condition including this condition being
imposed on the subsequent purchaser.

A CIP catalogue record for this book
is available from the British Library.

ISBN 978-0-7515-5496-0

Typeset in Caslon by M Rules
Printed and bound in Great Britain by
Clays Ltd, St Ives plc

Papers used by Sphere are from well-managed forests
and other responsible sources.

MIX
Paper from
responsible sources
FSC® C104740

Sphere
An imprint of
Little, Brown Book Group
100 Victoria Embankment
London EC4Y 0DY

An Hachette UK Company
www.hachette.co.uk

www.littlebrown.co.uk

Dedicated to Eve, Irene, Betty, and Rosemary
for generously sharing their stories about working in
an elegant ladies department store during a bygone era
when courtesy and first-rate customer service was expected from
all shop girls – especially at Heyworth's Fashions, Cambridge

Also in memory of two extraordinary men,
George and Herbert Heyworth, who elegantly attired
so many women in Cambridge and beyond

FOREWORD

This is a story that begins a hundred years ago. Or perhaps even before then, going back several generations to a family whose roots are found in the thriving cotton industry of Edwardian Lancashire. Although his forefathers may have made their living at the loom, George Heyworth – born towards the end of the nineteenth century – had greater ambitions. It is his story, and the story of the women who worked for him, that fills the pages of this book.

George Heyworth left behind the noisy and dangerous mills which deafened many workers and, within only a few years, became proprietor of an elegant department store in Cambridge. G. A. Heyworth and Co. was, for many years, a Cambridge landmark – thriving under the ownership of George and, later, his son, Herbert.

None of this success would have been possible without the women who worked at Heyworth's – the 'shop girls'. Dressed demurely in dark skirts and a crisp white shirts, they served their customers with the utmost deference and courtesy – the kind of service that many shoppers yearn for today. Yet beneath the surface of their immaculate and reserved appearance lay the fascinating lives which form the basis of this book.

These women were the backbone of G. A. Heyworth and Co, which counted the Marchioness of Cambridge, related by marriage to the royal family, among its distinguished customers. But those were days when people kept their private lives to themselves, and the shop girls and their inner lives would have been as invisible and inconsequential to a society lady as a servant 'below stairs'.

While many people are familiar with Selfridges and Harrods, John Lewis and Fenwicks, it is unlikely they will have heard of Heyworth's, which closed its doors in 1965. Even in Cambridge very few people remember it. But for the women who worked there, the memories are vivid.

I had never heard of Heyworth's, it closed long before I moved to Cambridge. My husband, Stephen, was a buyer at another popular Cambridge department store, Eaden Lilley, now sadly closed as well. After watching the wonderful television adaptation of Lindy Woodhead's book *Shopping, Seduction and Mr Selfridge*, I began to wonder what stories I might unearth in a lesser known department store. I did some digging and came across a former Eaden Lilley employee, Eve Collis (Gray). She told me that prior to Eaden Lilley, she had worked at Heyworth's, starting there in 1944 as a fourteen-year-old. As we spoke, I realised that perhaps Heyworth's forgotten story was one worth telling. Eve put me in touch with other another Heyworth girl, Betty Hume (Lipscombe), who in turn put me in touch with Irene Dean (Fiander) which set the ball rolling. Their stories form the backbone of this book.

Sadly, there are no surviving members of the Heyworth family to keep this stylish store's memory alive. Writing about it has been like bringing a ghost back to life. And I never expected that in the course of my research, I would unravel a closely guarded Hayworth family secret …

George Alfred Heyworth was the eldest of five children, born in 1887 to George and Mary Alice Heyworth, both cotton weavers. His grandfather John Heyworth (1820–1886) was a cotton manufacturer, and his paternal great grandfather John Heyworth (born

1798) was a warehouseman, while his maternal great grandfather Richard Lord (born 1797) was a power loom weaver.

It was a hard life in the mills. The hours were long; 6 a.m. to 6 p.m. during the week and 6 a.m. to 12.30 p.m. on Saturdays. The average wage for a weaver in north-east Lancashire in 1908 was between 23s 8d and 24s a week, £1.18 to £1.20 in today's currency. They were expected to run several looms at the same time, changing the weft in the shuttles, looking out for flaws in the cloth and so on. Weaving sheds were incredibly noisy and, at times, dangerous places.

George's first job in 1901, aged fourteen, was as an office boy in a mill. He stayed there for ten years. It was not a hard physical job like weaving, the job his ancestors had done for more than a century. George wasn't the only one of the Heyworth children to seek out professional employment, away from the loom. His sister May sought to better herself by becoming a schoolmistress, and his brother Herbert became a postman, before he was killed in action in 1916, aged just twenty-five. Only George's youngest brother James kept up the family tradition and became a 'tenter', an assistant to a weaver. George's infant sister Sarah died aged two.

In 1911, George moved south, securing an apprenticeship as a draper's assistant for Herbert James Hinds in Luton, Bedfordshire. At the time Luton had a thriving hat industry and was recognised as the centre of ladies hat production in the country. Heyworth's department store was later known for its bespoke millinery department, a service which distinguished the store from its rivals. Perhaps it was George's early experiences in Luton which led to this unique feature in his own store.

It is not known exactly when George moved to Cambridge, but the town (it did not become a city until 1951) was enjoying tremendous growth and prosperity as its boundaries expanded to take in more land from outlying areas. The ambitious young man may have been attracted by the business opportunities the booming town offered at that time.

In her book *Drapery Stores*, Claire Masset describes the first half of the twentieth century as 'the golden age of the department store', which is attributed to 'developments in window-dressing, advertising and retailing, combined with rapid changes in fashion, the emergence of new products and an ever increasing spending power'. We can imagine George Heyworth avidly following all this exciting news and making his own plans. He was a fast worker – by 1914 he was running a thriving business in Burleigh Street, Cambridge. It spanned three premises at numbers 8, 9 and 10 at the East Road end of the street. *G. A. Heyworth & Co Milliners, Ladies Complete Outfitters, Drapers and a provider of Specialist Baby wear* was boldly painted across the top of the premises.

Once George had settled in at Burleigh Street, the time was right to marry his sweetheart from back home, Elizabeth Ann Ashworth. Elizabeth was one of six children and her family also had a cotton weaving background; her father, Richard Ashworth, was a worsted weaver, and his father before him was a calico printer. They were married on 1 June 1914, and lived above their store in Burleigh Street.

Like the more famous Mr Selfridge, George was a prolific advertiser and promoter of his store. *The Cambridge Chronicle and University Journal*, for example, published eleven photographs of his well stocked premises in the broadsheet newspaper: *All Depts. Abloom with New Things*, the advertisement read, *Everything New in Ladies and Children's Wear and Home Requirements*. Astonishingly, one caption boasted that their millinery department 'now displays over 1,000 exclusive new hats, trimmed, semi-trimmed and untrimmed'.

*

A year after George and Elizabeth married, their son, Herbert George, was born on 2 August 1915. While the nation's young men were signing up to support the Great War, business continued pretty much as usual for the new shop keeper. George Heyworth does not seem to have had an active role in WWI. His war records show that he enlisted in 1917 when he was twenty-nine years and ten months. He was described as a 'very capable driver' and 'very reliable man' with a 'clean' conduct sheet. His military history sheet seems quite bare and does not show that he went to the front.

After fourteen years of trading in Burleigh Street, George Heyworth made a decision which transformed the future success of his store. He decided to move to one of the most prominent and affluent shopping areas in the centre of Cambridge. His new store was based at 53 and 54 Sidney Street and was leased for twenty-one years, trading as G. A. Heyworth & Co. The plush new premises offered two floors for shop display, a third floor for storage, living accommodation and a workroom, and a basement for further storage and dispatch.

Heyworth's was now positioned shoulder-to-shoulder with its rival stores, Joshua Taylor and Eaden Lilley, and could enjoy vastly increased footfall. It was a stone's throw from the bustling market place and close to the colleges.

I like to think that George Heyworth's decision to move had been influenced by Gordon Selfridge, who had links with Cambridge. The American-born entrepreneur had visited the flourishing university town in the mid-1920s, having been booked as the star speaker at a summer school held by the Drapers' Chamber of Commerce. George was still trading from Burleigh Street during Mr Selfridge's visit, and it seems unlikely George would have passed up the opportunity to hear Selfridge speak.

Lindy Woodhead refers to this visit in her fabulous book, *Shopping, Seduction & Mr Selfridge*, describing how Mr Selfridge spoke about 'new methods of merchandising, display and window dressing'.

The move to Sidney Street resulted in Heyworth's selling more select and exclusive fashions. Gone was the bed linen and towels of the previous store, instead George Heyworth's sights were set on trading as an upmarket ladies department store and millinery, selling beautiful clothes and hats to the well-to-do college wives who were now right on their doorstep.

Heyworth's was such an exclusive store that many of the shop girls featured in the book said they had never set foot inside it before their interview as their mother could not afford to shop there.

George Heyworth soon established himself as a pillar of the business community. He joined Cambridge Rotary Club in 1929 and was elected as President in 1952. When he was congratulated on his election by his predecessor, Mr A. H. Chapman, it was noted that 'there are few men who can be relied on with greater certainty to shed grace, kindness and hospitality on your meetings'. It is believed he was also a member of Cambridge Freemasons.

George's son Herbert, an only child, was educated privately at Bishop's Stortford College, in Hertfordshire, thirty miles from Cambridge. He went on to join the family business and was groomed to take over from his father. When war intervened and Herbert joined the Royal Artillery in Cambridge on 29 August 1939, aged twenty-four. He described his trade on the application form as 'general manager of a drapery store'. He joined the Light Anti-Aircraft Battery. Little is known about Herbert's war service, but we do know is that during this time, he met and fell in love with a pretty member of the Auxiliary Territorial Army, Canadian-born Pamela Coyle.

Pamela joined the ATS in Ditchling, Sussex, working as a short hand typist and became a 2nd Sublatern ATS Officer. She was posted to the Isle of Wight, which is where the couple most likely met. Thrown together through their war work, their romance blossomed and they married on 30 April 1942 in the Church of the Sacred Heart, in Hove, Sussex. Unfortunately, the marriage was short lived. For unknown reasons, less than two years after their marriage, Herbert left Pamela, who was then pregnant with their child. He was discharged from the Army on 6 January 1944 and returned alone to his parents' home in Cambridge. His discharge papers describe him as 'honest, sober and hardworking'. Meanwhile, Pamela remained in Hove following her discharge from the Army. She gave birth to their son, Paul John, in the Sussex town on 13 March 1944, just weeks after Herbert had walked out on her.

Back in Cambridge, Herbert picked up his old life. He returned to his former position at Heyworth's where he was regarded as an aloof and authoritative figure by many of his employees. But he had a different side to his nature too and was a caring and generous boss to the staff he favoured. No one knew about the wife and son he had left in Hove.

A veil of secrecy surrounds the reason for the break-up of the Herbert and Pamela's marriage, a secret which they both took to their graves. Herbert never once saw his son or made contact with him.

By extraordinary coincidence, both Herbert and Pamela remarried their new partners on exactly the same day – 10 April 1948. At the same time that Herbert became the new husband of Marjorie Bass, Pamela was tying the knot with Stanley Robert 'Bob' Hales, a mechanical engineer in Hove Register Officer.

The widowed Mrs Bass, a tall, striking woman, had been married to Lt. Eric Bass, a law don at Christ's College, who was presumed to have died in 1943 while a prisoner in Japanese hands. She had one son, Nigel, who was ten years old when his mother remarried. Nigel, who became a cardiologist and now lives in New Zealand, recalls Herbert providing support to his mother after the war when his father did not return from the Far East.

Herbert and Marjorie remained devoted to each other throughout their marriage. They had an affluent lifestyle and friends describe Marjorie as always being exquisitely dressed, wrapped in expensive fur coats in the winter. She was said to be a wonderful hostess with a great sense of humour.

One friend who went to their parties at their 'palatial' Spanish-styled home in Fen Ditton was Betty Lloyd and her husband Oswold. 'Herbert always seemed so terribly proud of Marjorie and they laughed a lot,' recalled Betty. 'She was always good fun and was very refined, more so than Bert.'

Describing their unique and lavish home, Betty says, 'It was incredibly big and people were keen to go there to have drinks just to see how nice it was. They had big Spanish pots around the place which they probably brought back from Spain where Herbert had a villa in Llafranc on the Costa Brava. It was an absolutely lovely place and had a wide verandah with arches and tried to look as Spanish as possible.'

The year after his marriage to Marjorie, Herbert relinquished all paternal rights to his young son Paul. An application was submitted to the Supreme Court of Judicature on 16 February 1949 by Bob and Pamela Hales, of Bitterne, Southampton, seeking an order for Paul Hales, aged five, to be officially adopted by Stanley Robert Hales and for his surname to be changed to Hales. The consent of his father Herbert was given to the court on 28 February 1949. The order was granted, and Paul grew up believing that Bob Hales was his real father. He remembers there being a distance between them, with his mother asking him to go to his bedroom to play or do his homework when Bob returned home from work so he could rest and have his meal undisturbed. There was no close father–son bond, although Bob was a very fair man and made sure Paul did not go without. Paul remembers being a happy child during his formative years. He bears no bad feeling against Herbert for his abandonment. His belief is that George and Elizabeth Heyworth did not consider Pamela good enough for their only son, despite their own humble beginnings.

On Paul's twenty-first birthday, his step-father told him that he was adopted. Bob thought that now he was 'officially a man', he should be told the truth about his background – or, at least, part of it. It would be another four years before Paul discovered the true identify of his biological father. He had become engaged was planning to marry in a Roman Catholic church. Paul needed to provide proof that he had been baptized in order for the wedding to go ahead. It was on his baptism certificate that he discovered the name of his biological father: Herbert George Heyworth. This was a major revelation, but, in many ways, he was still none the wiser; his mother refused to talk about Herbert, simply saying 'it's all in the past now'.

Paul accepted her reluctance to discuss it and put it to the back of his mind. It was only when my researcher's path led her directly to Paul's sister-in-law Margaret Moores, who was accessing the same genealogy websites, that he was able to get in touch with me and learn about his biological father for the first time.

I sent Margaret a photograph of Herbert with his wife Marjorie and his father George and mother Elizabeth to show Paul. It was the first time Paul had ever seen a photograph of his father and grandparents.

After receiving the photograph, Paul phoned me. He wanted to learn as much as possible about his father's life, and we agreed to meet. When we did, Paul pored over all the information and photographs which had been lent to me by Heyworth shop girls, and I told him what I had learnt of his father. He shared all the information he had gathered too. It was intensely emotional and, at times, Paul's was close to tears as he took in all the information that had been withheld from him throughout his life.

Paul later met some of the shop girls at a lunch in Cambridge and thoroughly enjoyed learning more about his father. He only wishes his mother had told him about Herbert, as of course he would have liked the opportunity to have tried to contact him. He feels he missed out on knowing his father.

Paul's career path couldn't have been more different to the life which Herbert and George pursued. Paul spent twenty-two years in the Royal Navy followed by two years on contract with the Omani Navy. He then became a Facilities Manager working for Body Shop International and Rentokil Initial until he retired.

Further insights into Herbert Heyworth have been provided by Bryan Saddington, the son of Heyworth's carpenter and handyman, Ron Saddington whose family he befriended. It is bittersweet to hear about the fondness Herbert had for Bryan, who was one month older than Paul. While Paul's twenty-first birthday was memorable for the revelation about his birth father, Herbert made Bryan's a day he would never forget.

Bryan, a fireman, remembers it well. He was celebrating at the Red Lion in Whittlesford with his fiancé, Pat, his parents and sister Janice, and a couple of close friends. They had feasted on prawn cocktail, steak and chips and black forest gateaux. Suddenly, a smiling waiter walked towards their table carrying a tray of out-of-season strawberries. The waiter announced, 'Mr Heyworth thought you might like these. He had them shipped in for you specially.'

Bryan was amazed at this unexpected act of generosity from his father's boss. It was an extraordinary gesture of affection towards the Saddington family and must have cost Herbert a fortune. It was particularly impressive as, unlike today, nobody then ever ate strawberries in spring.

Herbert and Marjorie spent a lot of time with the Saddingtons, even staying the night at theirs on occasion. Bryan reflects, 'They liked my mum's cooking, they liked the homeliness and sometimes I think it was nice for them to step off their pedestal and come back into a different world, and I genuinely think they enjoyed doing that with my mum and dad.'

In the course of researching this book I have spoken to many fascinating people whose stories have helped make Heyworth's come alive. People, like former employee Joan Darling, have made Heyworth's history so vivid and colourful. When Joan was planning her wedding in 1956, she was able to use her staff discount to buy two beautiful outfits from Heyworth's – an elegant charcoal grey suit for the ceremony, and a chic black suit for going away. I was thrilled to discover that Joan's daughter, Helen, still had the black suit and was kind enough to bring it along when we met. She told me that she also wore it as her own going-away outfit when she was married in 1990.

The suit is made from pure worsted wool, with a velvet collar. The jacket has a nipped in waist, shoulder pads and silver buttons and the skirt is a flattering mid-calf length. Above the Alexon label is a *Heyworth's Fashions* label – the name embroidered in dark red swirling letters. I could really feel the quality in the fabric, and even though the suit is now nearly sixty years old it looks as good as new.

Another shop girl who remembers the magnificent wedding dresses on sale at Heyworth's sold was Gillian Payton (Garner). Gillian joined the store straight from Cambridge College of Arts & Technology at the beginning of the 1960s with hopes of becoming a window dresser. But because they didn't have a vacancy for this at the time, the hopeful eighteen-year-old was offered a job in the fashion showroom. Keen to make a good impression on her first day, the new junior stepped forward to serve customers when they walked into the department and earned quite a bit of commission, unaware that she was jumping her turn could only serve if the first and second sales assistants were busy; it could have been a scene straight from the television series, *Are You Being Served?*

A short while later Gillian was transferred to the department where Heyworth's sold designer wedding dresses and exquisite ball gowns. It was her particular job to brush them down regularly to ensure they were immaculate. The bridal gowns were slashed to only £1 in Heyworth's legendary sales, resulting in lengthy queues from bargain seeking brides-to-be. Before too long, Gillian was able to transfer again – this time to her dream job in the window-dressing department. Like all the women interviewed for this book, Gillian's memories have been invaluable in recreating Heyworth's history on these pages.

As well as meeting many wonderful Heyworth shop girls, I was very fortunate to meet Sandy Tothill, the daughter of Herbert Heyworth's best friend, Richard Tothill, who ran Great Chesterford Country Club. Sandy believes the two men met in Cambridge in the 1930s and struck up a close friendship. They frequently visited Spain together, a country they both loved and spent many holidays together in their Mediterranean villas.

The Tothills, Sandy included, often joined Herbert on his extravagant flights to Paris. In Sandy's words, 'People go to Brighton for the day; we went to Paris.' And always in great style, flying in privately chartered planes from Marshall's Airport in Cambridge which Herbert generously paid for.

Sandy was also able to provide a tantalising suggestion of the pain Herbert felt about his divorced and estrangement from his son, Paul. She recalls a story her father told her, about a drive he and Herbert took through Brighton. Herbert suddenly burst into tears as they passed a church. 'Bert told my father that's where he had married.' She believes this was the first time he had been to Brighton since his divorce and he seemed unable to hide his emotions.

Around 1956, Herbert and Richard Tothill opened a Spanish-themed café called El Patio in Sidney Street, a few yards from Heyworth's. It was an overnight sensation – the first café in Cambridge selling frothy coffee made by a hissing Gaggia machine and serving continental food. It was hugely popular with students, and became a hang-out for musicians and intellectuals.

As the grey Cambridge sky filled with the loud explosive crackling sound of fireworks, a riot of bright fizzy colours on 5 November, 1965, Heyworth's closed its doors for the very last time. Herbert Heyworth kept his promise to find new jobs for his staff. At a farewell party, he was moist eyed as he thanked them for their loyalty and support to him and his father over so many years. He presented watches to long serving staff who had worked for the family business for twenty-five years or more. The recipients were children's wear buyer Mary Ryder; corsetry buyer Jean Pryor; office manager Jim Clarke; Douglas Dumper, the window display manager; Ron Sadler, from dispatch; and Herbert's dear and trusted friend, Ron Saddington.

Herbert died suddenly of a heart attack in Jersey in 1969. He was only fifty-three. After his death Marjorie continued to live in Jersey. Three years later she married Dan Morley, of Poole, Dorset. She was sixty-two and he was seventy-three and they lived in Bournemouth. Marjorie died in 2003 aged ninety-four.

Paul's mother Pamela and his adoptive father, Stanley Hales, were divorced in July 1980. Pamela died in July 2004 aged eighty-four.

*

Paul Hales is the nicest man you could meet. He now lives in County Durham with his wife Patricia. They moved there from the Worthing area with their eldest daughter Katie and son-in-law James as the family wanted to be close to their youngest daughter Sarah, husband Sean, and, most importantly their granddaughter, Phoebe.

This story began a hundred years ago, and to end it, I visited Sidney Street to see what now stands in the place of G. A. Heyworth and Co. Having been home to a number of different businesses since Heyworth's time, the large premises are currently divided between branches of Trailfinders, Ryman stationers and Office Angels. El Patio's now forms part of a Sainsbury store.

Heyworth's rival independent stores, Joshua Taylor and Eaden Lilley, have also long-since closed their doors. In their place also stand some of today's common high-street stores: Superdrug, W.H. Smiths and TK Maxx, to name but a few. It is a sign of the times, and makes me all the more glad that I found Eve and stumbled across the Heyworth's story. I hope it will live on for another hundred years.

Ellee Seymour
June 2014

EVE

1944

Eve is pictured third from left on the back row, next to the children's wear buyer, Elsie Stubbings, in the lovely hat. They were on a Heyworth staff outing to Marlow, Buckinghamshire

'We normally only take on grammar-school girls, but I'd like to offer you a junior's job. We'll give you a trial in our children's department.'

The words were music to the ears of the shy fourteen-year-old being interviewed by George Heyworth. Eve looked across at her mother, Gertrude, who had done most of the talking while her daughter sat quietly, responding with a brief 'yes' or 'no' to any questions.

'I normally only pay fifteen shillings a week, but I'll start you off with a pound a week,' he added, smiling at them both.

Eve thought she was being offered extra money because he felt sorry for her mother. Gertrude had told him about the hardships she faced as a widow and the man sitting opposite her listened with a sympathetic expression on his face.

'I brought up seven children on my own after their father died, and I've never had trouble from any of them,' she said.

Mrs Gray was dressed smartly and wore her best hat. She spoke in a very matter-of-fact way about her life; she wasn't seeking sympathy for the struggles she'd endured.

Mr Heyworth turned to look at Eve, a picture of innocence in her red school beret and a smart blue-grey coat. She smiled back at him, delighted with the generous pay and the chance of being a junior shop girl in such a smart shop.

'Thank you, Mr Heyworth. When would you like me to start?'

'How about next week?'

'Yes, of course,' she replied eagerly.

Eve had immediately warmed to the grey-haired, fatherly figure who was to be her boss. He was softly spoken and had a kind face.

'He's such a lovely man – he seems so kind,' she told her mother as they left the store.

It was the first time that Eve or her mother had ever set foot inside Heyworth's; the clothes on sale were far out of their price range. Eve wondered what it would be like working there with its posh customers.

The job offer was a huge relief for Eve and she counted her blessings that the visit to Heyworth's had proved successful. It was the last name on a list of three shops offering positions for school leavers which her teacher considered suitable for her.

The first name on her list was Joshua Taylor's, a large department store opposite Heyworth's. It also sold top-quality ladies' clothing and was a rival to Heyworth's. It had begun trading in Cambridge in 1860, but had opened its first store fourteen miles away in 1810 in the cathedral city of Ely. Joshua Taylor's had established a library in the store and had advertised for an assistant to look after its precious archive. As Eve had helped out in her school library, her teacher thought she would suit this post, but Eve quickly dismissed the idea. Although she'd liked school, she didn't feel she was very clever, and told her mum, 'It's not for me, I'll be bored working in their library.'

They walked around the corner to the second shop on her list, a ladies' underwear store called Etam in Market Street. Eve's heart skipped a beat when she took one look inside the door, overcome with dread. She stared at the sales assistants wearing long, black old-fashioned dresses and knew this was no place for her – the women looked like relics from the Edwardian era and Eve shuddered at the thought of working there. She was so sure of its unsuitability that she fled without even stepping inside to enquire about the vacancy they had on offer.

'I'm sorry, Mum, but I can't work there. It looks dead. I wouldn't be happy working with those old ladies. Let's see what Heyworth's is like.'

Gertrude wanted her daughter to be happy and could understand her reluctance to work with the old ladies at Etam, but she hoped their next stop would prove to be third time lucky for her youngest daughter. Heyworth's was a couple of minutes' walk away. Although Eve had never set foot in Heyworth's before, she immediately felt at home there and was relieved to have finally found somewhere to work where she felt she would be happy.

One question troubled Eve. 'What will I wear? I don't have anything smart enough.'

Eve knew Gertrude couldn't afford to spend very much, as every penny she had was budgeted carefully to pay the bills. Eve and her mother never went out shopping together, but for this special occasion Gertrude was happy to make an exception. They walked together to Frost's, in Norfolk Street, to buy a suitable dress for Eve's new job.

The final choice left Eve feeling disappointed – the dress her mother chose for her was not to her liking. It was a black long-sleeved woollen dress with a high sweetheart neckline. As she looked at her reflection in the mirror, she felt it made her look frumpy, far older than her age. But, as an obedient daughter, Eve never considered openly questioning her mother's choice of dress for her.

'It should keep you warm in the winter. You'll get used to it,' said Gertrude reassuringly.

Other girls from her school were starting new jobs too, working at Chivers' jam factory in Histon, a village just outside Cambridge, or at Pye's factory in Cambridge, where telescopes and height-finders were made for war planes. Some schoolgirls found jobs in offices, on the local telephone network switchboard, or, like Eve, in shops.

*

Eve was born in the Fenland village of Littleport, near Ely, and the family later moved to Darwin Drive in Cambridge, where her father William found work as a butcher. Her three sisters were called Peggy, Beryl and Marjorie, and her brothers were Bill, Ron and Derek. Eve was second youngest, and the youngest girl, with Derek being the baby of the family.

They were never well off, but Eve's hard-working father liked to give treats to his young family when he could and each Friday he brought sweets home for them after work. Unfortunately, poor health and heart trouble forced William to give up his job, but he soon found part-time kitchen work at Jesus College, part of the University of Cambridge.

When Eve was six, William's health unexpectedly took a turn for the worse when he developed a fever and had difficulty breathing. An ambulance was called. The last time Eve saw her father, he was being carried out of their house on a stretcher on his way to hospital. All the neighbours gathered round to watch.

'I'll be back,' he called out to his wife and family, waving as he was being carried away.

They never saw him alive again; William returned home in a coffin. He died of pneumonia aged forty, leaving Gertrude widowed with seven children to feed and clothe. Eve was only six years old and baby Derek only six months.

William's coffin was brought to the house, where it lay on the black leather sofa in the front room. All the children leaned over to kiss him on the forehead and pay their last respects. Eve shuddered as she felt the iciness of his marble-like skin against her lips.

Following the loss of the family breadwinner, Eve's mother, who was ten years older than William, scrimped and saved and miraculously made ends meet to feed and clothe her children, making sure they had all the essentials.

When Eve's shoe soles became thin, her thrifty mother carried out her own repairs to save money. She used a cast-iron shoe-form, a cobbler's last – which many families kept in their shed – that William had bought to hammer on new leather soles. If she didn't have any leather, she fitted the shoes with cardboard insoles to make them last longer until they were either repaired or replaced.

Despite her hard work looking after the family and home, Eve's mother always took pride in her appearance and everyone told her how smart she was. She liked to wear a hat like the best-dressed women. At home she always wore a long apron, the kind that wrapped around the waist and tied up at the front. In the afternoon she swapped her long apron for a little pinafore apron with a frill.

She cooked delicious traditional dishes, and Eve's favourite meals were liver and bacon or pork with sliced potatoes and gravy. She also loved her mum's scrummy steamed puddings. On Sundays they tucked into a roast dinner, and the rest of the day revolved around church. Eve wasn't allowed to knit or sew, the family treated Sunday as a day of rest, just as the Bible instructed. From the age of seven, Eve went to Sunday school every Sunday afternoon at the United Reformed Church, and then as a teenager she went to church in the morning and to a church youth group in the evening as well.

Eve knew little about her parents' lives. She knew her mother came from Banbury, but she had no idea how she had met her father, who came from Luton – it was never talked about.

She knew nothing about her mother's childhood and family, and it was several years before she realised her mother had lots of brothers and sisters. One of her uncles, whom she had never met before and knew nothing of, suddenly surprised Eve and her three sisters after their father had died by sending them each a pair of black leather boots for the winter. They had buttons down the side and the generous gift was much appreciated by all the girls. Eve could only think that he felt sorry for them, and they all thought how kind their mystery uncle was, knowing their mother could not have afforded to buy them. There was no spare money for extras, any luxury items or holidays.

Eve's mother was a proud woman who never showed her feelings or complained about her lot. She seemed unable to show affection to her children or to tell them she loved them; she never gave them hugs or cuddles, and sometimes turned her cheek the other way when Eve went to kiss her. When she was older, Eve would wonder what might have happened in Gertrude's childhood to make her unable to show her feelings.

Christmas Day was a big day for Eve and her brothers and sisters, and even though the family didn't have much money, they always woke to find their stockings were filled with an orange, an apple and some nuts. The seven children were also given three board games – one of them being shuffleboard – to share between them, and they spent many happy hours playing them on dark winter nights.

A year or two after Eve's father died, Eve was given a special present that surpassed all others – a beautiful doll's house. Every room was fitted with miniature furniture and she adored playing with it. She never found out who sent it, and her mother remained close-lipped on the subject.

The family later moved to a large rented house in Victoria Road, Cambridge. Gertrude took in a lodger to help make ends meet, and Eve's older sisters all paid their way too. Eve loved the new house, and spent her summer holidays playing in a nearby park, taking picnics of jam sandwiches and home-made lemonade. She would spend the whole day there, playing hide and seek, skipping and tag with her younger brother Derek, and friends from Sunday school.

Eve loved swimming and it was fortunate that Jesus Green Pool, Cambridge's biggest pool, if not the biggest lido in the country at

300 feet long, was only around the corner from her home. The sight of the glistening water on a hot summer afternoon was exhilarating, and hearing the sound of splashing and everyone having fun made it an irresistible attraction. Swimming was tremendous fun for Eve and her brother Derek, and they were the only children in their family who could swim, having been taught at school. They went as often as their mother could afford to give them the penny each to get in.

Unlike most of the other girls at her school, Eve didn't wear a uniform, as her mother couldn't afford to buy one. When Eve took up dressmaking in needlework class, she was able to wear school colours for the first time by making a red and white gingham skirt and blouse, and wore a smart red beret to complete her uniform. It made her feel really good to be able to dress like most other girls in her school for the first time and very proud that she had made something for herself to wear.

She often felt deeply embarrassed during school cookery lessons. If her mother couldn't afford to buy the ingredients she needed, Eve had no choice but to watch her classmates prepare delicious food, smelling the wonderful aroma of a cake, fruit pie or a savoury dish, while she washed up.

Bedtime was scary for Eve. She shared an iron-framed double bed in the attic with sisters Beryl, six years older than her, and Marjorie, three years her senior. Being younger than her sisters, Eve had to go to bed first. And because she was the youngest, she slept in the middle, which she didn't like, as she was squashed up. But at least it was the warmest place on cold nights when they cuddled up to keep warm. The winter nights were sometimes so cold that icicles formed inside the bedroom window, which Eve and her sisters would pick off and suck.

It was an old house full of creaking sounds, which made Eve's hair stand on end. As she lay in bed scared and alone, waiting for her sisters to come up, she heard strange sounds and her imagination ran riot, terrified in case it was the bogeyman.

'Who's that coming up the stairs?' she wondered, trembling under the blanket, and waiting for her door to open.

Eve was nine when the war started. She was petrified of the air raids – the sound of the warning siren made her shake like a leaf. Sometimes the siren went off once a week, sometimes twice a night.

When Eve's mother heard the shrieking sound of the siren, she would call out urgently to her children, 'Quick, quick, get down into the pantry.'

The pantry was located under stone steps in the basement and provided an ideal secure hideaway and makeshift air-raid shelter. Eve would obediently follow her mother down the steps into the basement, eager to escape the unbearable noise.

The pantry had thick concrete walls and Eve sat there in the dark, her hands pressed against her ears to block out the terrifying sound of heavy aircraft overhead.

The raids happened mostly at night, but sometimes in the day too, and Eve would quickly dress when she heard the sirens, ready in case she needed to leave the house. With one brother, Bill, away in the army and another, Ron, in the navy, and with her sisters at work, Eve cuddled up in the dark pantry with her younger brother Derek if it was a daytime warning. Sometimes they stayed hidden in the pantry for an hour, sometimes longer. They stayed there until the all-clear siren, and then Eve eagerly rushed up the steps in search of daylight.

'I hate it here. I hate being down in this basement,' she told her mother after one lengthy raid.

'We've got no choice. This is the safest place for us,' Gertrude replied.

'I know, but I'm scared, and I hate those sounds.'

Back in 1940, when Eve was ten, the whole of Cambridge, and particularly Eve's neighbourhood, were shocked by a terrible aeroplane crash in Histon Road, just around the corner from her home in Victoria Road and close to the park where Eve used to play.

Tragically, it had been caused by an RAF bomber returning from a raid on the Continent, which crashed into the terraced houses, killing three elderly women.

Eve joined her friends to see the aftermath and terrible destruction. There were mountainous piles of rubble where the homes had once stood, and the women's personal belongings were scattered on the ground with their smashed furniture.

And the war was still raging when Eve left school. Her young life was about to move into a new direction and she counted the days till she could start work as a junior shop girl at Heyworth's.

'See you lunchtime, Mum,' Eve called out cheerily to Gertrude as she walked out of her house.

She was due to arrive at Heyworth's at 8.45 a.m. sharp and was keen to be there on time on her first day.

Her mother, with her pinny tied up neatly around her waist, nodded as Eve left and wished her well.

Eve walked briskly into the town with her sister. Marjorie worked at Eaden Lilley's, a rival store opposite Heyworth's. It was regarded as more of a family department store, however, and not quite as upmarket. Marjorie had started at Eaden Lilley straight after school as a junior in the gloves, scarves and accessories department, and loved her job there. The two sisters walked across Jesus Green and arrived at their respective stores after fifteen minutes or so.

As they parted company, Marjorie wished Eve well on her first day. Eve stood and looked at Heyworth's. She felt shy and a little nervous as she entered through its staff entrance in Market Passage.

It felt strange to be opening a staff door, no longer being a school-child, but a junior on her first day at work.

Eve wasn't sure where to go, but she soon spotted a group of young shop girls who had also just arrived. She asked them coyly, 'I'm new – where should I hang up my coat?'

'Just follow me, I'll show you,' replied one of the girls with a bright friendly smile that instantly put Eve at ease.

Eve followed her to the basement, where she was allocated an empty locker, number 25. Eve removed her coat and looked around. She noticed that all the sales girls wore smart black skirts and a white blouse and looked very neat.

She suddenly felt very self-conscious, wearing her frumpy black dress that she felt made her look almost as dowdy as the old ladies who worked at Etam. She also wore smart new black shoes and girlish white ankle socks, as she didn't yet have stockings.

The shop was long and narrow, and the children's and babies' clothes were on the left side of the store as customers entered through the front door. An archway led to the accessories department, which stocked the latest gloves and scarves. Lingerie and hosiery were sold on the ground floor too, while gowns, dresses, coats and suits were in the fashion showroom upstairs. Eve had no idea about fashion and clothes, but she could tell by glancing at the stock and the price tags that Heyworth's was a place where well-to-do customers shopped.

Eve was taken to meet the childrenswear buyer, Elsie Stubbings, who was to be her immediate boss. She was a friendly-looking dark-haired woman in her late fifties or early sixties, and had smiling eyes.

'I'm Miss Stubbings, I'm in charge of this department. You must be the new junior,' she said warmly.

Eve nodded, beginning to feel more at ease by the woman's friendly manner and smile.

'Let me introduce you to the other girls. Miss Gray, this is Miss Hulyer, she is the first sales girl. Her real name is Mrs Smith, but as there is already a Mrs Smith in the store, we are calling her by her maiden name, Miss Hulyer.'

Miss Hulyer was a senior sales assistant in her fifties, and gave Eve a welcoming smile.

'And this is Mrs Dumper, one of our part-time sales assistants. Her husband also works here, as our window-display manager.'

Mrs Dumper seemed more aloof than the other shop girls; she had a superior air about her, and nodded briefly at Eve.

Mrs Dumper worked with another part-time senior sales assistant, Mary Ryder. Mrs Ryder had a young son and was able to leave work early in the afternoon to collect him from the school gate.

Eve was not the only junior; there was also Beryl Carter, who was seventeen, and Joan Beeby, fifteen, and an evacuee from Twickenham who had been sent to stay with a relative in Sturton Street, Cambridge.

Miss Stubbings handed Eve a soft brush and explained her duties. 'Mr Heyworth likes all the garments to be brushed and kept dust-free. Come and watch me carefully – this is how we brush them.'

Eve followed Miss Stubbings to a rail of children's woollen coats in vibrant red, blue, dark green and black. The sleeves were folded inside the cuffs. The coats had sleek black velvet collars and a nipped-in waist with a skirt that flared out. They were exquisite, the kind of coats young aristocrats wore; they were not the sort Eve's mother could have afforded for her children. Eve felt the softness of the fabric as she held the coat in her hand, ready to brush it.

'Here, you have a go,' said Miss Stubbings, after she had finished demonstrating the task, handing the brush to Eve.

Eve gently lifted the velvet collars and brushed off any dust. She went along the rail doing the same with each of the coats.

'Is that okay? Have I done it right?' asked Eve.

'That's perfect, they're fit for a prince!'

Eve also vacuumed and dusted the department and cleaned the glass counter until it sparkled. She had to start at the bottom and had much to learn before she could sell to customers.

'I don't mind at all,' Eve told her mother when she went home for lunch and told her about the chores she had to do. 'I like it there, I really do, and everyone is so friendly. It is tiring, though, standing on the wooden floor all day. My poor feet do ache so. I don't know if I'll ever get used to it.'

It was agreed that Eve would give her mum 17 shillings and six-pence each week towards her keep and keep the remaining half-crown for herself. She didn't mind at all; what she had left was more than enough for what she might want to buy for herself.

The six eldest children were all at work, but they returned home at lunchtime to have their hot meal of the day. It was eaten in different shifts to fit around their different lunch breaks, starting from midday. Eve always arrived home last, leaving Heyworth's at 1.15 p.m., and would tuck into liver and bacon or sausage and mash, followed by pudding, her favourite being spotted dick or steamed pudding.

When Eve returned to Heyworth's after lunch, she clocked in using what looked like an antiquated contraption that should be in a museum. The huge black clock, a yard in diameter, had one big brass handle in the middle. Around the edge were holes with numbers forming the clock face, and Eve had to swing the arm around twice and press the numbers to indicate the hour and minute at which she was clocking in.

Eve looked forward to being able to sell to customers, especially as the shop girls were paid a penny in the pound commission for every item they sold. But she knew she had to wait her turn in the pecking order. The senior sales girls had priority, starting with Miss Stubbings, and then second sales and third sales, so there was rarely a chance for juniors like Eve to sell and earn commission, as there were so many others in front of her.

'Your turn will come soon enough,' Miss Stubbings told Eve reassuringly. 'For now, you have to tidy up and put away all the garments the senior sales girls take out to show customers.'

The senior shop girls, keen to make as much commission as possible, worked very quickly, moving swiftly from one customer to another, bringing out different stock to show customers, and then leaving them out on the counter for Eve to tidy up afterwards. Eve never complained, and neatly folded it all, placing everything back in the wooden drawers in the glass counter or display cabinets, which had a lovely curved edge.

One of the department's popular lines were exquisite hand-made smocked dresses and romper suits, which were specially made to order by Miss Stubbings' sister Hilda. Her craftsmanship and embroidery was greatly admired and much sought-after by Heyworth's upmarket customers. Hilda worked hard to keep up with demand, even though the outfits cost 19 shillings – the equivalent of almost a week of Eve's pay.

The smocking was done on soft cream fabric that would be warm against the baby's skin, and the cross-stitching was in blue for a boy and pink for a girl. Smocking was very popular, and some dresses for children, such as the Lindsay Maid dresses, had deep smocking from the waist up to the top of the chest.

Eve loved to feel the softness and quality of the Diyella and Viyella baby clothing and the fleeced lining of the popular Chilproof vests, which were much in demand during the winter for children with chesty coughs. The vests were in short supply during the war, when wool was hard to get hold of – being needed to make uniforms for servicemen – so when they became available again, Heyworth's made sure they went to the most loyal customers first.

'Please only take orders for account customers for the vests, and as soon as they come in, they will be given priority,' Miss Stubbings instructed the sales girls.

Mr Heyworth often walked around the departments and had very firm views about how staff should behave at work: he liked to see them being busy at all times and not standing idle.

'I should tell you that Mr Heyworth does not tolerate slouching from his sales girls – keep busy or you'll be in trouble,' Miss Stubbings warned Eve when she started at Heyworth's.

George Heyworth was able to keep a close watch on the children's department through a large mirror fixed inside his office door. If he left his door ajar, he could see a reflection of exactly what Eve and the others were doing. This meant he could keep one eye on his paperwork and one eye on them, to make sure they weren't standing around wasting time. But the girls could also see his reflection in their own department's mirrors, which alerted them if he was on a walkabout and about to return to his office through their department.

Eve observed the gracious way in which George Heyworth welcomed customers, the politeness and courtesy he bestowed on them.

'Here, let me help you,' said Mr Heyworth, always the perfect gentleman, rushing to open the door for an elderly customer or a mother struggling with a pram.

'Can I offer you a seat?' he asked, leading them in and pointing to one of the chairs placed against the counter for their comfort.

Eve noticed that whenever Mr Heyworth entered or left the store, he always nodded and smiled, and acknowledged whoever was passing by, exchanging brief pleasantries, like, 'Good day to you,' or, 'What a fine day it is.' He was always polite to the shop girls too, and this made Eve like him as a kindly boss.

Around this time she was suffering from a recurring ache on the right side of her body, which made her feel sick and giddy. She had become very thin and pale, and Miss Stubbings noticed her walking around holding on to her side. She asked Eve what was wrong.

'I don't know what's come over me. I feel breathless and sick,' Eve told her boss, pausing for breath.

Miss Stubbings looked at Eve's pallor and the way she was standing bent over to one side; she could see she was not well. 'You must go and see a doctor straight away. A young girl like you shouldn't be feeling like this, it's not right. You may have appendicitis.'

Miss Stubbings always had a caring and protective way towards the shop girls, which Eve appreciated.

'I don't know whether it's appendicitis,' she replied. 'I'm certainly not eating anything to make it worse. I just don't know why I feel so poorly.'

George Heyworth heard about Eve's discomfort and offered some reassuring words. 'You don't need to worry about that. The doctors told me years ago that I had appendicitis, and I never had it out.'

Eve hoped he would prove to be right, but as the sharp pains and giddiness continued, she knew she could ignore it no longer, and took Miss Stubbings' advice to see her doctor. An X-ray resulted in an unexpected diagnosis. It was not appendicitis after all.

'You have a floating kidney,' the doctor told her.

Eve was stunned. 'What does that mean? I've never heard of it before.'

'I'm afraid your kidney drops down into the pelvis and it's something you'll have to live with,' he replied. 'We need to stop the kidney moving about and this can be done by wearing a special corset,' he added. 'It can be very successful.'

Eve was appalled. Because she was so thin, there was no spare flesh on her to pull in with a corset, and now she was being told she would have to be trussed up like a chicken on medical grounds. A flesh-coloured corset with bone stays was specially made for her to ensure it was the right fit and would pull in and support the float-ing kidney. It had laces at the back and reminded Eve of the undergarments that her grandmother might have worn in the olden days.

'Ugh, it's so ugly,' she said, looking at herself in the mirror, trying it on for the first time. She didn't like it one bit, but knew she had no choice. She clipped up the hooks at the side, having first tied up the laces to make sure it fitted tightly to hold her kidney in place.

Eve wore the corset every day until she put on sufficient weight to support the floating kidney unaided. She noticed that the dis-comfort worsened when she bent down to help fasten up the buttons on a child's coat. The worst of the pain stopped after a few years, though she continued to feel a nagging ache from time to time.

Eve also became fond of Miss Stubbings and the way she cared for the well-being of the girls under her charge. She was only too willing to repay Miss Stubbings' kindness by doing whatever was asked of her, and didn't mind running errands on her behalf. This included dropping off packages for Miss Stubbings' parents at their home in Chesterton Road, but Eve's mother didn't feel too happy about this.

'I thought you were there to be a shop assistant, not to run errands,' said Gertrude.

'I only changed some library books for her. I don't mind at all, and she's so kind to me. And I don't mind taking things to her par-ents – they're lovely people.'

It wasn't just Miss Stubbings who sent Eve on errands; Mr Heyworth did too. She always did as she was asked and never ques-tioned the reason why she was doing something.

'Miss Gray, I have a package here for you to deliver. Could you please take it this afternoon,' he asked the junior.

Eve took hold of the parcel, which was wrapped neatly in brown paper. She had no idea what it contained, and she didn't recognise the name written on it. The address she had been given was an almshouse in King Street, just a short walk from the store. When she arrived, she handed the package over to the tiny grey-haired lady who answered the door.

Eve later discovered that the woman used to be Mr Heyworth's housekeeper. Perhaps it had been her birthday, or maybe it was a gesture of goodwill from her former boss for a once-valued and trusted helper.

After working in Heyworth's for two years, the day that Eve had been looking forward to finally arrived. She was at last allowed to serve customers.

'You've come on very well,' said Miss Stubbings. 'We are very impressed with your dedication, hard work and loyalty. It's now time for you to sell to customers.'

'Thank you, Miss Stubbings. I'm really looking forward to it,' Eve replied, delighted that they were showing such faith in her. She had spent two years watching and learning from the senior shop girls, and she knew she was up to the task. She couldn't wait to start. She was familiar with the regular customers, including the snooty ones with haughty airs. These women preferred to be served by Miss Stubbings, rather than by one of the other shop girls.

'Look, it's Mrs Handley, the one with the posh voice,' one of the assistants whispered, alerting other shop girls when this particular customer's distinctive voice was heard in their department.

'Good morning, Mrs Handley, how are you today? How can I help you?' Miss Stubbings would ask. She was always very charming to all customers.

Eve dreaded having to serve posh customers. She felt uncomfortable in their presence and wished they could all be lovely, like Mrs Calder, the doctor's wife.

'She never looks down on you, and always speaks to you nicely,' Eve told Miss Stubbings. 'I wish all our customers were as nice.'

The shop girls were given personal account books to keep a record of their sales. They wrote down each item in the book and, after the final figure had been double-checked, it was placed in the cash cup with the payment and any war coupons, and sent to the cashier, who sat in a glass-windowed booth on the shop floor.

The prices were clearly set out. Children's coats cost seven coupons, and a smart coat with leggings, which had buttons up the side of the legs and a matching peaked cap, was ten coupons. A set of mittens and bootees cost half a coupon.

Watching the cash cup whizz around the store was great fun for children. They loved watching it soaring above their heads, darting off like a missile. They couldn't take their eyes off the canister as it sped upwards and around the corner, and then finally arrived at the cash desk, where the money and coupons would be taken out, and then returned to the assistant with a receipt.

Sometimes the cash cup got stuck, and needed a helping hand to get it moving again.

'Oh dear, it's got stuck on the corner again,' Eve said, watching the cash cup grind to a halt before nudging it back into action.

'Let me have a go – can I get it going for you?' a young child asked excitedly.

'Come on, then,' said Eve, taking hold of the child by his waist and lifting him up until he could reach the pulley and knock the cup into action.

Mr Heyworth's wife Elizabeth sometimes visited the store. She was very quiet, with a rounded figure and thick, round glasses. On the occasions that she called in, she liked to walk around the departments to see that everything was in order. Like her husband, she felt that the shop girls must be kept busy at all times and not stand idle.

She was particularly keen that the fashion floor was always fully staffed and frequently moved assistants there from other departments to help out if they were quiet, particularly during lunchtimes.

'I hope she doesn't ask me to go into fashions, I don't like it there,' Eve confided to one of the other shop girls. 'I don't know anything about it – I've only been trained in children's clothes.'

But sometimes she had no choice, and found herself working in the fashion showroom surrounded by sumptuous gowns and beautifully cut suits, thinking, 'I can't wait to get back to children's. This isn't the place for me. Thank goodness it's just for the lunch break.'

Heyworth's also offered a bespoke school-uniform-tailoring service for local public schools. This was used by well-to-do families with larger children who couldn't fit into ready-made uniforms.

If Eve was asked to measure up a child, she fretted about it. 'I'm no good at measuring up. I'm worried I'll get it wrong and it won't fit,' she told Miss Stubbings, anxiously.

'Don't worry about it. Someone else will always check it for you if you ask them. Make sure you do ask if you're worried, rather than get it wrong. You'll be fine.'

She had no choice but to go where she was sent, and took Miss Stubbings' advice, but never enjoyed measuring up.

One day Eve had reason to be grateful to George Heyworth's wife, Elizabeth. She was returning back to the store after lunch when the heavens opened and there was a thunderstorm, the noise of which terrified her: it was an unpleasant reminder of the air-raid sirens she had hated so much.

Mrs Heyworth saw Eve arrive in a distressed state. She was wet through and the older woman took pity on the shivering young girl.

'My, look how wet you are! Come with me and I'll dry you off.'

Eve nodded gratefully, explaining how she had been caught out in the storm. It left her shaken to the core. 'The storm started when I was walking across Jesus Green and I ran here all the way. It was a terrible thunderstorm,' said Eve, shivering and shocked from her ordeal.

'I can see you are very upset,' the older woman replied.

Eve followed Mrs Heyworth upstairs into part of the store she had never been to before. They walked up until they reached the roof, and then across a ledge across the top of the roof, finally reaching a door that opened into a former storeroom. It had been converted into a bedsit for Mrs Heyworth so she could rest during the day if she became tired.

Mrs Heyworth fetched Eve a towel and she took it thankfully, rubbing at her wet hair. The shy junior removed her wet coat to dry off in front of the electric fire.

'Just lie down for a minute till you feel better. I'll make you a cup of tea,' her boss's wife said kindly. 'Don't worry, we'll soon have you dry in no time.'

Eve looked around the room. It was a cosy little place, with flowers on a table and a single bed. Eve took off her shoes and lay down. She relaxed and slowly began to feel better after drinking the tea. After resting for half an hour, she felt well enough to go back to work.

'Thank you Mrs Heyworth, I feel much better. I'd better go down now,' she said, not wanting to make a fuss. She returned back to her department, feeling very fortunate to work for kind people who cared for their staff in this way.

When Eve first started at Heyworth's she wore white ankle socks, but once she had been there a while she decided it was time to buy her first pair of nylons. She knew she ought to wear stockings for work, as she'd been told that they must be worn at all times, including on hot summer days, with smart shoes.

As stockings were rationed for customers, Miss Stubbings came up with a suggestion. 'Just put your name down with the buyer in hosiery and you'll soon be allowed one pair a month. Tell her I sent you. Although account customers get priority, you'll get a pair soon enough.'

'I'll do that, I'd love some stockings,' said Eve, thrilled at the thought of getting the chance to feel grown up like the other shop girls.

Her turn soon came and her face lit up when she was handed her first pair of stockings. She couldn't wait to put them on and show her friends at the church youth club – none of the other girls there her age owned any, so she would be the first.

'Lucky you. How did you manage to get hold of them?' her friends asked enviously when Eve showed them off.

'I know I'm lucky to have them, I got them from work,' she grinned.

One of Eve's friends at her youth club, Joyce, was very excited and couldn't wait to share her good news.

'My brother Les is coming home after all this time!'

Les and his family lived around the corner from Eve, though she didn't know him very well. She had heard that Les had been captured and incarcerated at a Japanese prisoner-of-war camp for three-and-a-half years, and knew there had been terrible suffering in their camps.

It took some time before Les could face returning to his old youth club. When he did, he just sat there smoking a cigarette, keeping himself to himself. Nobody asked him what he had seen in the Far East, and Les said nothing. Eve saw him staring into space, alone with his thoughts.

Then after a year, and out of the blue, it was almost as if a spell had been broken. Les slowly began talking to people and joining in badminton, playing doubles with Eve and her friends at the club.

'He's nice,' Eve thought to herself, drawn by his kind manner, good looks and the way he had become attentive towards her.

At the end of youth club one night, her heart skipped a beat when Les suddenly asked her, 'Do you mind if I walk you home tonight?'

She was thrilled and replied shyly, 'Yes, that will be fine.'

The walk marked the start of a deep love that would last a lifetime for the shy shop girl.

IRENE

1948

The loud, persistent ring of the phone almost made Irene jump out of her skin. She wasn't expecting to hear it.

'Whoever can that be? Nobody ever rings here,' she wondered, as she walked towards the phone in the hallway.

Irene picked up the receiver tentatively, puzzled. A polite voice at the other end of the line asked, 'Can I speak to Mrs Dean, please?'

Irene replied, 'I'm sorry, she's resting at the moment.'

'I'm Mr Heyworth's secretary and Mr Bendall has given us her particulars,' the caller persisted.

It suddenly dawned on Irene that the call was meant for her. 'Sorry, that's me,' she replied, coming to her senses.

As a new bride living with her husband Peter's family, Irene was not used to being called Mrs Dean, and had immediately thought the call was for her mother-in-law, Gladys, who was taking an afternoon nap.

Irene was even less used to having personal phone calls at the house, as not many people she knew had their own private telephone. It had been installed in the house because Peter's father, Richard, worked as a Post Office engineer and there were occasions when he needed to be reached for emergencies. Although he had since died, the phone remained in the house, but it was rarely used by anyone – it was virtually an ornament.

'Yes, I gave Mr Bendall my particulars,' Irene told the caller, recalling the discussion with her hairdresser earlier that day.

'Well, Mr Heyworth would like to see you at ten o'clock tomorrow morning. Is that convenient with you?'

'Thank you, I'll be there,' confirmed Irene, scarcely able to believe the speed at which the message had been acted on.

At twenty-six, Irene was already an experienced sales assistant and had been a buyer for the Edwin Jones department store group in Dorset where she'd lived before she married. Now, recently married to Peter and living in Cambridge, she found being a housewife dull, and had confided this to her hairdresser, Frank Bendall, during her appointment that morning. They were also neighbours.

'How are you getting on?' he'd asked Irene, while rolling up her brunette hair.

'To be quite truthful, I'm bored. I've got nothing to do,' she'd replied.

'So why don't you take a job?' he asked.

'Well, Peter might not like me to,' she said.

'Oh, come on. These days that sort of thing has changed. What do you do?'

'I was a buyer in fashion and accessories for a department store.'

'I'm going to lunch with the Rotarians today. Write down what you do and I'll see if I can put a word in,' he offered.

Irene wrote down details about her experience at Edwin Jones, and included her phone number, but didn't give it another thought – until the phone rang later that afternoon.

Irene now faced a dilemma – should she tell Peter about her interview at Heyworth's? She decided to keep it to herself, just in case he tried to persuade her against it. Irene badly missed her work and buying beautiful ladies' accessories. With her mother-in-law cooking their main meal of the day, there really was nothing for her to do, and she was thrilled to have this unexpected opportunity.

The following day Irene dressed in her best suit, blouse and smart shoes, and wore a hat. She was slim, very attractive and elegantly dressed, and wanted to impress Mr Heyworth.

She felt confident at the interview, and liked Herbert Heyworth. He offered her a job straight away, but there was a hitch. 'We don't have a vacancy for a buyer at the moment. I'd like you to be in our gown showroom until one comes up. Would you agree to this?'

Irene agreed readily – it was better than staying at home all day. Mr Heyworth explained that the accessories buyer, Miss Hayward, was coming up to retirement, and Irene could have the job when she left.

Irene had never been to Heyworth's before and liked the fact that it was a small, family-run ladies' department store, much smaller than the large store she had worked at before. It had a more intimate, friendly feel about it, while retaining a formal and professional air. She felt she would feel happy working there with the beautiful outfits and accessories.

After leaving the store, she called in at Lloyds Bank, where Peter worked as a cashier. She wanted to tell him her good news and hoped he would approve. She went up to his counter, and when he saw his wife dressed in her best suit, his jaw dropped. 'Where are you going?'

Irene replied mysteriously, 'It's where I've been …'

And then she couldn't hold back any longer and blurted out, 'I've got a job!'

Peter's face fell. But when Irene told him that she would be earning £8 10s a week, his face lit up. It was hard to turn down that kind of money.

'That's fantastic news, darling. Congratulations!'

'It's just that I'm so bored sitting at home all day doing nothing. And the extra money will come in handy,' Irene told him excitedly. 'I start next week.'

*

Irene was one of six children born in June 1921 to Nora and Harry Fiander in the picturesque village of Canford Magna, Dorset.

She had an idyllic, carefree childhood and was a bit of a tomboy. Being born between her two brothers, Ronnie and Philip, she spent more time running around with them, climbing trees and swimming in the river, than playing with her elder sisters, Ivy, Phyllis and Nora.

When Irene was three, her father started working as a groom and gardener for the distinguished landowner Sir Arthur Read on his estate in nearby Kingston Lacy. The house had beautiful gardens with espalier fruit trees trained up the walls. A three-bedroomed cottage came with the job and the family lived there happily.

Although they were poor, they always had a meal on the table and clothes to wear. Despite money being tight, Irene's house-proud mother never complained. She was a very quiet woman who never raised her voice or got cross with her large brood. Irene inherited her mother's patience and gentle manners – a quietness and calmness – having learned from her the benefits they can reap.

Sometimes Irene went to Sir Arthur's big house with her mother. Nora was friendly with the nanny who worked there looking after his children, Lady Helen and Master James. Lady Helen was around the same age as Irene, and the nanny passed down her young charges' unwanted clothes to her.

'Thank you, this is beautiful,' said Irene's mother, accepting the clothes gratefully. The nanny had given her a brown-and-white gingham dress with a broderie anglaise trimming around the neck and bottom. It became one of Irene's favourite dresses, and the nanny continued to send her Lady Helen's cast-offs after Sir Arthur Read and his family later moved away.

Irene and her mother only ever visited the servants' quarters. Her mother was also friendly with the parlour-maid who worked there, a girl called Alice, who once scared the living daylights out of Irene.

The servants used a black paraffin stove for heating, and when the four-year-old Irene went near it one day, Alice called out, 'Don't go near that. There's an old bogey man in there!'

Irene leaped backwards, terrified of what might happen if she ventured too close to the stove. Alice had only intended to warn her so she didn't burn herself, but Irene remained frightened of black stoves for a long time afterwards.

The experience did not put Irene off liking Alice, who thrilled her by asking her to be her bridesmaid. It was a very special occasion for a young child and an opportunity to dress up like no other day. Nora plaited Irene's hair the night before so it would be wavy on the day. When the plaits were removed and Irene slipped into her shell-pink bridesmaid's dress, she felt like a little princess: it was the prettiest dress she had ever worn, and a day she would never forget.

At the Victorian-built village school, Irene listened keenly, enjoyed learning her lessons and excelled at gymnastics. Her talent was spotted by a teacher, who sent her and some other girls for extra coaching with a local celebrity, an actress called Madge Beaumont, who lived nearby in the picture-postcard village of Stapehill.

Madge, who was in her late thirties, was the most flamboyant and glamorous woman Irene had ever seen. She wore very feminine long, floaty dresses and a big, wide-brimmed hat over her blonde hair and was unlike anyone else Irene knew.

Madge trained the girls, gesturing theatrically, to perform gymnastic displays and maypole dancing in the garden of her home, raising funds for the poor 'waifs and strays' she actively supported.

It was exhilarating for Irene to be in the company of such a star. Irene's mother was musical too, and played the piano, but their family sing-songs were mostly confined to Christmas, when they all gathered round and sang with gusto.

When Irene was seven, Sir Arthur Read sold his estate and

moved away, and her family moved on as well, to a hamlet in nearby Canford Bottom. Her father decided this was an opportune moment to train for a new job, something totally different with prospects. Harry joined Dorset County Council and studied for three years to become a surveyor, passing his exams with flying colours, and staying on with the council to develop his career.

Their new home sat on the edge of a wood and they had no running water, only a spring well; a path led from their house through the wood to the well, where they would fill their buckets. Neither did they have gas or electricity, using paraffin lamps downstairs, and carrying candles to bed at night.

Irene and her siblings collected fruit for their mother. In late summer they gathered an abundance of blackberries from the hedgerows, which Nora turned into delicious blackberry and apple jam and blackberry jelly. The hedges were filled with the succulent, dark fruit and, best of all, they were free! There were dozens of jars neatly stacked on a shelf in their very large pantry, labelled with the names of all the different fruits Nora preserved to last them through the winter months: strawberry, raspberry, gooseberry and damson jams sitting alongside their favourite blackberry preserves.

But Nora didn't like cooking in the kitchen in summer, finding it too hot to bake there. Instead, Harry found a stove with an oven that could be used outdoors, and put it in the outdoor washhouse where the copper was kept. Nora cooked there when the weather was warm, with the door wide open for the fresh air to circulate freely.

Nora hardly ever had the chance to put her feet up, except on Sunday afternoons, when Harry would take a deckchair into the woods for her to rest in the cool shade. She never complained about her tireless domestic duties; it was a labour of love for her family.

Saturday night was bath night and the family took it in turns to use the tin bath in the washhouse. Irene's father spent the weekend filling the copper with water for Nora to heat for the Monday wash, making repeated trips to the well to collect enough. When Irene left for school on a Monday morning, she waved goodbye to her mother, who was already busy working in the washhouse. When school had finished, she returned home to see her mother still hard at work with the washing, making sure the linens were spotlessly white. When everything was dry, she used a flat iron to make their laundry crisp and immaculate before putting it all away.

Irene helped with the dusting, and her mother, a perfectionist, would check her work afterwards, running her fingers along the surfaces to make sure Irene had done a good job.

As a child, Irene spent many happy hours running around the centuries-old Fox and Hounds pub in Wimborne, run by her grandmother, Maggie Toomer. When Harry helped out there, Irene joined him and loved running up the winding, creaking staircase that opened into three bedrooms, one room leading through to the other two. The beer barrels were stored along the passageway, and the pub had lots of nooks and crannies for Irene to play hide and seek. It was a popular pub with locals, who could satisfy their appetites with bread, cheese and pickles with the beer if they felt peckish.

On bank holidays the family would often head to the beach, catching a bus to Bournemouth, six miles from where they lived. They'd trudge through the crowds to find a spot to spread out their picnic, sit back and soak up the sun in deckchairs. Irene's father would tie a handkerchief – knotted at the corners to stop it blowing off – round his head to protect it. Irene and her brothers and sisters loved those idyllic days on the beach, making sandcastles with their buckets and spades and paddling in the sea, hoping the day would never end.

At fifteen, although Irene had loved school and enjoyed learning, passing her entrance exams for grammar school, it was decided that she'd have to leave, as her parents couldn't afford to buy her the uniform she'd need.

Irene wasn't sure what she wanted to do next, and considered becoming a hairdresser. After discovering that she'd have to pay for her training, she dropped the idea. She wanted to earn money, not pay to learn a trade.

Instead she started work at Corfe Mullen Dairies, where they boiled up milk in big vats to make thick Devon cream. Her duties were in the teashop, but she didn't enjoy it. Being the youngest, she was at everyone's beck and call and quickly got fed up. She wanted to do something more interesting.

Her mother spotted a newspaper advertisement for apprentices at Edwin Jones' department store in Poole. Their head office was in Southampton, but they also had branches in Bournemouth, Poole and Weymouth.

'I think I'll apply and give it a go. It sounds interesting and it's got to be better than what I'm doing now,' Irene told her mother.

Irene's application was successful and she was ecstatic to be offered an apprenticeship by the company at their Poole store, which traded as Bon Marché; it was the biggest store in the town. She was told she would earn 2s 6d a week for the first year, doubling to 5 shillings for the second year and 7s 6d for the third year. The working day was long, as the shop closed at 7 p.m. on Mondays, Tuesdays and Thursdays, not until 8 p.m on Fridays, and 9 p.m. on Saturdays. Wednesday was a half-day.

Irene was sent to work in the hosiery and gloves department, and knew instantly she had made the right decision. She liked fashion, colours and matching outfits and accessories, and couldn't have chosen a more perfect job. As a young child she had always liked pretty clothes, and now she was in her element, surrounded by departments full of the latest fashions and stylish accessories.

Poole was seven miles from Irene's house and in order to reach it, she cycled two miles to Wimborne, where she caught the train into Poole. The journey took no more than twenty minutes in total if she didn't have to hang around waiting for the train. However, coming home in the evenings always took longer.

As she sat at the station platform in Poole waiting for her train home one evening, she was surprised to be approached by Mr Stone, the store manager. It was 7.50 p.m.

'What are you doing here this time of night?' he asked the new junior.

'I missed the earlier train because it left at five to seven, so I'm waiting for the next one at five to eight,' she told him. She had finished work at 7 p.m. that day.

'Well, come and see me in the morning,' he told her, before stepping into his carriage.

Irene fretted all night, worried what the store manager was going to say to her. When she went into his office the following day, he surprised her by saying, 'From now on you can go home a quarter of an hour early every night to catch your train. We can't have you sitting on that platform for an hour.'

As the youngest junior, Irene was expected to carry out the most menial tasks. Miss Proudley, the department's twenty-year-old buyer, told Irene, 'Just watch me and the other sales girls and you can learn from us that way.' She learned how to tidy up after the older shop girls, replacing all the stock that had been taken out and shown to customers, as well as making sure that all the fixtures with garments on display were in order.

One of her jobs was to meticulously put stockings that had been shown to customers back in their packets, with the sheerest stockings requiring the most delicate handling so they did not snag on a fingernail or ring.

Irene got on well with Miss Proudley, who was soon to be married. When Miss Proudley noticed that the collar on her dress was wet one day, she asked Irene to press it with a flat iron. She was still wearing it at the time, and Irene was unsure how to do this.

Heating up the flat iron, Irene placed it straight on the fabric – and heard Miss Proudley let out an agonised cry.

'You've burned me!'

'I'm so sorry,' she apologised profusely, feeling mortified. 'I didn't mean to.'

Irene hadn't thought of placing her hand underneath the collar and holding it out to shield Miss Proudley's skin. She looked aghast at the burn on her neck.

'I'm getting married in a month's time. Now I shall have a big scar on my neck, which everyone will see,' Miss Proudley lamented.

'A month is still a long way away, and I'll see what concealer we can use to cover it up,' replied Irene, who was crestfallen.

Thankfully some New Skin concealer did the trick, and when Miss Proudley's big day arrived, the one-inch scar was barely visible, much to Irene's relief.

One day a customer Irene knew called Hetty came in to Bon Marché and made an unexpected suggestion: 'I've got a brother who I'm sure would like to meet you.'

Hetty, who worked in a munitions factory, liked Irene and also thought a lot of her younger brother; she believed the two of them would get on well. Irene agreed and was introduced to Hetty's brother outside the shop on her way home from work one evening.

Leslie Race was eighteen and walked Irene, who was sixteen, to the station, where she caught her train home. They arranged to meet again. The young couple hit it off and a romance developed. They spent carefree afternoons strolling in the beautiful park in Poole, where a band played, or they went to the cinema.

Leslie was very nice looking, very smart and worked with a firm of butchers. He was quiet and considerate and would always see Irene home on the train if he met up with her after work, walking the two miles from her house to Wimbourne to catch the train back to Poole, where he lived.

Her parents approved of their daughter's suitor and, after a year's courtship, Leslie popped the question when Irene was seventeen, first seeking Irene's father's consent: he readily agreed. Now engaged to be married, Irene thought she would spend the rest of her life with Leslie and that they would live happily ever after.

But it was not to be. Leslie had signed up for war work with the Royal Navy. When he was posted on the *King George V* battleship, he became seriously ill with lung problems. He was put on shore in Aberdeen and admitted to hospital for urgent medical attention. Irene raced there with his anxious parents, catching the sleeper train to be with her fiancé as soon as possible. When they arrived, Leslie was barely conscious. He died the following night from tuberculosis, just a few months after they'd got engaged. Leslie was just twenty; he'd been Irene's first love, and she was devastated.

Irene immersed herself in work to recover from her grief. She had noticed that the shop girls didn't stay long at Bon Marché, especially as many were recruited for vital war work. In 1939, within two years of her starting there, all the senior assistants in her department had moved on and, at the age of eighteen, Irene became a buyer.

It was a rapid promotion, but Irene quickly grasped her new responsibilities, relishing her sudden ascent up the career ladder. The buyers ordered stock for Bon Marché via a central Edwin Jones' wholesale operation, which the company also owned. The wholesaler was based in Southampton in the same premises as Edwin Jones' large department store, thirty miles from Poole. Irene made regular trips there to place her orders for the Poole store.

One morning in the early 1940s, Irene set out on a buying trip to Southampton, thinking it would be no different from her usual buying days. She needed to replenish the shop's supply of silk stockings, which was running low. She could still get rayon and the warmer lisle and woollen stockings for their regular customers, as well as rayon-plated lisle stockings, which had a glossy sheen on them. But the shortage of silk during the war meant pure silk stockings, which women craved, were scarce.

When Irene reached the warehouse, she was totally unprepared for the terrible sight confronting her. She stopped dead in her tracks and looked around in disbelief. The premises had been bombed the night before and reduced to a smouldering pile of rubble. The attack was so recent that news of it had not even reached the store in Poole before she set off on her journey that morning.

'I can't believe it. Where is everyone?' she gasped.

She looked around and spotted some police officers, who directed her to the nearby Dolphin Hotel where the Edwin Jones staff had sought refuge.

'Thank goodness nobody was hurt or killed,' she said. 'I had the most terrible fright when I saw that the building had been burned to the ground.'

It was still very much business as usual, despite the bombing, as staff had scrabbled in the rubble to salvage any stock they could get their hands on. Irene placed her order, although she couldn't get as much stock as she'd originally planned. She was relieved that her journey had not been wasted, and the order was dispatched the following day.

Poole was falling victim to the bombing as well and, during one ferocious attack, the windows at Bon Marché were shattered. Fearing another bombing, a rota was set up for shop girls to guard the store. One Wednesday afternoon when the store closed early, Irene and other young shop girls were asked take their turn, spending the afternoon and night there so they could save as much valuable stock as possible if it was hit.

The girls had practised fire-fighting on the beach at Sandbanks, where a ramshackle shed was put up with an old settee inside. This was set on fire, so they could extinguish the blaze with a bucket of water and a stirrup pump.

Despite the training, Irene was terrified when her turn came to stay at the store, her heart thumping and her ears straining for the sound of aircraft overhead. She desperately hoped the German bombers would stay away. Fortunately, they made it through the night unscathed.

The following year, on 13 October 1941, Irene left Bon Marché. She was twenty and felt it was her turn now, like many shop girls before her, to volunteer for war work. She believed that if she didn't, she would be called up and put in a women's munitions factory, when she had set her heart on joining the Women's Auxiliary Air Force.

She applied and her wish was granted when she was assigned to the WAAF's equipment section. After training, her first posting was to a balloon centre in Titchfield, Hampshire. Large tethered barrage balloons were used to defend against low-level aircraft attack and Irene provided the crew with the equipment needed.

In March 1943 she was transferred to RAF Scampton in Lincolnshire with the equipment section, where her unit issued the air crew with essential items needed for flying missions. She was assigned to distribute one particular item: it would be either clothing or pilots' watches, as well as navigation equipment or even special parts for the aircraft. As she handed over the item, she never knew where the missions were going to take place, or whether she would see the crew alive again.

She loved her war work and the people she met. One Sunday evening she was invited into the sergeants' mess for drinks. One of the officers in charge of the photographic section offered Irene a challenge: 'If you can drink two double whiskies I'll give you ten shillings.'

Irene accepted the challenge without giving it a second thought, full of bravado and keen to win the money, even though she had never drunk whisky before in her life.

The officer handed her the measured whiskies, she threw back her head, pouring the alcohol straight down her throat without any hesitation, one after the other.

'That was an easy way of making ten bob,' she told the officer, who laughed and handed over the money. She couldn't believe how easy it had been – and she was still standing, too!

But when she walked outside, the alcohol hit her like a brick. She was dizzy and unsteady on her feet, feeling sick and wretched. She couldn't undress herself when she reached her hut and lay on her bed watching the ceiling spinning around. She had never felt so ill in her life. The experience remained firmly in her mind and she vowed that she would never touch another drop of spirits.

In May that year, the men from 617 Squadron lined up before her and other women in her unit: nineteen planes and their pilots needed to be equipped before embarking on their latest secret mission. So secret were the plans that the battle order pinned up on the RAF noticeboard that day was entitled 'Night Flying Programme' to make it seem like a normal training run to the men.

The crews were informed of their mission – codenamed Operation Chastise – only four hours before the planes took off for Germany's Ruhr Valley. They had been assigned to fly the daring 'Dambusters' raid.

Irene knew none of this as she and the other girls handed over the equipment. They later learned of its success, how their brave pilots had caused catastrophic flooding and wiped out scores of armament factories. But the success came at a high price; fifty-six of the 133 crew who left Scampton that day didn't return: fifty-three were lost and three were taken prisoner of war.

Some of the girls from Irene's section were faced with the heart-breaking task of sending the personal belongings of the dead crew to their families and returning their equipment to the store. It was the most devastating duty they were faced with, and Irene was thankful that it was not part of her work. For this reason, the girls in the WAAF tried not to fall in love with one of the aircrew. They knew the risks involved with the airmen's work; that one night you would be out with them, and the next day they could be gone for ever.

Irene couldn't help having a soft spot for one of the airmen, an Australian navigator called Archie. One day she received sad news: Archie was among the crew who didn't make the return journey back to Scampton after flying off on another daring mission. It was devastating, but Irene knew this was the cold reality of war, and it didn't do for the girls to get attached to the pilots, however handsome they were.

After the Dambusters raid, Irene and her comrades at the WAAF were moved away from Scampton, for fear of reprisal air attacks. They set up base in a village about six miles away called Welton, sleeping in little huts with only a coke fire in the centre, which they gathered around, shivering for warmth in the winter. Their outdoor wash-hut had only primitive facilities and Irene had to wash in cold water each day.

While washing there one morning, Irene noticed that her chest was covered in red spots. She had no idea what it could be. As she had planned a trip home to Dorset to see her brother, who had been hit by a sniper in Germany while serving with the Dorsetshire Regiment, she thought she'd get her spots looked at then by the local doctor.

On the packed train home to Dorset, Irene found a seat. The man sitting opposite kept staring at her. Eventually he asked, 'Have you looked in the mirror lately?'

'No, why do you ask?' replied Irene, having no idea what he meant.

'Well, you look just like a turkey cock!' he replied. 'You're covered in spots – your face is all red.'

Irene dug into her handbag for a compact mirror. She was appalled to see that the spots had worsened considerably and she was now anxious to be seen by a doctor as quickly as possible. By the time she arrived back at Wimborne, she had developed a raging temperature. Her anxious mother immediately called the family doctor, an ambulance was called, and Irene, feeling very weak and feverish, was carried out on a stretcher and driven to Alderney Isolation Hospital in Poole, a hospital where servicemen and women were treated.

'I'm afraid you've got measles,' the doctor told Irene after examining her. 'You'll need to stay here and recuperate.'

'Oh no, how could that have happened? I have no idea where I could've caught it from,' said Irene, aghast at the diagnosis.

Although measles could be fatal, Irene wasn't worried, believing she was in good hands. Soon after she was admitted, her anxious mother and sister came to visit, but were not allowed on the ward. Matron told them firmly, 'Sorry, you can't see Irene. Measles is very contagious.'

They could only look helplessly at Irene through a window. Irene smiled back feebly and mouthed some reassuring words, 'I'm all right – don't worry about me.'

Her days were spent resting under the watchful eye of matron. After a week, Irene was relieved to see the spots had vanished. She felt much better, much more like her usual self. Matron, noticing how Irene's complexion had cleared up, suggested to her patient, 'It's a lovely day, why don't you go outside?'

Irene nodded and stepped outside. It felt good to feel the fresh air on her face after being confined to bed for a week. Within moments she was joined by a handsome young man. Matron had also gone up to him and made the same suggestion, saying, 'There's a lovely WAAF outside. Why don't you go and say hello?'

The man introduced himself as Peter Dean, and the pair went for a walk across some heathland. Peter had dark hair, grey eyes and a warm smile that captivated Irene.

As they walked, Peter told her that he was a lieutenant in the Royal Marines, stationed at Westcliff-on-Sea in Essex. While escorting a prisoner from the Marines to Hamworthy in Poole, he noticed he was covered in spots and was sent to the same hospital to recover. Every day for the next week they took a walk arm in arm, and Irene realised she was falling for Peter, attracted by his gentlemanly ways and lovely voice, his sense of humour and his dashing, handsome looks. She hoped Peter felt the same way.

Now, at the end of their second week at the isolation hospital, they were both fully recovered from their infections and the time had come for them to go their separate ways. Although they had only known each other a week, it was a terrible wrench to be parted. It was March 1944 and they were still in active war service.

'I'll write to you – we'll see each other again,' Peter promised, as they said farewell.

As Peter held her and they kissed, Irene hoped with all her heart that he would return safely from the war.

'I'll write to you, too. I shall miss you so much,' she told him, her eyes moist. They had no idea when they would see each other again.

A short while later Peter was posted thousands of miles away to Burma. Allied forces in the British Commonwealth, the United States and China were fighting against Japan with the Allies, who were preparing to launch large-scale offensives into Japanese-occupied Burma.

Irene worried about him constantly. Peter kept his word and wrote to Irene almost every day, pledging his love and describing his life in Burma and the harsh conditions he endured. It made harrowing reading for Irene, back in Scampton, whose love for Peter continued to grow during his absence.

Peter did not hold back his feelings. On 6 January 1945, Irene received an airmail letter from him that made her the happiest woman in the world. It sealed the love they both felt for each other and she knew they would be together for ever.

The front of the letter was stamped with the usual security warning, 'Think before you write'. Irene opened it eagerly and read the heart-touching words from the man she loved:

My Very Own Darling,

Quite an event this afternoon, I received a letter from you – the first mail I have had since Xmas. I was very glad to hear that my mail was reaching you again, sweetheart.

Now to tell you what has been happening to us in this part of the world. As I said in my last letter, we've been working hard getting our craft seaworthy again, storing up ammunition, food and water. We worked at this until we were sick and fed up with the sight of it.

But last night when we packed up we had our craft on top line.

Then the trouble hit us. During the night we 'stopped' a cyclone and boy did it rain and blow. I've been in some gales before but nothing like last night. The rain just lashed our cabin and we were more or less soaked. Late for breakfast this morning, so we had no food. That in itself was bad enough, but worse was to come. When we got down to the jetty we found much to our horror that all out craft had broken adrift. We found three on the beach, two more piled up, others floating out to sea and my particular craft moored alongside a warship. Apparently the crew had salvaged her early this morning and were trying to claim her as a prize. Needless to say that didn't work. Things were in a shocking state and we were right back where we started. However, something had to be done, so we set to work to get things put right again. We had dinner on board – corned beef, cold beans, cheese and ship's biscuits and water whilst still slogging away.

Then, at 1.45 I was told that my craft had to be ready to move off at 3. Back to camp we rushed, packed all our gear and got back on board again, only to be told that the move had been cancelled. Once again we trailed back and unpacked once more. That is the state of things at the moment darling and we are keeping our fingers crossed in the hope that it doesn't blow up rough again tonight.

Have had a cold water bath this evening – quite an achievement. I am ashamed to say that we haven't had a bath now for over two months. Apparently out here one is expected to wash in about 2 pints of water daily. After working all day on the craft, putting all our stores on board and also down in the engine-room, you can appreciate darling that we aren't very clean and at times we've had to wash in water from a ditch.

Certainly sweetheart, living conditions couldn't be worse than the ones we are existing under at the moment. It certainly makes one appreciate the comforts of home.

The savings campaign is going on fine. This year I have spent 3/- on 100 English cigarettes and 16 packets of chewing gum. Quite cheap, don't you think sweetheart.

Well darling that just about brings me to the end of my news – such as it is. Now to answer your letter.

Yes darling, I would love you to act as my nurse, but on thinking, it would be best if you stayed back in England. I have seen what happens to the majority of white girls who come out here and I thank God that you are back there safely and waiting for me. As I said before darling, it is a great comfort to me to know that you are there thinking about me and praying for my return. May that joyful day when we meet again be very soon and then we can take up our courtship again. By the way darling, do you think you could put up with me and become Mrs Dean? I only hope so, as that is one of my greatest longings in life.

As for the question about the photograph sweetheart, I promise that as soon as we reach civilisation again I will have it taken and send it on to you. I know that you appreciate that I can't do anything about it in this desolate spot.

I will write to you as often as I can my dearest one, you know that you are forever in my thoughts. I pray that God may take care of you for me and that we may enjoy our future together, just you and I.

In case you have forgotten darling, let me reassure you that I love you with all my heart and ask nothing better than your whole love in return.

Goodnight, my precious one.

<u>All</u> my fondest and dearest love,

Ever your devoted,

Peter xxxxxxxxxxxxxxxxxxxxxxxxx

Irene's eyes filled with tears as she read Peter's loving words and tender proposal. Although they had only spent a week together before being parted, Irene knew without any doubt that Peter was the man she wanted to marry and spend the rest of her life with. It had been a fortuitous coincidence that their paths crossed at the same isolation hospital, thanks to the matchmaking of a kindly and romantic matron who thought they'd make the perfect couple.

She wrote back immediately, accepting his proposal, telling him she was the happiest woman in the world and couldn't wait till they saw each other again. Within months she was wearing his engagement ring. It had been delivered to her personally by a fellow marine who had returned to England to resume his work as a police officer.

Irene clasped the ring tightly against her heart. Peter had bought a gold nugget and yellow topaz stone in Bombay while on leave and had had the ring made there. It had been presented to her in a round cigarette tin and was the most beautiful ring she had ever seen.

After the war ended and Irene was demobbed, she returned to her old job as a buyer with Edwin Jones in Poole, counting the days till she could be reunited with her fiancé. Her dream came true in May 1946 – two years and two months after they had parted.

Irene had already met Peter's mother and sister, Rita, who shared a house in Cambridge. After the couple got engaged, Peter's mother wrote and invited Irene, who was still at Scampton, to spend Christmas 1945 with them. Gladys had not long been widowed at the age of fifty-three, her husband had died of a heart attack while Peter was in Burma. Rita worked as a nurse at Mill Road maternity hospital in Cambridge and both women warmly welcomed Irene into their home in Cherry Hinton Road, keenly exchanging the latest news of Peter in the Far East.

Soon after Irene had been demobbed, the day Irene had longed for arrived: Peter was demobbed too, and returned to England. Gladys had made a special request to Irene, which she felt she couldn't turn down. 'Would you mind if we had Peter to ourselves for his first two days back home? His father died while he was away and we need some time on our own together.'

Irene understood and agreed. She had waited all this time, and could wait another two days.

Peter planned to meet Irene at Cambridge station. Although tremendously excited, she felt slightly apprehensive too, after all, they'd only actually spent a week together, and had conducted the rest of their relationship through letters.

Her train arrived early. She looked around the station and couldn't see Peter. Rather than wait, she decided to jump into a taxi and go to his house. They had only driven a few yards out of the station when Irene spotted Peter. He was dashing down the road and she asked the taxi driver to stop immediately.

Her fiancé looked even more handsome in his blue uniform than she remembered. Her heart was racing as Peter jumped into the taxi next to her.

'I've waited for this moment so long,' he said. 'You're more beautiful than I remember you,' he told her as they embraced.

Irene knew instantly that she had made the right decision in agreeing to be his wife; she was happier than she could have imagined in her wildest dreams.

'I'm so happy to see you too. It's been so long,' she told him smiling, her heart thumping. 'Now the war is over, we need never be parted again.'

It was now their work and homes in different towns that kept them apart, with Irene living in Dorset and Peter resuming his work as a cashier with Lloyds Bank in Cambridge, 155 miles away from his beloved.

They met up whenever they could, but because it could take up to eight hours to travel between their two homes, they only managed to see each other infrequently. These special days were often spent enjoying the beautiful surroundings of palm-fringed Torquay, and the resort became their favourite.

Their big day was set for March 1948, two years after Peter returned home from Burma. Irene, who was twenty-six, looked radiant in her long pale pink embossed satin wedding dress. She chose this shade instead of white as she had a pale complexion and wanted to wear a dress with some colour. She had a tiny figure, and although she was 5 feet 4½ inches, she weighed only 7 stone 6 lb and had a slender 24-inch waist. A halo of carnations in her hair and a bouquet of carnations completed her wedding ensemble.

That day Irene felt she was the happiest woman in the world, married to a wonderful man who was handsome, romantic and clever – and could make her laugh too.

The happy couple honeymooned in Torquay, which already held many special memories for them, and began married life in Cambridge, living with Peter's mother and sister. They never considered living anywhere else, as paying their lodgings would help Gladys financially and they'd be able to save up for their own place at the same time. A regular routine soon emerged, with Peter's mother happily cooking a hot lunch each day while Irene provided the tea – something light, such as scrambled eggs on toast. They all pooled their war rations to cook more satisfying meals. But Irene soon began to feel restless and bored, missing the buzz of working. She had never considered what it would be like to be a housewife, despite how much she loved Peter.

Neither had it entered her head to look for work – until the day she went for a hair appointment with Frank Bendall. She was very grateful that he offered to put a word in for her at his Rotarians lunch.

When the call from Heyworth's came later that day and she nearly jumped out of her skin, Irene knew she desperately wanted to be a shop girl once again.

'When can you start?' Herbert Heyworth asked her.

'Next week if you like,' she replied, thrilled that she'd be returning to the work she loved.

BETTY

1949

B etty could have wept with joy.

'Mrs Lipscombe, the job is yours. We look forward to seeing you next Monday.' Herbert Heyworth smiled at the smartly dressed woman sitting opposite him.

'Thank you, Mr Heyworth. I'm very grateful,' replied Betty, a broad smile lighting up her face.

Betty had never wanted a job so badly. After a short-lived, painful marriage, she had taken her eight-month-old baby daughter, Jennifer, and gone back to live with her parents.

She needed a job quickly to pay for their upkeep and was hopeful that her previous experience as a shop girl would help her get her foot in the door at Heyworth's ladies' department store in Cambridge, one of the most upmarket stores in the town.

Betty rushed home to share her good news with her mother.

'I'm going to work in their millinery department; I start next week,' she said.

'Oh Betty, that's such wonderful news. I'm so happy for you,' Mabel told her eldest daughter, delighted at her success. 'You know I'll look after Jennifer – don't worry about her.'

Betty looked across the room at her father. He said nothing; he didn't even look up from his newspaper, but this didn't surprise Betty. Lewis never had a kind word for his daughter, while her mother was the opposite – she was all softness and love, which helped make growing up with a cold and distant father more bearable.

Mabel adored her chubby granddaughter with her golden smile. Jennifer was the easiest baby to look after, too; she was always happy and gurgling contentedly. Mabel couldn't resist picking up her grandchild in her arms and cuddling her, enjoying the silky softness of her skin. And, of course, she wanted to help Betty in any way she could, following the collapse of her daughter's marriage.

'Thanks, Mum. I really appreciate it. And I'm so grateful to Irene for suggesting me to Mr Heyworth for the job,' said Betty.

Irene Dean lived around the corner from Betty with her husband Peter, a bank cashier she'd married the previous year, following a wartime romance. After starting at Heyworth's as a shop girl in the fashion showroom, Irene had become pregnant within months of starting her job, but was thrilled to return to the store as their accessories buyer when her baby, Patricia, was three months old. She felt bored and restless stuck at home.

Jennifer and Patricia were born within three months of each other and the two women soon struck up a friendship. Jennifer was always a picture of glowing contentment, in sharp contrast to Patricia, who yelled and pulled at the straps in her pram.

Irene knew Betty was looking for a job and immediately thought of her when she heard about the vacancy.

'Heyworth's is looking for someone to work in their millinery department, would you be interested?' Irene had asked. 'I mentioned you to Mr Heyworth and he said he'd like to see you.'

'Oh yes, I would,' replied Betty keenly, even though she knew nothing at all about hats. 'I've worked in a shop before, so have experience.'

Betty knew how much Irene enjoyed working at Heyworth's and was keen to find a job as soon as possible to provide for herself and her baby daughter while living under her parents' roof. Her father had made it plain that she could not live there without paying for their keep, and she fervently hoped that Heyworth's would be the answer to her prayers.

Shop work had been her main job since leaving school at fifteen in 1939. She was used to working with high-class clientele too – the kind who shopped at Heyworth's – as she had been taken on as a junior at Cambridge's finest grocery store, Matthew's, suppliers to the university as well as the townspeople. She'd then signed up for war work but returned to Matthew's again after being demobbed.

Betty was slightly apprehensive, as she had never set foot in Heyworth's before her interview; it was far too posh for her and her mother. But Betty knew she was a hard worker and was determined to succeed – for Jennifer's sake – even if it meant that at twenty-five she'd have to start at the bottom of the ladder again as a junior, working alongside other juniors much younger than her.

Betty put her father's harshness down to the long hours he worked. He'd never been able to show her love or give her a kiss, or offer a kind word to her as she grew up.

His strict ways were a contrast to his pleasant appearance. Lewis was a nice-looking man, tall, fair-haired and with blue eyes. He was born in the Cotswolds and served with the Royal Flying Corps during the First World War as a driver. After the war he was unable to find work in the Cotswolds, where his father had been a carpenter, but in 1922 began working as a driver for a flour-mill company in Coventry, and was transferred to Cambridge when they opened a mill near the town's railway station.

Lewis found lodgings with Betty's grandmother, Elizabeth, who had bought a new house and let out her back bedroom to bring in some extra money. She was a wonderful woman, standing at only 5 feet 2 inches, and had three children – Lily, Mabel and Walter. It was dark-haired Mabel who caught Lewis's eye, and they later married.

Lewis worked hard to provide for his family, scrimping and saving his wages. His boss was a demanding and mean-spirited man. During the winter months when the ground was covered in snow, Lewis had to climb a slippery wooden ladder, its rungs covered in ice, until he reached the loft, where he picked up heavy bags of flour, flung them over his shoulder and tentatively carried them down the perilous rungs to load up on his lorry. Lewis could easily have slipped and worried that he might lose his grip and fall. But his boss had no sympathy, speaking sharply to Lewis and other workmen if they complained: 'There's a queue at the gates if you don't like it. There's always someone else who will do your job. Just get on with it.'

During the summers Betty looked forward to joining her father in his cab on his delivery trips around the country; it was one of her few happy childhood memories with him. Lewis didn't use maps to find his way from A to B – he used pubs as familiar landmarks, making a mental note of every pub he passed en route. If asked for directions, he would say, 'It's the first left past the Red Lion, or turn right at the Fox and Hounds.' This proved valuable knowledge in the Cambridgeshire village of Sawston, where there were fourteen pubs on the high street – it would have been impossible to direct people there without referring to them!

Mabel never knew how much her husband earned; he never told her. Even up until the day she died, she still didn't know. Lewis would be paid on a Saturday afternoon at the end of his morning shift, when he finished work for the week, and he handed Mabel the housekeeping when he returned home that afternoon. Come each Saturday morning, the housekeeping money was virtually all gone. Betty's worried mother fretted about how she could put a hot dinner on the table that lunchtime, their main meal of the day, ready for when her husband returned home from work hungry. 'I don't know what we're going to have for dinner today because I've only got sixpence in my purse until your father gets home.' Somehow she miraculously managed to stretch it out and cook a tasty meal with half a pound of sausages for the three of them.

Betty came home from school one day and asked her mother for one penny. 'It's for the starving children in Ethiopia; we're having a collection.'

'Well I haven't got a penny to spare,' replied her mother, who struggled each week to put food on her own family's table.

Betty was desperate for the penny, and eventually her mother found one to give her, as she refused to give in. It made Betty feel so proud when she could hand over the money to her school teacher the following day.

By carefully squirrelling away his money and saving hard, as well as receiving a legacy from his father, Lewis had enough money to put down a deposit on the house next door but one to Betty's beloved grandmother at 5 Derby Road.

When Betty was seven years old, she was thrilled to have a baby sister, Joyce, join the family. As they grew up, their father knew how to strike fear into their young hearts. He kept a stick by his chair and would flick it through the air, making a sharp whooshing sound as a warning if he felt they were misbehaving; this threat always worked, as the sight of it in his hand sent shivers down their spines, though he never struck them with it.

Betty could not understand why her father was so harsh with them. He seemed so different from his gentle sister, her maiden aunt, Amy. Every birthday she popped a ten-shilling note in Betty's birthday card, but Betty never kept the money. As soon as she opened the card, the money was quickly taken off her by her father. He gave the crisp note to her mother, who used it to buy shoes or clothes for Betty; she was never able to spend her birthday money as she wished, or save it. There were no presents for Betty from her parents.

Betty always enjoyed visits from Aunt Amy, who would sometimes stay with them during her holidays. If her kindly aunt heard Betty's father being unkind to her, she would see the hurt look on her niece's face and scold her brother, saying, 'Lewis, stop picking on the young girl.'

Her pleas fell on deaf ears. Nothing anyone said made any difference, and Betty felt she could never do anything right in her father's disapproving eyes.

At Christmas their stocking was stuffed with the familiar orange and sugar mouse, a penny coin, and, if they were lucky, a packet of crayons and a colouring book. When she was eight, Betty asked for a pair of shoes to wear for church. They went to church every Sunday morning and to Sunday school in the afternoon. She wore her best Sunday clothes, which she hung up in the wardrobe as soon as she returned home. Betty had set her heart on owning a pair of black patent ankle-strap shoes, the same as the other young girls wore at Sunday school. She crossed her fingers and fervently hoped that her wish would come true.

When the day arrived, she excitedly ripped open the present handed to her. She could not believe her eyes. A feeling of immense disappointment welled up inside her as she looked at the longed-for gift in her hands. Instead of the black patent shoes she had dreamed of wearing, she had been given brown leather shoes instead. She was devastated.

'Why have I got brown shoes instead of black?' asked Betty, with a sinking heart, the disappointment clearly etched across her face.

'Because they'll clean up better. Black patent splits, but with brown leather, you can put polish on and clean them,' her father told her, oblivious to the distress he had caused. Betty was mortified. She had no choice but to wear them. Her father had to be obeyed and she never dreamed of challenging him or complaining.

While Sundays were spent at church, Betty ran errands for her father on Saturdays. It was her job to take their radio accumulators to a depot to be charged; an accumulator was like a battery, which provided the power to pick up the airwaves. It cost sixpence to charge them up and they had two, so that one fully-charged accumulator could be used when the other one had run out.

Betty's house had no electricity, just gas wall lights downstairs and a candle in her bedroom. She liked to watch the shadows on the wall that the flame created. When Betty carried the candle upstairs at night, she held it with a steady hand and was always very careful, particularly if a draught made the flame flicker, in case it caught on something close by and started a fire. When she was a child, her parents came up and extinguished the flame each night, but when Betty was older and was trusted to do this herself, she pressed the burning flame together with her thumb and first finger to extinguish it, careful to do it very quickly so she did not burn herself.

When electricity became available in the 1950s, Betty's father only agreed to provide it downstairs, saying firmly, 'You don't need electricity upstairs in the bedroom.' He thought that was a waste of money.

Betty enjoyed school, but as her parents could not afford to pay for the uniform and books she would need at grammar school if she passed her exams, she was not encouraged to stay on. At the end of one summer term, she brought her school report home in a brown envelope and placed it on the table. Her father picked it up and read the teachers' comments, where they described Betty's work as 'adequate' or 'could do better'.

But there was one subject at which Betty excelled – physical education – and the teacher had written: 'excellent, good team leader'.

Betty was thrilled to receive such high praise, but her father thought otherwise. He slammed the report down furiously on the table and told her, 'That's all you're bloody fit for – jumping and jigging about!'

Despite her hurt feelings, Betty hid her frustrations. She never dared answer her father back, and always accepted his word.

Betty's love of sports soon included swimming. When she was around thirteen years old, she loved to walk to the River Cam in Newnham, where the river banks were flanked with weeping willows as it wound its way to Grantchester. It was a beautiful spot, popular with families out having a picnic. She would watch the kids swimming there and one day decided to take the plunge herself and join them.

A tributary that led into the River Cam was enclosed for public swimming. Changing huts were placed on each side of the bank; on one side for boys and the opposite for girls. Betty could hear the squeals of laughter and splashing sounds as she approached the swimming area, known locally as the Snobs, where she handed over her admission fee; there was an additional charge for swimming lessons.

The temperature of the river's water was displayed at the entrance of their 'pool', running alongside meadowland called Sheep's Green. The stream was slow moving, and during a good summer the water warmed up beautifully. At the beginning or end of the season, the river was chilly and Betty shivered as she dipped her toes into the water.

Betty couldn't afford to pay for lessons, but she watched and listened closely as the swimming teacher shouted out his instructions, and that's how she learned to swim. She watched as a boy strapped a harness around his waist and held tightly on to a long pole that the instructor held out; he walked up and down the river bank, pulling the child along. The boy gingerly lifted his feet off the bottom and reached his arms out in front of him, splashing them in and out of the water, thrilled that he could stay afloat with his doggy paddle, and having the time of his life.

Betty soon mastered the strokes and was as proud as punch that she had learned to swim without any tuition. She was tested by the instructor, who watched her successfully swim 15 yards, and presented her with a certificate to mark her achievement.

'Look, Mum, Dad! I've passed my swimming test. Here's my certificate to prove it!' she told them, her chest swelling with pride. While Betty's adoring mother heaped praise on her daughter, there was no acknowledgement at all from her father for her moment of glory.

Children always swam in the stream under the watchful eye of an instructor, but after they could swim 50 yards, they were told they could progress to the main river. Betty didn't do enough swimming to pass her 50-yard swimming test.

'I don't fancy going in there anyway,' she told her mum. 'All the boys keep jumping off the bridge into the river!'

Betty was two months short of her fifteenth birthday when Britain declared war on Germany on 3 September 1939. Her father built an Anderson shelter at the end of the garden to protect them from bombings, which struck Cambridge from the following year.

In June 1940, ten people died in a bombing raid that flattened houses in Vicarage Terrace and, within months, other parts of the town were demolished by bombs too. On 15 February 1941, Betty heard the terrifying sound of the siren warning them of imminent attack, and the family fled for shelter. It was three months before the London Blitz.

The previous month, two people had been killed during air attacks in Mill Road and a month later the bombers struck close to Betty's home. The reason for this was clear. Betty lived a stone's throw from the cattle market at the top of Cherry Hinton Road, which German bombers were targeting that evening. During the war it was being used as a holding depot by British military for their anti-aircraft tanks and army vehicles, and the enemy wanted to wreck it.

'Go on, get down to the bunker,' Betty's father shouted urgently, listening to the siren's persistent wailing sound.

'I don't like it down there! I'm not going. It's damp and dark and horrible!' replied Betty stubbornly.

She dived under the dining-room table instead. Lewis called out, 'Well, make sure you stay there, then. I'm just going to check on Mrs Chapman.'

Whenever the rising and falling sound of the siren went off, Lewis dashed to check on their elderly widowed neighbour, a friend of Mabel's. Mrs Chapman's son was serving in the army and her daughter was married and living elsewhere. When the piercing siren made its screeching sound, Lewis showed a rarely seen thoughtful side by escorting the elderly lady to his house.

She took shelter in a cupboard under the stairs, sitting on a chair until it was all over. Betty's mother joined her, and the two women huddled together. They listened, terrified, to the droning sound of the overhead aircraft and the whistling noise made as incendiaries were dropped. It sounded very close; too close for comfort.

Mrs Chapman and Mabel also refused to use the Anderson shelter. They'd tried it a couple of times, but felt trapped inside and preferred their own hideaways in the house, believing they would be safe and protected if the ceiling collapsed. The women, Joyce and Betty were left in the house as Lewis went out on fire-watch duty, looking for incendiaries.

They would remain in their positions until they heard the all-clear sound, a single, continuous note, confirming that the skies were clear of enemy aircraft.

They discovered just how lucky they had been soon after the most recent raid. One of the bombs had exploded in a garden around the corner in Cherry Hinton Road – just a few yards away from Betty's home. Miraculously, nobody in Derby Road died. Others were not so lucky that night. Eleven people died during ferocious air attacks in her neighbourhood – in Cherry Hinton Road, Hills Road and Cambridge Place. The Germans had missed their target, the nearby cattle market.

Betty surveyed the damage incredulously, shocked and shaken. Their windows had been blown inwards, and it was impossible to walk down Cherry Hinton Road and Derby Road, which resembled a ploughed field, with the gardens blasted out. Betty couldn't wait for the day when she could sign up and do her bit for the war.

When it was time for her to leave school, aged fourteen, her mother found her a job at the end of the road in Golding's grocery shop; it was Betty's first shop job.

'It will suit you just right – it's only down the road,' her mother told her, and Betty obediently complied.

The Goldings were a joyless couple in their sixties, and looked ancient to Betty. They had no children so were not used to having young girls around the place and Mrs Golding expected Betty to work hard for her pay, instructing her coldly, 'We expect you to clean the shelves and inside the house, too. And don't forget to do a good job with the brass taps.'

Betty couldn't stand her job, or the Goldings. She endured it for a few weeks, until she could take no more. She felt she was being treated like a skivvy, and it wasn't real shop work at all. She also wished she could work with other young people, instead of spending the whole day with an old couple, and working her fingers to the bone for them.

'I hate it there. I'm not going back,' she told her mother one day, deciding she'd had enough and could face it no more.

Her mother understood, saying, 'Go into town and see what other job you can find.'

It was fairly easy to find new work. She found a junior's job at Matthew's, a prominent grocery store in the heart of Cambridge, facing Trinity College. Her tasks involved making endless trips to the storeroom and filling up the shelves. It was so very different from Golding's corner shop, and she felt happier there working with people her own age. Matthew's had an air of refinement about it, with a high-class clientele.

Before Betty started work at Matthew's each morning, she had another job to complete first – a newspaper round she had taken on to earn more money. At the end of the week she handed over the bulk of her earnings to her mother; if she had earned 12 shillings, her mother would have 10 shillings towards Betty's keep.

As Betty experienced her first taste of independence, she was becoming increasingly unhappy at home. Her father seemed unreasonably strict: he'd made it clear that wearing lipstick was forbidden, even though Betty hadn't considered wearing it. He thought only 'tarts' wore lipstick, and told her he wouldn't have any of that 'muck' in his house.

Betty felt she could only be happy if she left home, and there was only one way she could do this: by signing up for war work. She counted the days to her seventeenth birthday in November 1941 and, as soon as the big day arrived, walked into the recruiting office in Cambridge to enlist.

'I've come to sign up. I want to put my name down for the Auxiliary Territorial Service,' she told the officer sitting at his desk.

He looked at her youthful face. 'How old are you?'

'I've just turned seventeen,' she replied.

'Well, you need to be seventeen and a half to sign up. Fill in this form and we'll contact you then.'

Betty was not expecting to be told this. She felt hugely disappointed: she'd been sure the sign-up age was seventeen. She left her details and walked out despondently. She told her parents about it when she went home that day.

'Are you sure you know what you're doing?' her mother asked her, worried at the thought of Betty signing up so young.

'I've made my mind up and I'm going to sign up,' Betty replied firmly. Her father couldn't have cared less.

The following May she received the letter she was longing for. Her face lit up as she read that she could now join the ATS, the women's branch of the army. She was asked to book a medical with an army doctor in Cambridge, which she passed, and was later instructed to report to a training centre in Northampton – a railway ticket was included.

Before she joined up she went to stay with Uncle Ernest, an engineer, in Kew Gardens, for a week's holiday. She was very fond of him, and he delighted her by giving her 10 shillings. Betty was lost for words, deeply touched by his generosity. It was the first time she had ever had such a large sum of money to keep for herself, even though she had worked hard since leaving school. And, unlike the 10 shillings her Aunt Amy used to send her for her birthday, her father would not get his hands on this note.

Betty returned home and eagerly packed her bags, preparing to leave for war. She felt more upset at leaving her generous uncle behind than her distant father, who had never once showed her such kindness.

When Betty left for her training camp, Mabel hugged her daughter tight. Betty felt sad about leaving her mother and sister behind with her hard-hearted father; she didn't know how Mabel had stood it for so long. Lewis could be severe with Mabel, though Betty never heard them argue. She was a dutiful wife who always had his meals on the table, but he never showed any appreciation.

When she was a teenager, she told her mother, 'Mum, I'll never get like you – I'll never bow down to a man like you do.'

Betty never heard her mother criticise him once; she remained silent if he was cross, showing her sympathy to Betty later on, if she had been upset by him. In those days most women did not leave their husbands and children if they were unhappy at home; they knuckled down and accepted their life, with its imperfections.

'Please take care, I shall miss you so much,' Mabel told her daughter lovingly, as she let go and watched her walk down to the street until she faded out of sight.

Her father didn't say a word; she could be going to Timbuktu for all he cared. Although Betty expected no different, it still hurt to know that he couldn't even wish her well when she was going off to do her bit for her country – and he might never see her again.

As she set off for the railway station, her mind switched to the journey ahead. She was excited about joining the war effort, and pleased to be leaving the unhappiness at home behind her. But she was nervous about taking a train on her own, as she'd never done this before.

Her journey went smoothly, and on the train she met many other young girls who had also signed up. They were all picked up by lorry at Northampton, and were driven to the ATS training centre for their basic training.

Here they were issued with their kit: a dress uniform of khaki tunic suit with brass buttons and epaulettes; battle dress – khaki trousers and shirt; thick denim overalls; and brown shoes. Her underwear included three pairs of bloomers, but Betty grinned when she saw them and exclaimed, 'There's no way I'm wearing those!'

The girls were set exams to determine what sort of war work they'd carry out. Some were made cooks or clerks, but Betty had the excitement of joining an ack-ack battery. The women were never told why they were assigned to different tasks or how well they'd performed in the tests, and neither would they have dreamed of asking about it, or questioning a decision made by their commanding officer.

Ack-ack stands for the letters AA from the British Army's First World War phonetic alphabet. AA meant anti-aircraft, and Betty was commissioned to work as a height-finder.

After three weeks in Northampton, she was given forty-eight hours' leave and returned home. Her dear mum was thrilled to bits to see her daughter walk through the door in her smart uniform – but her father didn't bat an eyelid.

Her battery was moved around different parts of the country. After Northampton, she was sent to Arborfield, near Reading, where her six-week training began. The men in her battery operated the five guns, while the women operated the predictors and height-finders.

Her task was to feed information into a huge predictor machine measuring 7 feet wide: data about the height, range and speed of enemy aircraft flying overhead. This vital information was then passed on to officers in the operations room, where they pored over maps to plan attacks on enemy aircraft.

From here she was posted to the outskirts of Manchester. Coventry had been bombed in 1940, and her battery was sent to protect Manchester against enemy attack.

It was thrilling work. Betty was delighted that she had not ended up with a dull job as a cook or clerk, preferring to see some action and have a more challenging role.

From Manchester she was posted to isolated parts of the coast – to Weybourne in North Norfolk and Bude in Cornwall – to learn more about the techniques required to feed in the range and speed quickly and accurately, using a viewer to spot the aircraft. The information was transmitted electronically to the gun, and they practised firing at moving targets, with Betty calculating the measurements required to shoot it down.

Nothing much happened in Manchester, but there was plenty of action on the Medway in Kent, where Betty was later sent. Here, in Chatham, the sky was filled with ferocious doodlebugs, a bomb with wings, which looked like an aeroplane but had no pilot. They kept flying until they ran out of fuel, then fell to the ground and exploded. They were launched from the French coast and aimed at London. Droves of them were fired at a time, intended to destroy the capital city.

At first nobody at Betty's camp knew what they were. They were mystified and looked up at the sky in utter confusion.

'Don't fire,' they were told, baffled by the fire coming from the back of the overhead missile. The object was not on their signal range, and they could see it was not a German plane. At one point they thought it was a British plane coming home after being attacked.

When Betty's battalion realised what they were and launched their attack on the doodlebugs, heavy shrapnel from their weapons fell on Chatham and Rochester, resulting in complaints from local people that they were causing more damage to their properties than enemy bombs.

It was decided Betty's unit should leave, and they were posted to the Isle of Sheppey, where they continued to attack the doodlebugs. It poured with rain for days and the ground was a quagmire. Betty sat in her ancient First World War tent and listened to the doodlebugs flying overhead, praying they would miss her camp.

Despite the risk to her life, Betty had no regrets, and never regarded her job as very dangerous; it was something that had to be done. She was happy and loved every minute of what she did. It was exhilarating to be given such important war work, contributing to the launch of an enemy attack and watching as the guns struck back, using the data she'd supplied. Sometimes Betty saw the planes crashing down, which gave her an immense thrill.

'We've done it, we got one down!' she yelled with delight following a successful attack.

Betty's love of sport, in which she'd excelled at school, was put to good use in her work. She was ranked as a private, but decided to try for promotion to corporal. To earn her stripes, she needed to show leadership skills by giving the ATS girls PT classes.

Dressed in an orange Aertex vest and dark brown shorts, Betty spoke encouragingly to them after breakfast. 'Come on girls, let's get up and go out running.'

She tried her best to enthuse and persuade them to join her outside for exercises, but her requests fell on deaf ears.

'Oh no, we're not coming. We can't be bothered,' they replied, worn out by their days of hard war work.

Despite the reluctance of other girls to join in, Betty succeeded in passing her test for promotion and was rewarded with two stripes and the rank of corporal. But far from this being a cause for celebration, it led to difficulties for Betty. The other girls in her battery felt she was no longer one of them. She was shunned by her friends, who gave her the cold shoulder. It made Betty unhappy and gave her second thoughts about her promotion.

She decided to turn it down, resolutely telling her commanding officer, 'I don't want to accept the stripes; I'd rather have my friends.'

Betty was also worried that she'd be posted to another area with a different battery, which was often the case when someone rose up the ranks. She decided she didn't want to give orders; she wanted to be one of the girls. She never regretted her decision.

She knew she'd made the right move in joining the ATS and had never been happier in her life. She hardly missed home – apart from her mother – and thoroughly enjoyed being immersed in challenging war work instead of shelf-filling.

*

Following D-Day, the ack-ack batteries were disbanded and Betty was given another test to determine what war work she should do next. It was now 1944, and it was decided she should learn how to drive. But it would not be in a car.

'However am I going to drive that thing?' said Betty in disbelief, staring at an old ambulance from the First World War.

You had to step up high to reach the cab of the monstrous-looking vehicle, and it had no windows, so drivers were open to the elements. There were no indicators, so Betty had to use hand signals. She also had to double-declutch when changing gears. Trying to reverse around a corner was incredibly hard, as Betty tried her best to manoeuvre its heavy and almost rigid steering. There was a tarpaulin cover on the back of the vehicle with a large red cross. Driving this relic was a very scary experience, but Betty had no choice, as no other vehicles were available: all the best equipment had been shipped across the Channel for D-Day.

Her determination paid off, and she was thrilled to pass her driving test. She was posted to Catterick Camp in Yorkshire, a major garrison headquarters where every branch of the army was based – the Engineers, Signals and Guards, as well as the Air Corps, where they had a shortage of drivers. It was also a prisoner-of-war camp. The sprawling site spread for many miles, as far as the eye could see, and thousands of military personnel were stationed there. This huge holding centre was like a town, with its own shops and post office, and all sorts of different war personnel who'd been sent there to learn new types of war work.

One of Betty's first tasks was to drive to Richmond Station in an Austin military van, picking up new people who arrived for the camp and delivering them to their different regiments. She nipped about in the van, which had a canvas roof, fitting six people in the back – often making two or three journeys a day to keep up with the troops arriving, and driving them back to the station when they left Catterick for other postings.

One day Betty was told by her superior officer, 'We need you to drive the Roman Catholic padre to mass each day.' Each morning she collected him in her two-seater Austin bug with a canvas roof, one of the standard vehicles for getting around, and took him to the Roman Catholic church in Catterick.

Betty discovered that being a driver was not as easy as she hoped, and she needed to learn about car mechanics too to get the car started each morning. During the winter, when temperatures plummeted below freezing, the car's radiator froze up. To prevent this happening, she drained the radiator every night, but in the morning when she wanted to fill it up with water, the water taps were frozen. She used hot rags to warm them up before the water poured out.

Driving the padre and officers was a job she greatly enjoyed and it gave her unique insights into life at the camp that most others could not see, especially meeting the Italian and German prisoners. The Italian prisoners lived on farms in Yorkshire, where they worked the land while the British men fought in the war. They slept in huts and wore heavy brown uniforms with a big orange circle on the front and back, making them easy to spot if they tried to escape.

'They wouldn't get very far anyway – they're in the middle of nowhere here,' she thought, watching them work on the land.

One officer from the Guards, who was due for retirement, was asked to stay on to take charge of these prisoners. Betty drove him around the farms to check on them, and if any of the farmers reported an escape attempt, he took the information back to HQ.

While the Italian prisoners were able to live and work in the community, the German prisoners at Catterick were held under tight armed guard. Their camp had an outer perimeter, from which the British guards watched them, and an inner perimeter where the Germans were kept. Very few people were allowed access.

One day the padre asked Betty if she would like to accompany him inside the perimeter.

'Oh, yes please,' she replied quickly, realising this was a unique opportunity to see German prisoners close up. No other ATS girls had ever been inside; she would be the only one to see what it was like there. On that day, an important inspection of the whole camp was being made.

'Leave it with me, I'll ask for permission,' he replied. The request was approved by an officer; Betty was fascinated to see what the German camp was like, and it would be the first time she had seen a German, too, other than pictures in the newspapers!

Betty parked her car and walked alongside the padre, wondering what the German prisoners would look like. Betty and the padre were accompanied by a very upright German officer. As they entered the huts, one of the Germans called out, *'Achtung!'* Everyone stood sharply to attention. Betty froze on the spot. She glanced around the hut. There were hundreds of prisoners, captured in North Africa and other countries nearby.

'They're so young,' she thought as she gazed at their teenage faces, 'They only look about seventeen years old.'

Fleetingly, she thought that they were no different from our own boys. She noticed how some of the officers appeared very arrogant by the way they stood and behaved with an air of calm confidence, which she had expected of them.

The prisoners lined up for their special inspection. Everywhere she looked in the hut was spotless. The bunk beds were neatly made and the prisoners were immaculate. Their living conditions appeared good – the same as those used by Betty and other military personnel; they did not seem to be treated any differently in that respect. They were well fed too, with three meals a day.

She walked past a hut that the prisoners used as a barber's, and on the grass outside, they had cut the shape of a pair of scissors, so it could be easily found. Betty discovered they had other creative skills, too. Some of the prisoners who were good with their hands made lovely crafts from ivory toothbrush handles, like bookmarks, which they sold through the perimeter fence for cigarettes or money when their guards weren't looking.

They also had their own theatre in one of the huts, where they staged plays, and one prisoner had been provided with a tight-rope to practise his tight-rope-walking skills.

Although it was extraordinary for Betty to witness these unusual scenes, she took them all in her stride as part of her job. She felt the men were being well looked after and were just like the British soldiers in many respects.

Betty usually wore trousers when driving around, but one day she was asked to wear a skirt for a special assignment; she made sure her shoes were their shiniest, too. The mission was to drive a junior commander, one of their highest-ranking women officers, to all the ATS camps in Yorkshire to see how their women were getting on. Betty used a little Transit van for the commander and her aide: it wasn't a posh vehicle, despite her high rank.

It was like royalty arriving wherever they went, as if the red carpet was being rolled out. The tour lasted a week and, on the final day, Betty received a call asking her to go straight to the junior commander's office.

'Oh no, what have I done now!' she fretted, worrying that she might have somehow upset her.

Betty entered her office with fear and trepidation. She saluted her senior officer, standing upright, nervously waiting to hear the reason she had been summoned.

'You've been driving me around all week – how do you think you got on?' the officer asked Betty.

'I think I did well,' Betty answered straight back.

'You did do well. In fact, I'd like you to be my permanent driver!'

Betty was stunned; she hadn't been expecting this.

'Thank you, ma'am. I would be delighted to,' she replied without any hesitation.

One of the perks of this new job was joining the junior commander in the officers' mess for coffee and food – far superior to the ordinary mess food she was used to!

Training to be a driver had given her some fabulous experiences and memories, which she would treasure for ever. Driving was a skill she now shared with her father – yet she'd never be able to speak to him about it.

It was almost a year after the war before Betty was demobbed and returned south to Cambridge. She brought her uniform home with her, a herringbone suit in cream and black with a little red stripe running through it, as well as the pint-sized mug she'd been issued with. It took her several weeks before she could get used to drinking from a cup and saucer again.

After the constant activity at Catterick, life felt flat in Civvy Street. Betty's mother was overjoyed that her daughter had returned home safely, while her father hadn't changed at all, and barely acknowledged her existence.

'I think I'll have a holiday before I start work again,' she told her mother.

'You've earned it,' her mother agreed.

She spent a week relaxing at Southsea on the Hampshire coast with a neighbour who was demobbed from the ATS at the same time. Betty mulled over her future plans and reminisced about some of her wartime experiences.

It was difficult returning home to start with. Betty had loved every minute of the four years she spent with the ATS. She'd learned so much and felt it had been the making of her. She had spent her twenty-first birthday there, drinking beer with the chaps from the transport section in a pub. She had seen and done the most amazing things while serving her country, and she knew she would miss it badly. But it was time for her now to move on.

It didn't take Betty long to find work. At first she returned to the grocery store, Matthew's, where she'd worked before joining the ATS. She worked with Mr Jacobs in the wine department, though she knew nothing about wine, and didn't even like the taste of it. What Mr Jacobs didn't know about wines wasn't worth knowing, and Betty soon became an expert on the best wines and spirits, confident enough to serve their special account customers from the university.

After a while a friend told her about an office job at Telecom, a subsidiary of Pye's, a pioneering Cambridge engineering company, which made forty thousand wireless sets a year. She joined them as 'a chaser', driving a colleague to factories to make sure all their components were ready for production.

Betty loved dancing, and Cambridge had many fantastic dance halls where live bands played. During one night out dancing she met Jennifer's father, whom she married. When things didn't work out for the couple, she felt she had no choice but to move back in with her parents.

It was not an easy decision to make, knowing how difficult her father was. And Betty knew she'd have to provide for herself and her baby daughter.

When Jennifer was two months old, Betty found work to keep them both. She took a job in a nearby factory, punching holes into metal sheets to make washers. She was bored and hated every minute of it, but was grateful to have found work and that it was close enough for her to cycle home each lunchtime to breast-feed her daughter.

Irene surprised Betty with a visit one day. Betty had first spotted

Irene in the neighbourhood when both women were pregnant at the same time. Betty saw Irene cycle along Cherry Hinton Road on her way to work at Heyworth's, heavily pregnant. Both women soon started looking out for each other and chatting about their pregnancies. Betty was delighted to make friends with another woman the same age – mid-twenties – whom she could confide in and exchange baby news.

In fact, both families had known each other for many years. 'I've known Peter all my life. We grew up round the corner from each other,' Betty told Irene.

Irene had just finished work at Heyworth's that day, when she called in at Betty's to tell her about a possible job in the millinery department. Betty was very grateful to be offered the chance to escape from a job she detested.

At the interview Betty explained she had a young baby to support, and felt a huge wave of relief when Herbert Heyworth told her, 'The job is yours.' She was thrilled to hand in her notice at the metal factory. Once again she was going to be a shop girl, undeterred that this time she would be ten years older than most juniors working at Heyworth's.

ROSEMARY

1957

Rosemary Northfield slipped into her slim-fitting dark grey skirt and white blouse and groaned as she looked at her reflection in the mirror.

'Oh dear, do you think I look frumpy in this?' she asked her mother. 'Still, not to worry, it's only for work.'

'You look fine. You've got to make a good impression on your first day. You know how strict they are at Heyworth's,' Sophia Northfield told her daughter.

Rosemary felt very grown up in her new work clothes. She was also very excited – not only was she starting a new job, but it was also her fifteenth birthday.

Blue-eyed Rosemary had three brothers so, as the only girl, was her mother's pride and joy. She was bubbly and vivacious and always had a broad smile on her face, framed by her short wavy fair hair.

She liked wearing pretty clothes, pastel-coloured twinsets that were all the rage and bright dresses with wide, floaty skirts pinched in at the waist. She felt old-fashioned in this new work outfit, complete with black shoes, which had a small Cuban heel. It was not her usual style of dress at all; much more formal than she was used to.

'I'll be all right, Mum, don't worry,' said Rosemary cheerily, as she left for her first day at Heyworth's.

Rosemary had never set foot in Heyworth's before her interview. The smart clothes they sold cost more than her mother could afford so they usually shopped at Frost's in Norfolk Street, a traditional store in a cheaper area of Cambridge; it was there that Rosemary had bought the dark grey skirt.

She had originally planned to be a hairdresser, signing up for a six-month course at the Cambridge College of Hairdressing when she left school. After a while she felt unsettled and questioned whether hairdressing was what she really wanted to do. She loved fashion and told her aunt, Sylvia Arnold, a cleaner at Heyworth's, that she was thinking of giving it up and doing something else.

'Why don't you come and work at Heyworth's?' her aunt suggested.

'That's a good idea! Do you know if they have any vacancies at the moment?' Rosemary asked.

'I don't know, but I'll find out and let you know.'

The following day Sylvia told Rosemary, 'You're in luck! I asked about a junior's job and they *have* got something – they're looking for someone to train in the millinery department.'

Rosemary's face lit up. 'Thanks, Aunt Sylvia – that's great! I'll give it a go.'

An interview was arranged with the manager, Mr Clarke. Rosemary couldn't help but feel nervous as she faced him, answering his questions about why she wanted to work there. She told him her Aunt Sylvia had suggested the job and Rosemary liked the idea, although it was a bit different to the career she had originally planned.

Rosemary quickly got over her nerves and found it easy to respond to Mr Clarke's easy-going manner. As she began to relax, she told him how much she enjoyed following the latest styles and thought she would enjoy working with ladies fashions. She confided in him how she thought that one day she would design clothes, how she pictured the styles in her head.

Rosemary knew that the interview could decide her future and career and answered his questions the best she could. Her determination to succeed paid off and she was thrilled when she was told that the job was hers.

She was excited to tell her aunt that she'd got the job and elated to be working in one of Cambridge's most upmarket department stores.

If she'd needed further persuasion to give up hairdressing, the pay she was being offered decided for her. Her wage as a trainee hairdresser was only £1 a week, compared to a whopping £1 9s as a junior shop girl. Rosemary decided it was too good an offer to turn down and that was it for her hairdressing course.

On her first day at Heyworth's, as Rosemary stepped over the threshold, she looked around at the beautiful clothes on display, instinctively feeling that she'd made the right choice.

'This is something different – I think I'm going to like it here,' she thought, looking around the latest styles on display.

Rosemary had two specific duties: to work as a junior sales girl on the shop floor under Betty Lipscombe, who was the millinery buyer and head of department, and to assist Mrs Pugh, the milliner, who made hats to order in the attic workroom.

Betty took Rosemary under her wing, showing her the correct way to brush their lovely hats using a soft brush. She pointed out the deep wooden drawers where the hats were stored carefully with tissue paper and held like delicate objects. There were head-turning, fabulous hats for every occasion, mostly small, close-fitting hats made from straw, felt, satin and velvet, and trimmed with bows, feathers, ribbons and short veils for the popular pillbox hat. Berets were in vogue with the younger customers, stocked in a wide choice of colours for those who preferred less formal headwear.

After her first day at work, Rosemary returned home excited to tell her family how much she'd enjoyed it. Her mother had made a cake for tea to celebrate her birthday.

Rosemary knew nothing about hats and rarely wore them, except for a special occasion like a wedding. Now she was surrounded by a great array of stunning headwear and quickly discovered there was more to them than she'd realised.

As the third sales assistant and the new junior, Rosemary learned by watching the more experienced shop girls serving customers, observing their polite approach and the helpful way they attended to the women. She was not allowed to serve customers straight away, and she busied herself tidying the displays and putting hats away that the senior sales girls had taken out to show customers.

Rosemary liked and respected Betty. She felt she was learning the ropes quickly under her watchful eye and could see she was always on the ball, giving clear instructions and being fair to her, too. Sometimes, though, they did get their wires crossed.

'Miss Northfield, could you please tidy the display on the counter?' Betty asked her young junior.

Rosemary, keen to impress, tried to respond to requests to work on any new tasks straight away. But if she was busy and replied, 'Just a minute,' Betty would sigh with frustration.

'I can't do everything straight away. I've only got one pair of hands,' Rosemary muttered under her breath, wanting to first finish off the job in hand. She knew that whatever she was asked to do had to be done to perfection, and she didn't want to rush anything and then be criticised.

Rosemary also appreciated the guidance given by a senior part-time sales assistant, Mrs Culpin, who had a distinctive purple rinse in her hair. She didn't say very much, but if Rosemary was stuck, she knew she could rely on Mrs Culpin for advice. She showed Rosemary how to pack hats neatly in their pretty boxes so the tissue paper fell over the edge of the box. The boxes came in an assortment of lovely fondant colours, like soft bluey-grey and yellowy-cream.

Mrs Culpin's purple-tinged hair puzzled the shop girls.

Rosemary, with her hairdressing training in mind, asked the woman, who was in her early sixties, 'You've been putting hair rinse on, haven't you?'

'Why yes, I have. It's the blue rinse I use – it's meant to tone down my grey hairs,' she replied smiling. 'I quite like it!'

At the time, bleached blonde hair was very popular – the kind of hairstyles worn by Hollywood stars Marilyn Monroe and Jayne Mansfield and copied by countless women around the world. Sometimes women put a blue rinse on top of their bleached blonde hair to tone down the brightness of the yellow, giving it a silvery tinge. Rosemary remembered asking her hairdressing teacher why putting a blue rinse on yellow hair didn't turn it green, but she was assured the special chemicals they used would stop that happening.

Because Mrs Culpin's hair had some grey in it, the blue rinse she used gave her coloured hair a purplish sheen and a distinctive look of her own.

Like the other shop girls, Rosemary followed Heyworth's strict dress code and rules for personal appearance. They weren't allowed to backcomb their hair into the popular beehive style, it had to be neatly brushed. Unlike some of the other girls, Rosemary didn't mind – her hair wasn't long enough for a beehive anyway. She was always careful to arrive for work smartly dressed and well groomed. She heard how girls had been told off for wearing sandals in the summer, and neither was it acceptable to wear a coloured blouse – only white or cream would do.

If Herbert Heyworth swept through the department and felt displeased with the appearance of any of the shop girls, he referred the matter to his manager, Mr Clarke, asking him to deal with it.

'I don't mind what you do in the evenings. But in the shop, rules are rules,' Herbert Heyworth told his staff firmly. He expected his high standards to be adhered to without question.

*

Rosemary grew up in a strong, close-knit family with three protective brothers, Graham, Barry and Christopher.

She was very close to her mother Sophia, who was one of twelve surviving children. Sophia's mother Kate gave birth to sixteen babies, two of whom died after being born prematurely, another died after choking on its dummy and the fourth died from a childhood illness.

Sophia had married Bill on 15 February 1939 and Graham was born the middle of the following November. She frequently had to quell whisperers and rumour-mongers following his birth, telling people firmly, 'I was not pregnant before I got married!'

The couple began married life while Britain was at war. Cambridge was targeted by German bombers and after one ferocious attack near their home, word got around that a German pilot had parachuted down and landed near St Matthew's vicarage. Sophia and Bill lived just yards away. Everyone was terrified, locked themselves in their homes and switched off their lights, afraid the German might burst in.

They were locked safely in the house one night when Sophia heard the loud thumping sound of boots running along the road. In a moment of blind panic, she scooped up baby Graham, who was only a few months old, and placed him in the bottom drawer of her chest of drawers. She hid the drawer under the bed to protect him, in fear of the German storming the house. Sophia held her breath and waited, listening intently for the sound of footsteps, which faded down the road. Finally she lifted her baby from his hiding place and cuddled him. Nobody ever found the German airman.

Bill, a small man of 5 feet 8 inches, served as an engineer with the Royal Anglian Regiment, who were based in Bury St Edmunds, Suffolk, just across the Cambridgeshire border and were due to be sent to Dunkirk. Shortly before the boat was due to leave,

Bill became unwell and feverish. He noticed a swollen lump on his arm and was seen by an army medical officer who told him, 'You've got a carbuncle and it's poisonous. You can't go out with your regiment.'

The 'carbuncle' was a large abscess, which looked and felt very sore, and the pus had to be drained to stop the infection turning lethal. Bill had no choice but to stay behind and recover from his painful ailment. His regiment sailed off for Calais as planned and he wished them luck with their dangerous mission before they parted.

Within hours he was told the most devastating news – the boat he was due to have sailed on had sunk. It had been attacked in the Channel. All his comrades perished; there were no survivors.

Bill was stricken with overwhelming feelings of guilt and grief for losing so many friends, while his life was spared. The shock hit him terribly and he wept for days. He couldn't believe that he was still alive while his comrades had died. The guilt remained with him for years after. If ever the war was mentioned in conversation, he would mutter 'that could have been me'.

Despite this terrible event and the lasting impact it had, Rosemary's father did his best to put on a brave face and didn't show his feelings to his children – life went on as normal for them. Sophia felt restless after the episode with the German airman. She no longer felt safe in her home, as it had frightened her so much and still played on her mind.

'I want to move house. I don't feel safe here any more. What if the German is still around?' she pleaded with Bill.

Bill had little choice but to agree and the family moved to a nearby street, Caroline Place, where Rosemary was born at 9.30 a.m. on 8 March, 1942. When the labour pains began, Bill sped off on his bicycle, frantically searching for the midwife. Midwives were hard to find in wartime.

By the time he found Nurse Dorrington and they dashed back home, their healthy baby daughter had already arrived in the world. She'd been delivered by Sophia's sister, Aunt Lou, on the sitting-room floor. Sophia held Rosemary in her arms, the umbilical cord still attached. Luckily, Aunt Lou had helped deliver babies before and the birth had gone smoothly.

Rosemary was an easy baby and the apple of her parents' eyes. Sophia found work in a bicycle and pram shop called Ward's, on the corner of Norfolk Street, and she and Bill saved hard each year to buy their children's Christmas presents. One year they bought a bicycle and a doll's pram from the shop with their savings.

Instead of the expected whoops of delight from Rosemary, who was given the pram, she was crestfallen and shunned the gift, telling them, 'I want the bike instead!' Her eyes had popped out after seeing the gleaming bicycle her brother had been given and she wanted one too.

Her brother added to the confusion by pointing to her gift and stating, 'I want the pram!'

Although Rosemary was very much a girlie girl, a small part of her was also a cheeky tomboy, and she enjoyed playing with her two brothers, Graham, who was two years older, and Barry, two years younger, and their friends. Her brother Christopher, the baby of the family, was eight years younger than Rosemary.

Sophia kept her family in order with a firm hand. If something was wrong, she didn't beat about the bush and would always speak her mind, while Bill was very placid. After the war ended, he joined a printing company.

Sophia was dealt a devastating blow when both her parents died young, aged fifty-six, within a year of each other, leaving their four youngest children orphaned. After Sophia's father Charles died, her mother was grief-stricken and died the following year on exactly the same day. The family said she had died of a broken heart. Once

Charles had gone, and because she had relied on him so much for everything, Sophia's mother Kate never bothered to look up any more, even though she still had children to care for.

It was decided that the orphaned siblings would be separated and sent to live with their older brothers and sisters, who were married and settled. Margaret, who was eleven, moved in with Rosemary's family, while Doreen, ten, Phyllis, thirteen, and Reg, sixteen, found new homes with other close family members.

Rosemary, who was four years old at the time, loved the extra fuss and attention from the new family member and became very close to her aunt Margaret. With Sophia working, Rosemary looked on Margaret as another mum, as she was always there doing things for her. She took her out on her mother's bicycle, placing her in a child's seat at the front, while Rosemary hung on tightly to the handlebars, her cheeks flushed pink from the fresh air.

As well as cooking and helping with the household chores, Margaret loved dancing and spent many hours bopping along to the latest hits with her young niece, teaching her dance steps and giggling. Rosemary's love of dancing grew even more after she joined Joan Slipper's Dance School, where she learned to tap dance and had acrobatic lessons, too, mastering the technique of back flips and somersaults. She was able to show off her dancing skills at a Christmas show at the New Theatre in Cambridge, looking every inch like Shirley Temple in her tap shoes and skirt, with a big red bow on her wavy hair.

Rosemary could see her smiling parents and her aunts in the large audience as she tap danced to *The Teddy Bears' Picnic*. At the end of the concert, the sound of the loud applause made Rosemary feel proud of her first public performance. It was an outstanding success and her beaming family showered her with praise.

Rosemary idolised her young aunt Margaret, and wanted to be just like her – even to smoke Woodbine cigarettes like she did.

'Can I have a fagiette?' Rosemary asked, watching her seventeen-year-old aunt puff away. She was still only four at the time; it was common for young women to smoke in those days, but perhaps not quite *that* young.

Rosemary had made up her own name for cigarettes – she'd heard her father call them 'fags', and the word 'cigarettes'.

'Do you *really* want a fagiette?' Margaret asked, laughing.

'Yes, I do,' Rosemary replied, firmly. She was curious to know what it felt like to smoke.

Margaret lit the cigarette and passed it to Rosemary. She placed it on her lips, breathed in and shuddered in revulsion.

'Urgh! It's horrible!' she said, spitting out the horrid taste of tobacco which remained on her lips. She thought it was the most disgusting smell and taste she had ever experienced. From that day on Rosemary never touched another cigarette.

When Rosemary was five years old, the family were living in a council house in Hills Avenue, where most of the children in the neighbourhood were boys and so she tried to join in with their boyish games. They set up a pile of bricks on the road and threw a ball at the pile, much like skittles. Rosemary's job was to fetch the cricket ball for the boys – they wouldn't let her have a turn at throwing. But one day, frustrated, she picked up the cricket ball and decided she would have a go at throwing. She took aim and hurled the ball with all her strength at the pile of bricks, but the ball bounced straight back in her mouth, cutting it badly. There was blood pouring down her face.

A wailing Rosemary was taken to hospital by her anxious mother, straddled on her child's seat on the front of her mother's bicycle. Sophia pedalled as fast as she could to Old Addenbrooke's Hospital where Rosemary's cut was stitched up. She still played with the boys afterwards, but not quite so vigorously.

One day Sophia returned from Cambridge cattle market with a tray of eggs among her other groceries. But there seemed to be a soft chirping noise coming from one of the eggs. Sophia leant closer and heard the faint sound again.

'I think one of the eggs has been fertilised,' Sophia told her daughter with a big grin. 'Let's see if it will hatch.'

Sophia gently picked up the egg, wrapped it up in cotton wool and placed it on a baking tray in the warm gas oven.

'Why are you doing that?' Rosemary asked incredulously.

'I want to see if the chick will hatch from the warmth of the oven,' her mother told her.

Sophia kept popping back to the oven to check on the egg. Then, after a while, she opened the oven door and picked up a tiny yellow fluffy chick. Rosemary was amazed, thinking her mother was a magician to produce a chick just by placing an egg in the oven.

The chick was nurtured and loved by the children who adopted her as a pet and named her Henrietta. Henrietta lived in the greenhouse at the end of the garden and was adored by all the family. Rosemary and her brothers enjoyed feeding her potato peelings and scraps of food. Sophia sometimes added cod liver oil to the chicken feed to provide extra nutrition so Henrietta would be plump and healthy and produce fat eggs.

Barry, who was nine years old, was particularly fond of Henrietta. Rosemary would watch her brother go up to the hen and say, 'Henrietta, can you lay me an egg?'

He returned to the greenhouse two or three hours later and always found a fresh egg had been laid, which he ate for breakfast the following day.

They'd had Henrietta for about two years when the children were given some very upsetting news. Sophia stunned them by announcing that Henrietta's egg-laying days were to come to an abrupt end.

'We can't afford to buy another chicken for Christmas Day, so we'll have to eat Henrietta,' Sophia told them sadly.

The children were devastated. On Christmas Eve Sophia and Rosemary scooped up the hapless flapping hen and took her to their neighbour, Mr Gleeson, who lived two doors away. They watched as he broke her neck. Eleven-year-old Rosemary found it very upsetting. When she returned home with her mother and the lifeless hen, Sophia and Rosemary started plucking the plump poultry, preparing it for their festive dinner. They each held one of Henrietta's legs as her head hung over the dustbin and started removing the feathers. They had plucked the legs and were removing the feathers from the breast when Henrietta began twitching and sprang back to life. She leapt out of their hands and spun around the kitchen floor, jerking and flapping, then finally flopped in a lifeless state on the floor.

Rosemary screamed. It was the most alarming and distressing sight she had ever witnessed.

'Oh my goodness!' said Sophia, shocked to see that Henrietta appeared to still be alive. 'It must be a nerve that's still active and has made her go into spasms.'

'It's horrible,' cried Rosemary, who couldn't face touching Henrietta again.

Barry was even more upset. He cried and cried at the loss of his pet hen.

'I'm not eating Henrietta. I'm never going to eat chicken again!' he declared. And he kept his word. On Christmas Day, Henrietta was served up on the table for dinner. Rosemary and the rest of the family managed not to let Henrietta's dramatic death spoil their Christmas. But she was never replaced and they never had another hen as a family pet.

As a child Rosemary spent many happy hours splashing about in the River Cam in Newnham, a beautiful part of Cambridge with meandering meadowland and sweeping weeping willow trees. A stream that fed into the river was a popular children's swimming area, the Snobs, where Rosemary learned to swim. It was an idyllic setting leading to 'paradise island', a strip of land on the Cam where Rosemary and her friends made dens and hunted for treasure, returning home exhausted afterwards and in need of a hot bath to clean up.

Rosemary enjoyed their big family get-togethers, too, when there was always lots of fun and laughter. They didn't need a special occasion to meet up. Sometimes at weekends the large family gathered for a picnic at one of Cambridge's many beauty spots, spreading their rugs on the grassy bank by the river where they feasted on home-made cakes and sandwiches filled with jam, meat paste, or sardine and tomato paste.

Rosemary felt sorry for her mother, who would never go swimming or wear a bathing costume if they went on the beach on a family day out. It was her toes she wanted to hide from the world, not her figure. Sophia had been injured in a terrible accident when she was only eighteen, while working at Chivers' jam factory in Histon. She had stepped into a lift, the old-fashioned kind with metal grid gates that opened from side to side. Somehow her foot became trapped in the metal gates as it was shutting, severing three of her toes. Sophia was in unspeakable agony and spent several months in Old Addenbrooke's Hospital recovering. She was self-conscious about the deformity for the rest of her life. As a young woman she had loved wearing high heels and going ballroom dancing. She had loved swimming too. But after the accident her life was never the same. She was no longer able to wear high heels and shunned the dance floors she had once loved so much, and became very self-conscious about her disability. She could never wear open-toed sandals either, too embarrassed by the appearance of her foot.

'You couldn't keep me off the dance floor before I had the accident,' she told her daughter.

'Poor Mum, what a terrible thing to happen,' said Rosemary sympathetically. 'I can't imagine what it would feel like not to be able to dance any longer.' Rosemary herself loved rock 'n' roll and, as she got older, spent weekends at one of Cambridge's many dance halls dancing to live bands.

Rosemary was very fond of her aunt Sylvia, who also worked at Heyworth's. Their paths didn't often cross, however, as Sylvia had usually left before Rosemary arrived. By then she was on her way to her next cleaning job, as she worked at two other businesses, as well.

One day when Rosemary did bump into her aunt, she heard how Sylvia had been lucky to escape unscathed from an explosion in Heyworth's basement. Aunt Sylvia had been cleaning when there was a deafening sound. Terrified, she fled up the stairs in panic, worried she may have been in danger. Once she reached the top of the stairs, she breathed a huge sigh of relief, glad to have reached safety without being injured.

She discovered the cause of the explosion had been the gas boiler. When Sylvia arrived for work at 7 a.m., nobody else was in the store except Henry, who worked in dispatches. It was his job to light the gas boiler in the basement each morning. On this day, he switched the gas on but forgot to light it. When he later remembered, he struck the match and walked towards the boiler, causing the terrifying explosion. He was lucky not to have been hurt.

'It was terrible. I thought I had burst my eardrums. I was only standing a few feet away from it,' she told Rosemary, shuddering at the memory. 'It could have been much worse. We're lucky no real damage was caused.'

'Cor, that *was* lucky. It must have been really frightening. You had a very lucky escape,' Rosemary sympathised.

Marjorie Pugh, Heyworth's stylish milliner who was in her mid-forties, was a perfectionist. She was a petite woman with impeccable manners and was always beautifully made up; she was very fond of bright lipstick. Rosemary helped out as and when required.

'Mrs Pugh needs a hand in the workroom – can you go and help her, please?' Betty would ask Rosemary.

Rosemary was only too happy to join Mrs Pugh in the attic workroom. She walked up two flights of steps, the second flight becoming very narrow as they reached the top. The workroom was small and had only one tiny window. It became unbearably hot and stuffy during the summer. A number of different sized wooden head-blocks were on the shelves; they were used as a mould to shape a brim or crown of a hat. The fabric was placed on top of the block, cut to size and, with the aid of a steamer, was gently stretched and manipulated into shape by hand.

Felts and furs, satins and velvet fabrics were laid out on shelves ready to be shaped. The fabric had already been pre-cut, ready for Mrs Pugh to apply her skills and follow the instructions from customers about the style and finishing touches they required. The shelves were stacked with decorations for the hats, such as delicate netting, as well as ribbons and bows, jewels, flowers and feathers in a huge variety of colours. The customer came in for a fitting to check it was the right size before the hat was decorated.

'We have an order from the Marchioness of Cambridge,' Mrs Pugh told Rosemary one Friday afternoon. 'She'd like to collect it next Friday to wear that weekend for the races.'

Betty had called Mrs Pugh down to speak to their distinguished customer in the millinery department. Lady Cambridge handed her a large box full of pheasant feathers, instructing the milliner to make her a new hat and decorate it with the plumage. Mrs Pugh put the box on a shelf in her attic workroom, planning to start work on the hat the following Monday. In the past she'd made many stunning hats for Lady Cambridge to wear at the races in Newmarket and Royal Ascot, where they were admired by members of the royal family when she joined them in the Royal Box. She was one of their most distinguished and valued customers.

Rosemary was hugely impressed, as she'd never met anybody connected to the royal family before, let alone helped make a new hat for them.

'The feathers came from the pheasants on her estate and she wants us to use them on her new hat. There are plenty to choose from,' added Mrs Pugh.

The following Monday when Rosemary entered the attic, the stench coming from the room was unbearable. She soon discovered where it was coming from – the box of pheasant feathers given to them by Lady Cambridge was crawling with hundreds of maggots.

They were faced with a chaotic situation. After the feathers had been plucked, flies had laid eggs on a few tiny pieces of pheasant flesh left on some of them, and the warm attic room had provided the perfect breeding ground. The maggots were crawling down the wall and into their precious stock. As it was a very warm September day, the sight and smell in the airless workroom was disgusting, making Rosemary's stomach heave.

She was very worried. 'What are we going to do, Mrs Pugh? The Marchioness will be in soon to collect her new hat.'

Mrs Pugh remained calm. 'We'll have to start by getting rid of the maggots and then I shall have to put my thinking cap on.'

'I've never known such an horrendous smell. It makes me feel quite sick. Those maggots are disgusting,' said the junior, feeling queasy.

Rosemary's aunt Sylvia was called in to fumigate the room. She scrubbed the room from top to bottom with disinfectant until it sparkled. They had cleared the contaminated shelves and thrown out any maggot-infested stock.

Once the workroom was spick and span, and free of foul-smelling infestation, the milliner began wondering what they could do to make sure their very special customer had her new hat on time.

Mrs Pugh had a brainwave. 'I know, let's buy some feathers from Eaden Lilley's!'

'That's a good idea. I'll go over and see what they have. Let's hope they have something suitable,' Rosemary offered.

Eaden Lilley was at the end of the passageway that ran alongside Heyworth's, and had a well-stocked haberdashery department.

Rosemary dashed across and found they had just what she needed. She returned to the workroom with a selection of large feathers very similar to those brought in by Lady Cambridge. She felt jubilant: a great weight had come off her shoulders now that she knew that Mrs Pugh could still make the hat for their client with royal connections.

'They're perfect, that's a big relief,' Mrs Pugh said with delight. 'I shall start on it now.'

Mrs Pugh placed the felt around the wooden block and cut the base of the hat, steaming it into shape. The feathers were styled to dramatically sweep across the front of the hat and over the wearer's forehead. It was exactly what Lady Cambridge had requested.

When Lady Cambridge came in to collect her new hat the following Friday, Mrs Pugh held her breath as she handed it over. She watched Lady Cambridge place it on her head, and look at her reflection in the mirror.

Then she turned to Mrs Pugh and said, 'That's wonderful, thank you very much. It's perfect. I knew I could rely on you.'

'I'm delighted to hear it. I'm so pleased you like it,' Mrs Pugh replied.

The milliner went upstairs and told Rosemary the good news. 'What a relief. Lady Cambridge couldn't tell any difference!'

'I'm so pleased,' Rosemary replied, relieved that their hard work had paid off.

Lady Cambridge was never told about the mayhem her feathers had caused. Nobody at Heyworth's breathed a word about it, not wanting to alarm or embarrass their valued customer. Mrs Pugh knew that Heyworth's couldn't let her down and was proud of the endeavours they took to make sure that Lady Cambridge could have the new hat she had set her heart on.

Rosemary was always spellbound as she watched Mrs Pugh at work. She thought it was fabulous the way she took a swathe of satin and swirled it around the mould for a new hat, creating stunning headwear. Sometimes she made a skullcap out of muslin and covered it with twisted silk and flowers. During the summer months, the hats had small brims to provide some shading and in winter berets were popular, which Mrs Pugh made by placing a flat piece of felt around a wooden block and manipulating it into shape with her hand, and the steamer.

Mrs Pugh's skills were in great demand by the dons' wives, who needed special hats to match new outfits for a university function, or a visit by the Queen or other members of the royal family, a regular occurrence at the university. The price was around two guineas, which seemed a fortune to Rosemary; it was more than a week's pay for her. But it seemed to her that older people wore hats more often than younger women, so they tended to have the money to spend and didn't flinch at the price.

If there were no customers in the millinery department and work was quiet, Rosemary, who liked showing off, had fun trying on the hats on display in front of the other shop girls.

'Does this one suit me?' she'd ask mischievously, smiling and admiring her reflection in the mirror.

'Oh no, you need to put it this way,' they'd reply, giggling, adjusting the hat on Rosemary's head and enjoying the impromptu fashion show, but nervous that they'd be discovered.

In Mrs Pugh's workroom, Rosemary made wedding headdresses

for brides and bridesmaids to complement the wedding dresses sold in Heyworth's bridal department. She threaded silk flowers and beads for a garlanded halo, while Mrs Pugh added flowers to the headdress on a bride's veil.

Rosemary couldn't resist trying on the bridal headdresses either, smiling at her reflection in the mirror, fantasising that one day she'd meet her Mr Right and wear a beautiful veil like this for her own wedding, dressed from head to toe in white. But she was still only sixteen and waiting to meet the man of her dreams.

She was thrilled when she learned that there would be wedding bells for her friend in the knitwear department, Eileen Robson, who was marrying a policeman called Roger Dent – and Rosemary was invited to the wedding

'I'd love to come!' she told Eileen, accepting the invitation. 'I love weddings.'

A born romantic, Rosemary was excited about her friend's Big Day. She could see how happy the couple were together. Roger didn't look like a policeman to Rosemary – she didn't fancy the thought of going out with a uniformed policeman herself – but Roger was a plain-clothed detective and worked with CID.

Other friends from Heyworth's were going too, including her boss Betty Lipscombe and Mary Ryder, who was in charge of the childrenswear department. They all wanted to look their best and placed orders with Mrs Pugh for new hats especially for the occasion.

Mrs Pugh made Rosemary a small, elegant, white fur hat to wear with her smart navy and white suit. A double string of pearls hung around her neck and a pair of white gloves and white clutch bag completed her outfit. All the shop girls looked equally splendid in their finery. Mrs Ryder's hat was made from satin and had a distinctive twisted sheath at the side.

'You all look wonderful. I bet I know where your hats came from,' the radiant bride told her beautifully attired friends.

All the shop girls felt a million dollars at the wedding, knowing their hats were one of a kind, made by the best milliner in Cambridge. There was nowhere else in Cambridge which provided this unique service and Mrs Pugh's skills were much sought-after.

Rosemary was very sociable and quickly made friends with the other shop girls. Her warm, outgoing personality also made new colleagues feel at ease. Judy Mortlock hadn't been at Heyworth's long when Rosemary started chatting to her in the canteen. It was an effort to reach the room where they spent their breaks. Staff had to climb to the top of the building and across the rooftops to a door that led them into a former storeroom, now converted into the canteen.

By the time they arrived, they only had a few minutes to enjoy their hot drink before having to return to work – their fifteen-minute break being strictly counted. As well as tea and coffee, the canteen also sold cigarettes, and a shop girl could put the cost of their cigarettes on a slate and pay for them at the end of the week when they were given their wages.

One lunchtime Judy was sitting in the canteen, quietly enjoying her lunch. When she saw Bill, who worked in the basement stores, tucking into his sandwich, she recoiled in horror.

'Whatever have you got there? It looks disgusting!' she asked him curiously, watching Bill tuck into his sandwich which had white gristle-like chewy stuff hanging from the side.

'That's my chitterling sandwich. Do you want to try some?' he grinned, pushing the pig's intestines towards her.

'Yuck, that's horrible. Get it away from me,' she said, shooing his hand away in disgust.

'Ah, they've lovely, come on and try them,' he teased Judy, who quickly turned the other way.

It made Rosemary's stomach churn when she heard about Bill's offal sandwich.

'I'm glad I didn't see it! I couldn't have faced that,' she told Judy, squirming.

Judy was fifteen when she joined Heyworth's underwear department, working under Kathy Twin. As the new junior, Judy was third sales, ranked after the first and second sales girls who attended to customers first.

Like Rosemary, she learned by watching, and soon familiarised herself with the stock, learning where the vests, panties, nightdresses and dressing gowns were stored.

'Keep your eyes open and you'll learn everything you need to know by watching Mrs Pointer, Mrs Ladd and Mrs Dumper,' Miss Twin had told her, pointing out the senior shop assistants.

Judy was naturally quiet and shy, but found she came out of her shell once she started serving customers, and loved her newfound confidence. Before she came to Heyworth's she had never seen the kind of old-fashioned underwear that their older customers preferred – the directory knickers and bloomers and thermal vests with built-up shoulders. Heyworth's had its regular customers who came in each winter and bought their thermals and long johns. Judy thought they were very quaint and old fashioned.

Judy preferred the look and feel of the silk and satin underwear, the French knickers that were all the rage and which their more glamorous customers preferred to wear. On Thursday mornings a group of women regularly came in. They met up for coffee in Cambridge and then visited Heyworth's where they all had personal accounts. This meant they could take home their chosen purchase and pay for it at the end of the month. The women browsed around the lingerie, picking up items and asking Judy to show them their latest ranges of underwear from the drawers. She brought out a wide selection of undergarments for them to choose and waited patiently for the women to make their selection. Their answer was always the same: 'I'd like to take them home on appro.'

Within the next couple of days the women each returned every item and found an excuse for them being unsuitable. This happened regularly and Judy moaned about it to Rosemary.

'They've been in again today and taken home some French knickers on appro. I know they're not going to buy anything. I don't know why they do it,' she told Rosemary.

'It's really annoying, because there's nothing we can do and Miss Twin says we have to let them take the stuff home because they are account customers. I have to spend so much time with them as well, and be polite and helpful, and yet it's all a waste of time.'

'It's not right,' said Rosemary sympathetically. 'I'd be cross about it too if I was messed about by time-wasters.'

'I like serving the men who come in,' Judy added. 'They always take my advice and are grateful for my suggestions. They don't bring their shopping back like these women, unless the size needs changing.'

Judy found that the men she sold Christmas gifts to were much easier to please compared to this group of troublesome women. The men stood by the counter looking sheepish, uncertain what to buy for their wives or girlfriends, eyeing up the silk and satin lingerie on display.

'What would you recommend?' the hapless men asked Judy.

'What size is she?' the shop girl would say.

The men were clueless about these essential vital statistics. 'She's about your size,' they replied, feebly, using their hands and making an outline of female curves to demonstrate the size of their beloved's curves. 'Or she's the size of the assistant over there,' they'd say, pointing to another shop girl in the department.

Judy heard this many times, and it always made her smile and stifle a giggle. But she always felt a great sense of satisfaction when the men left the store delighted with the gifts she'd suggested, particularly those who left it very late. It was not unusual for some men to rush in at the last minute on Christmas Eve, gasping, 'I hope you haven't sold out – I hope I'm not too late to buy a special lingerie set.'

'I'm sure we can find you the perfect gift,' Judy would reply helpfully, keen that they should not leave empty-handed and disappointed.

On Saturdays, Rosemary and Judy eagerly slipped out of their black and white work outfits in exchange for a fashionable dress with a large swirling skirt or a twinset and pencil skirt.

Judy couldn't afford to buy clothes from Heyworth's and most of their styles were too old for her. Her favourite shops were Jennifer's, Vogue and Modiste. Jennifer's sold separates, Modiste sold dresses, while Vogue, which stocked mostly expensive, beautiful dresses, often had some that were affordable for her, too.

'Where shall we go tonight?' asked Rosemary, always excited at the thought of a night out dancing.

'How about the Rex? That's my favourite,' Judy suggested.

'Yes, that's a great idea!' agreed Rosemary.

Sometimes they were joined by other shop girls, including their friend Jean, who everyone thought was the spitting image of Audrey Hepburn. Her elfin face, large wide eyes, porcelain skin and chiselled cheekbones made heads swivel when people mistook her for the beautiful Hollywood star. Shop girl Judy Parker also came along sometimes. She loved jiving, like Rosemary. The two girls had both gone to the same school in Cambridge and were surprised and delighted to later be reunited at Heyworth's.

However, this particular night, Rosemary and Judy Mortlock went alone to the Rex, a hotspot for live bands near Castle Hill. The venue was popular with American GIs stationed in and around Cambridge after the Second World War. Sometimes fights broke out between them with the local lads, and Rosemary was not keen on the Americans and their bragging.

There was a great atmosphere at the Rex when Rosemary and Judy entered the ballroom, the music was playing loudly and the shop girls soon started tapping their toes and swinging along to the music.

As they danced, they were soon joined by some local boys, including one called Bill who danced with Judy. The girls smiled and giggled all night as they jived to one tune after another, until it was time to go home.

Rosemary and Judy set off alone and walked home part of the way together before parting, with Rosemary shooting off towards her house.

'It's been a wonderful night. I'll see you on Monday,' she said cheerily, waving good night to Judy. Just before they parted, the girls suddenly heard footsteps running up behind them. Judy turned and saw Bill, the boy she had danced with that night.

She smiled. Bill was tall with dark hair and was dressed in a smart double-breasted suit. They had hit it off on the dance floor, despite their age difference; she was coming up to sixteen while he was twenty-three.

'I didn't realise you lived in Chesterton. I'm going that way too,' he said. 'Can I walk with you?'

Judy nodded in agreement and Rosemary took her road home. It wasn't until the following Monday that Judy could tell Rosemary about her new admirer. Bill had recently come out of the army and was working for a company that recycled milk bottles.

'Will I see you at the Rex again next weekend?' Bill had asked Judy when they reached her home. Although Judy liked Bill, she was not swept off her feet by him. But she agreed to be there, nevertheless.

'He seemed really nice, but I'm not sure about him,' she said. Rosemary had had some admirers too, but she had not met anybody special yet. Judy and Bill, meanwhile, were both great dancers and their romance grew on the dance floor.

EVE

1944

Eve stopped dead in her tracks and gasped with amazement. It was her first day back at work after the New Year – and the first day of the sales.

'My goodness, I've never seen anything like it!' she said, her eyes following the long line of bargain-hunters that vanished out of her sight around the corner down Market Passage.

'Excuse me, can I come through? I work here and I just want to get in through the staff door,' she told the waiting crowd, which had blocked the entrance. She tentatively edged her way through them, relieved when she was finally able to clock in.

Even as an inexperienced junior, before she was allowed to sell to customers, it was always all hands on deck during the sales, Heyworth's busiest trading time of the year. Eve was expected to serve customers too, joining the line-up of shop girls at the back of the queue. They formed their own line inside the store, starting with the first, second and third sales assistants and ending with youngest juniors, like Eve. The shop girls would serve all the customers in turn, to ensure they were not disappointed after their long wait. Heyworth's still prided itself on providing a first-class personal service to its valued customers, even during the chaotic sales.

The floor walkers, managers and porters – any of the men who worked there – dressed in their best suits for the first day of the sale and ensured the queue was kept in order. They patrolled outside, speaking to customers to find out what they wished to buy, writing the request on a piece of paper. The customer at the front of the queue would be led into the store, and the piece of paper handed to the next available shop girl.

'Miss Gray, this customer would like to see the black coat in window two. Could you please show it to her?' The windows were numbered, and the shop girls knew exactly which garments were displayed in them.

The shop girl stayed with the customer until the purchase was completed, however long it took, and regardless of the length of the queue outside. The assistant then returned to her line-up in the store, ready to serve the next customer. 'This is the personal service which Heyworth's prides itself on and which our ladies are accustomed to on the first day of our sale, our busiest day of the year,' Miss Stubbings had explained.

'Are you ready now Miss Gray?'

Eve nodded and joined the line of shop girls queuing up inside, ready for the doors to open and for the rush to begin. As a shy junior, Eve felt uncomfortable serving clothing in departments where she had no specialist knowledge. She knew nothing about corsets or tweed suits, and was worried in case she was asked a question she couldn't answer.

'I know what I'll do: I'll linger with the customer. I'll drag it out as long as I can before returning to the queue,' she told herself.

The first day of the sales was always the busiest, and Eve felt chuffed that she had coped with all the sales requests from customers, asking for advice when she needed it. She glanced around at the rails and drawers, which had been almost stripped bare in every department – but now the shop was ready to display the new spring range.

Eve had a special favour to ask Miss Stubbings. She had to pluck up the courage to ask.

'I'd like to have a Saturday off so I can be bridesmaid for my cousin Jean. I've never been a bridesmaid before and it would mean so much to me.'

She hoped that Miss Stubbings could twist George Heyworth's arm, as Eve had been a model employee who had never asked for a special favour before.

'I'll do my best. Leave it with me and I'm sure Mr Heyworth will agree,' Miss Stubbings replied.

Eve felt optimistic. Her gold taffeta bridesmaid's dress had just been completed, hand-made by her aunt. Eve had never worn anything as beautiful before, and she was excited; it was much fancier than any dress she'd ever owned and the thought of wearing it was thrilling.

Although Miss Stubbings' response had sounded hopeful, George's final answer was devastating for Eve.

'I'm sorry, Miss Gray. Mr Heyworth won't let you have the day off. I tried my best, but he said he can't make any exceptions, as the other girls would then ask for Saturdays off too, and then where would we be?'

Eve's heart sank and she fought back the tears welling up inside her. She felt terrible letting her cousin down.

'I'm so sorry Miss Gray, I know how disappointed you must be feeling,' Miss Stubbings added consolingly, seeing how upset Eve was.

'It's not fair, especially as my dress is already made and the wedding is only a couple of weeks away. I can't believe he won't give me the day off,' said Eve, disappointment etched on her face.

'I had hoped he would make an exception, but I'm afraid he wouldn't. He was afraid of setting a precedent,' said Miss Stubbings. Eve had no choice but to accept the decision.

George Heyworth began spending less time in the store after his son Herbert returned from the war and took over the helm. It was not a change Eve favoured. Whereas Mr Heyworth senior had always been very polite and considerate towards his staff, including the most junior shop girls like Eve, she noticed that Herbert had a more abrupt manner, which she didn't like. While George Heyworth used to chat amiably to his staff, his son didn't bother with them unless he wanted to know something. Eve had very little to do with him the whole time she worked there.

She saw him barge through the door and swing through, regardless of who was behind him – unlucky for them if it slammed shut in their face. He never held it open in the same way for others like his father did.

Eve felt that Herbert Heyworth showed more respect and interest in speaking to the buyers and took little interest in the childrenswear department, preferring to spend time in the glamorous ladies fashion showroom, where beautiful evening gowns, expensive fur coats and the smartest suits were on display. Eve always did her best to avoid him and keep her head down, and always made sure she was busy if he was around; she knew that Herbert, like his father, could not tolerate slouching.

Eve was happy with the girls she worked with and their friendship, and that was what mattered most to her – she didn't let Herbert Heyworth worry her.

Les and Eve still enjoyed their Monday evenings at the church youth club, where they played badminton doubles together. Eve didn't feel she was nearly as good as Les. He excelled at the sport, and could have played for the county. He was happy playing matches against his friends, however, and didn't want to take it seriously.

The United Reformed Church had played an important part in both of their lives. Before the outbreak of war, when Les was nineteen, he became Scoutmaster for the new church Scout troop, and he was made a Sunday school teacher.

When war broke out, Les immediately volunteered for his father's old regiment, the Royal Field Artillery, where he had served as a saddle-maker during the First World War. But the unit was full and Les decided to wait for his call-up, turning down an offer to join the Artillery for six years, saying, 'I'm not that green!'

Instead he joined the Local Defence Volunteers (Home Guard) and guarded the electricity power station one night a week, where his duties included helping the stokers shovel coal into the furnaces. He was the only person who was provided with ammunition for his rifle and was shown rifle drill by one of stokers, who had been in the Guards regiment. The following year he joined the RAF.

Les kept his wartime experiences to himself and never discussed the living nightmare he'd endured in the Far East. Eve never pressed him on this, and neither did anyone else. What mattered to her was that she really enjoyed his company, even though he was years nine years older than her, and she was only sixteen.

When Les walked Eve home, they just chatted as friends and there was no hint of a romance at first, though the seed had been sown and Eve knew she had a soft spot for him because of the warm glow she felt when she was with him. When they parted company at the end of the evening, Les simply said 'goodnight' at the front gate, and then walked straight off home.

One evening, as they walked back to her house, instead of leaving as usual without saying anything in particular, Les spun around and surprised Eve by asking, 'Would you like to go to the cinema next week?'

Eve readily accepted. When they arrived at the Tivoli cinema, Les found some seats at the back that had their own curtains, which could be pulled around them for privacy. They were popular with couples.

'Let's go and sit in the back in the cubbyhole,' said Les. They held hands throughout, though they kept the curtains open. The river ran alongside the cinema and it had been known to flood the seats in the front known as 'the pits'; it was far more romantic to sit in the 'cubbyhole'.

At the end of the evening, when Les dropped Eve off at her front gate, he said, 'I've had a wonderful evening. Shall we go to the cinema again?'

'Yes, I'd like that. I really enjoyed this evening. Thank you for taking me,' she replied shyly.

Eve knew that when she went out with Les, she had to obey her mother's strict rules and be home by 9 p.m. sharp. Once, when she had been walked home by another friend from the youth club, she had been in trouble with her mother for being home fifteen minutes late. She didn't want to risk upsetting her again, and kept a close watch on the time to be sure of arriving home punctually.

Eventually, Les felt the time had come for Eve to meet his mother, Florence. The two women hit it off immediately, chatting over a cup of tea and getting to know each other. It was not long after they met that Florence confided in Eve about how Les had reacted when he returned home from the Far East.

'One of the first things Les did when he came back was paint his bedroom dark blue. I didn't like it one little bit. It's not your usual colour for a bedroom, but it shows you where his mind must have been. He still can't talk about it.'

'Poor Les,' replied Eve, nodding sympathetically. 'I know he doesn't like to talk about those days.'

Eve's mother Gertrude had also taken an instant liking to Les, despite her initial reservations about the nine-year age difference. The couple rarely argued, but one day, after a minor tiff, Eve returned home from work to find a posy of freshly picked forget-me-nots on the windowsill.

'Where did they come from, Mum?' asked Eve.

'Well, how would I know? I doubt they were intended for me,' she replied.

It dawned on Eve that Les had left them there for her by way of an apology, a gesture that Eve could not fail to be moved by, and the couple soon made up.

'Les spoils you rotten,' Eve's mother said, noticing his romantic gestures towards her youngest daughter. But Gertrude had a soft spot for Les, knowing that he had suffered terrible atrocities as a prisoner of war. She ruffled her children's feathers by buying bananas – something of a treat – only to tell them firmly, 'No, hands off, they're for Les!' And nobody disobeyed her.

It was a sure sign that Les had won Gertrude's firm approval, and her affection for him increased by his willingness to help with any jobs that needed doing.

Les couldn't put a foot wrong, and Gertrude grew even fonder of him when he took Eve to choose a special birthday gift.

Eve had never had her own bike, and used to borrow one belonging to a friend if she needed to go anywhere. As her seventeenth birthday approached, Les knew that this would be the perfect gift for her.

'Come on, let's go and choose a bicycle together. I'd like to buy one for you – then we could go out on bike rides together,' he said.

'Oh Les, that would be wonderful,' she said.

Together they went to a shop in Chesterton Road and Eve spotted a gleaming black Raleigh bike.

'That's the one I like,' she said. 'It's perfect.'

The bicycle had gears, a large wicker basket, a shiny bell and lights. It had all the extras she needed and was everything she had ever wanted.

'I know it must cost a fortune, but it's the best present I could ever have had. I can never thank you enough.'

Eve stood on her toes to reach up and kiss him chastely on the cheek, a warm wave of love surging through her body. Although she was 5 feet 6 inches tall, he towered above her at 6 feet, and she felt very protected by him.

'You deserve the best,' he replied lovingly.

'I can't wait to go out on a bike ride. I could make a picnic,' Eve offered. 'Let's cycle over to Grantchester at the weekend. It's not too far and it's so pretty there.'

'But it's January – it's far too cold for a picnic,' Les replied, amused by her enthusiasm. 'We'll go there in the spring.'

'All right, I'll hold you to that. But I'm going to go for a quick ride now.'

Eve perched tentatively on the seat and reached for the pedals and handlebars. After a quick adjustment to the seat, Eve spun off to test out her present, ringing her bell and waving behind to Les.

Eve's mother reproached Les when they reached her home. 'Les, you do spoil her. You shouldn't spend so much on her,' she gently chided him when she saw the special gift.

'It gives me pleasure to buy it for Eve and to make her happy. You're all so very kind to me.'

When the soft glow of April sunshine arrived, Eve kept Les to his promise for their picnic at Grantchester.

'Let's go on Sunday afternoon. The weather's so lovely now and I'm really looking forward to cycling there through the meadows,' Eve urged Les, who readily agreed.

Eve was very pleased to see that the weather was bright and dry when the day of the picnic arrived. She happily busied herself preparing sandwiches and packing cake, fruit and tea for their picnic, which she placed in the sturdy wicker basket on the front of her bicycle.

Poignantly, Grantchester, a quintessentially English village with thatched cottages, meadowland and the meandering River Cam, had once been the home of Rupert Brooke, the First World War poet. He died aged only twenty-seven in April 1915, after becoming ill on board a troopship bound for Gallipoli.

Eve thought of this as they arrived there, laying out their picnic on the grass in front of the river. She knew his famous poem, 'The Soldier':

> If I should die, think only this of me:
> That there's some corner of a foreign field
> That is for ever England.

Eve wondered if these sentiments struck a chord with Les, reminding him of his dark days as a captive thousands of miles away in the Far East, when perhaps there were days when he gave up hope of returning home.

The village was only three-and-a-half miles from Eve's home, and on a very picturesque route. As Eve and Les set off, winding their way along the famous Backs in Cambridge, past the towering King's College Chapel and university buildings, they didn't have a care in the world.

When they arrived, a little breathless, they paused to take in the view before them. Grantchester Meadows was a green, dream-like scene of nature at its most perfect, where even the grazing cattle appeared mellow and content. They listened to the birdsong and, smiling, they gazed into each other's eyes and clasped hands.

'Let's sit under that willow tree,' said Eve, pointing to a quiet spot close to the river.

They leaned their bicycles under a tree and lay back on the grass, looking up at the bright blue sky above them.

'I love it here, it's so peaceful,' said Eve, she couldn't remember feeling happier.

Grantchester was a popular picnic spot with many Heyworth shop girls. It was one of the most romantic places in the area and for many years had attracted courting couples. Eve loved the quaint-ness of the village, a corner of England where time stood still, and they could sit on the riverbank watching students pass by on their punts, feeding the swans as they gracefully glided along.

'I know, I need to pinch myself to make sure I'm not in a dream,' replied Les, his arm cushioning Eve's head.

Eve's heart skipped a beat. 'You make me so happy too, Les,' she said.

As time passed, Les began confiding to Eve about his terrible three-and-a-half-year ordeal as a prisoner of war. When he was twenty, he'd signed up as an airframe fitter for the RAF and volunteered to go over-seas. He had no idea that he would return home a broken man.

Les sailed from Liverpool on 7 December 1941, the day that Japan bombed the American fleet in Pearl Harbor, and that was the last his family saw or heard from him. Nobody at home knew what had happened to Les, though they heard of atrocities in the Far East that were too horrible to speak about. Les worked in the dock-yards at the notorious Habu camp, watching his friends die at the hands of their brutal captors.

Les weighed only 4½ stone when he was finally freed from the camp, his life hanging by a thread. After being rescued, he was taken in by a family in Australia, and spent six months with them, slowly recovering and building up his strength again, before returning to Cambridge. Although he had put on weight, the invisible mental scars were harder to heal.

He had left home an excited young man and returned as an old man who didn't know what to say to his own family. He couldn't even face the minister at church, the Reverend John Buckingham, who visited him on his first day back home. Les pleaded with him to be left alone.

'I don't want to talk about it at all. I'm not ready to come back to church yet. I want to be on my own.'

Rev Buckingham understood. 'There's no pressure for you to speak or come back. You'll find your own way in time. We'll be here for you when you're ready.'

Les was finally persuaded to return to the church eighteen months later. He bumped into a member of the congregation when out walking.

'Come on, Les, come back to church. We all want to see you there. We miss you,' she pleaded in a friendly way.

'I'm not sure. I just don't know what to say to people. I don't know if I'm ready for it yet,' he replied.

'Why don't you give it a try and find out? We really do want you back.'

'All right, I'll come along to the club next Monday,' Les reluctantly agreed.

It was because of his return to the church youth club that Eve and Les were now out together on their bikes enjoying a picnic. Eve waited patiently for Les to open up in his own time and talk about his ordeal. She had a wise head on young shoulders, but when he finally began to tell her stories about the acts of cruelty he had witnessed, about the inhumane punishments handed out to prisoners, who were forced to stay in the sun all day and not allowed to help or pick up their comrades if they fell down, she was at a loss for words.

As they sat out in the spring sunshine in their Grantchester meadowland, he told Eve how they were starved. 'Some of them killed the Commander's dog and cooked that one day – they'd eat anything they could get their hands on.

'The officers were the worst: the higher the rank, the more they'd fight over the food on the floor. But the privates, they didn't do that. They looked after themselves and didn't bother about anyone else.

'You don't expect to see your old schoolmates there, but that's what happened. I was at Cambridge Central School with Ronald

Searle, and there he was, with me in Habu camp in Innoshima. He used to write notes and draw pictures of the camp, which we hid.'

'Poor you, I can't bear to hear how terrible it was,' Eve told him.

Les then rolled up his trouser leg and pressed his finger into the flesh on his calf. It left a deep indentation like a crater opening up before her very eyes.

As she gasped, he told her, 'That's because of beriberi. We all suffered from it because of the poor diet.'

It was almost too awful to comprehend. Beriberi was a common disease among the prisoners of war, caused by dietary deficiencies. It caused weakness and pain in the limbs and in many cases caused kidney failure.

Les described how he had spent his twenty-first birthday at the camp – and the surprise card he was given by fellow inmates.

'Here you are, Les, this is for you. Happy birthday, mate, wish you could have been somewhere else for it,' one of his comrades said, handing him a rolled-up sheet of paper. Like Les, he was a bag of bones, but he had a big grin on his face as he gave Les the scroll. It was a card they had secretly made for him and signed.

Using carefully concealed coloured crayons, and drawing on the back of a large Japanese sheet of paper intended for some form of accounts, an artist in the camp had drawn Les's beloved Boy Scout motif beautifully and the words, 'The Pen Is Mightier Than The Sword'.

Les was deeply touched and treasured his hand-made card, bringing it back to his Cambridgeshire home. Eve was stunned by such heroism and thoughtfulness from Les's campmates, that despite their terrible suffering they did their best to mark the occasion and make Les's birthday special.

'A penny for them. What are you thinking?' asked Eve.

'I'm just thinking I am the luckiest man in the world,' he replied, smiling. Eve was pleased that, in spite of everything he'd been through, Les had been able to find some peace with her.

'Come on, let's go and feed those swans.' And they raced over to the river to throw in their crusts, the swans gathering round and reaching up to take the food from Les's hand.

'What we'd have given for a crust of bread like this in camp,' he said, watching as the swans stretched out their long necks to scoop the bread up.

Like the other shop girls, Eve enjoyed trips organised and paid for by Heyworth's. The latest one to be announced had particularly caught her attention – a visit to the theatre to see the comedian Max Wall in a play at the Cambridge Kinema Theatre in Mill Road. Wall had recently been invalided out from the war, and he appeared regularly on television. His expressive, rubbery face attracted legions of fans around the country, including Les.

'Of course I'd like to see him – he's my favourite and always makes me laugh so much. I can't wait!' he told Eve enthusiastically, when she invited him to join the Heyworth party. Mr Heyworth paid for them all. Although he had his funny ways, Eve noticed how generous he was in paying for staff outings.

Throughout the play, Les nearly exploded with uncontrollable laughter. His big belly laughs made heads spin around and attracted the attention of Miss Richards, the straight-laced buyer from millinery, who was sitting nearby.

Every time Les roared, she glared at him, a big, disapproving scowl on her face. Although Eve couldn't help laughing along with Les, Miss Richards clearly didn't share Max Wall's wacky sense of humour, and looked at them sternly. The louder Les laughed, the sterner her face became, which made Les want to laugh even more.

'How can anyone come to see Max Wall and not laugh? You'd have to be pretty miserable,' he whispered to Eve.

'That's just the way she is,' Eve said, trying not to laugh out loud. 'She's very fussy and particular at work. She gets really cross if she sees people touching the hats without her permission. She can be very sour, but don't worry about it.'

'It's one of the best nights I've ever had! I'll always remember it,' said Les, taking Eve's arm as they left the theatre.

As well as enjoying Heyworth's work outings to the theatre and seaside, the shop girls were sometimes invited to meet up with Miss Stubbings to have a gossip, share a picnic and enjoy a carefree afternoon after the store closed early on a Thursday. Despite the age difference between the girls and Miss Stubbings, who was approaching sixty, they always had a wonderful time, full of smiles and laughter.

'Would you like to come down to the caravan on Thursday afternoon?' she asked Eve. 'We can take the boat out as well.'

Although Miss Stubbings was head of her department, she had a very open and friendly manner, which her staff warmed to. She didn't put on airs and graces, but was still able to command the respect of her shop girls and retain an authoritative air.

Eve felt pleased to be invited along with the older shop girls. Lil Hulyer had come along, as well as Beryl Carter, Betty Hancock and Mary Ryder. They all changed quickly out of their work clothes – black skirts and white blouses – into pretty floral dresses and cardigans.

Miss Stubbings kept a small caravan in a field near the village of Fen Ditton, which sloped alongside the River Cam on the outskirts of Cambridge. It was a picturesque spot, and, like Grantchester, an unspoilt English village where weeping willows lined the riverbank and the birds serenaded them.

'I love it here, it's so peaceful,' said Eve, sitting on the grass and looking up at the cloudless sky. 'I hope we can go on the boat today.'

'Why don't we go now?'

Eve and her friends headed for Miss Stubbings' rowing boat, which was stored in the field, and pulled it along to the river's edge, dropping it gently into the water. Taking the oars, they rowed up and down the river, enjoying the peace and tranquillity of the countryside. Eve closed her eyes and sank back into the boat, feeling the warm, soft breeze on her skin.

When they returned to Miss Stubbings, her boss was keen to hear the latest about Eve's romance with Les. After Eve told her, Miss Stubbings stunned Eve by saying, 'Well, I never! Isn't that a funny thing? There's something familiar about your Les. I'm sure we're related – there's a connection between him and my family.'

Eve gasped. 'I can't believe it – wait till I tell Les. Fancy you being related to him!'

When Eve asked Les and his family about this, it turned out to be true – there was a link between their two families.

One sunny Sunday afternoon, Les invited Eve to cycle over to Grantchester for another picnic.

Eve was only too happy to agree; it was one of her favourite places to visit with Les. As they sat by the edge of the river, she watched other couples stroll by arm in arm, enjoying the warmth of the sun. Students in their college blazers and boaters skilfully steered their punts by, the gentle sound of rippling water soothing Eve and Les as they sat on the grass.

Eve gazed at Les, and thought how lucky she was to have found him. He stared back, before looking down, and it seemed to her that he was struggling to find the right words.

Then he said simply, 'Eve, will you marry me? I love you and want to spend the rest of my life with you.'

Eve was overjoyed and had no hesitation in responding.

'Yes, of course I'll marry you!' she replied, feeling tenderness welling up inside her. 'I love you too.'

Eve's mother was delighted when she heard the news.

'We are not going to rush it, Mum, I'm not eighteen yet,' Eve reassured her.

'I'm so pleased for you both. What wonderful news! Les is a lovely man. You couldn't have anyone better,' said Gertrude.

The exciting news soon spread around Heyworth's and the shop girls gathered to admire Eve's platinum engagement ring, which was engraved with two small leaves and had a diamond in the middle. Herbert joined the well-wishers. 'Miss Gray, may I congratulate you on behalf of Mrs Heyworth and myself. I wish you both every happiness,' he told her, smiling.

Eve and Les weren't in a hurry to get married, but their plans unexpectedly changed within a year. Eve's sister Peggy made a suggestion that brought their wedding date forward.

'Instead of you and Les waiting till next year, why don't you get married now and live here with Mum? It will save her getting another lodger in and having to live with a stranger.'

At first Gertrude wouldn't hear about it. 'She's far too young! There's plenty of time for her to get married,' she insisted.

Eve and Les considered Peggy's idea and agreed with her.

'It makes sense, Mum. Why should you take a lodger in if Les and I can stay here with you? And it means Les and I can save up more. We know you could never afford to stay in this big house all on your own. And anyway, I'll be eighteen soon!'

Eve's mother eventually relented and they began to plan for the big day. When Eve opened the curtains on her big day on 9 October 1948, the air was thick with fog. Although it was autumn, Eve had hoped the sun would shine – and fortunately it did, in time for the 2 p.m. service.

Eve looked radiant in her full-length satin bridal gown with dainty flowers embossed on to the fabric. The long-sleeved dress had a sweetheart neckline and a row of pearls hung around her neck. It didn't matter to Eve that her wedding dress had been borrowed from Les's sister, Phyllis. It was a stroke of luck that Phyllis had a dainty figure like Eve, and the dress fitted like a glove.

Eve's brother Bill walked her down the aisle, her long veil cascading down her back. Her bridesmaids were her school friend Freda Carter, a seamstress at a Cambridge tailoring shop, Les's sister Joyce, who worked in the Co-op offices, and Les's eleven-year-old niece from London. Freda and Joyce wore blue taffeta dresses, which had also been borrowed, and the younger bridesmaid wore pink. Their dresses matched the bouquet she carried – pink carnations and blue scabious, along with her lucky horseshoe. The veil was held in place with a halo of flowers.

As Eve walked down the aisle, Les could not resist turning around to glance at her. Dressed in a navy double-breasted suit, white shirt and striped tie, he smiled at her. Eve felt happier than words could describe. She smiled back as he softly told her, 'You look beautiful,' when she reached him at the altar.

Knowing that Gertrude was hard up, Les offered to pay for the food at the reception, which was held in the Victorian-built Overstream House, a popular social venue close to their home in Victoria Road.

'You don't need to worry about that. I'll pay for the reception; we'll make sure it's a special day for Eve,' he promised her.

'Bless you, you are a good man,' Gertrude replied gratefully.

A generous supply of cakes and sandwiches were provided, as well as trifle – Les's favourite.

Les's brother Cyril, who worked at the Savoy Hotel in London as a toastmaster, gave the happy couple a very special treat. He asked the Savoy's chef to make a three-tier wedding cake, which would have cost a fortune to buy.

The guests gasped with delight when they saw the jaw-dropping cake, covered in white icing, with bride and groom figures perched on the top.

'Is it real? I can't believe it. Nobody could get hold of dried fruit to make a wedding cake during the war,' the disbelieving guests said.

'Oh yes, it's real all right. Just goes to show it's who you know that counts,' replied Les, winking at Cyril.

Eve's mother told the guests how they very nearly lost the cake. It had been placed on their sideboard the night before the wedding, but the thundering traffic passing by made the house shake so much that the top tier slid off – thankfully, she had managed to rescue it in time!

Guests savoured every mouthful. It's not every day that they got the chance to eat a cake made by a chef at one of London's top hotels!

'I can't remember the last time I tasted anything as good as this,' said Eve.

After the reception, Eve and Les set off for their honeymoon in Clacton, with their fifty wedding guests following them to Cambridge railway station to wave them off.

As the train moved off and they collapsed into their seats, Les took Eve's hand and asked, 'What does it feel like to be Mrs Collis?'

'Wonderful! It's the best feeling in the world,' she replied.

Eve and Les had originally planned to go to Bournemouth for their honeymoon, but as the wedding had been brought forward a year, they couldn't afford it.

Instead, they took up an offer from one of Eve's mother's friends.

'I know it's not what you'd hoped for, but you should get away for a few days' honeymoon, and my friend said you can stay with her friend, Elsie Stone, in Clacton. She'll look after you,' Eve's mother suggested.

Mrs Stone was a tiny old lady and welcomed the newlyweds

when they arrived at her two-up two-down terraced house just off the seafront.

'You must be ready for a cup of tea. Here, let me show you your room first,' she said.

They followed her up the narrow stairs to the tiny spare room. There was barely room to walk around the furniture. It wasn't what they'd planned for their honeymoon, and their hearts sank.

'Never mind Eve. We'll save up to go to Bournemouth next year,' Les promised when he saw Eve's downcast gaze.

Very little happened in Clacton in October; it was well past the end of the summer season. To make matters worse, it rained almost every day. Clacton felt like a ghost town as Eve and Les walked arm in arm along the deserted seafront sharing an umbrella, ducking and diving from the heavy showers.

With no attractions to visit, Eve and Les took cover in the cinema almost every day, and feasted on fish and chips. Despite their disappointment, Eve was just happy to be married to Les and she knew they had their whole lives ahead of them. When Eve returned to Heyworth's after her honeymoon, there was an announcement that took Eve by surprise.

'I'm leaving Heyworth's. It's time for me to retire,' Miss Stubbings told the shocked shop girls. 'I've handed in my notice.'

'Oh no – it just won't be the same here without you,' Eve said, wondering who would take charge of the department.

Miss Stubbings didn't have the same comfortable close relationship with Herbert Heyworth as some of the other buyers, and didn't want to work with him after he took over running the shop. She felt awkward with him and didn't like or respect him in the same way she had his father, George.

'I can't work with Herbert, but I shall miss you all very much,' she told her assistants.

Eve felt sad as she reflected back to the wonderful afternoons they had shared on her boat and in her caravan during their Thursday afternoons off. She thought about the close bond that Miss Stubbings had with her shop girls, and how she had trained her from her first day, when she was only fourteen.

'I want to wish you well for the future,' Eve told her. 'I'd like to thank you for being so kind to me over the years, and for everything you did for me.'

Eve could only think of one question – who would be the next buyer and head of the childrenswear department? And what would it mean for Eve?

IRENE

1948

The elegant Irene Fiander, Heyworth's accessories buyer

It didn't matter to Irene that her new job was as a lower-ranking sales assistant. She was just glad to be back at work. Herbert Heyworth had told her she'd be offered a position as an accessories buyer when the present buyer retired – which would be soon – and she was happy to bide her time until then.

'You'll be known as Miss Fiander, as we already have a Miss Dean here. We can't have two sales girls with the same name, it'll be confusing,' she was told. She didn't mind at all: she was still getting used to being called Mrs Dean.

It was early summer. Dressed immaculately in her black suit, Irene glanced around the fashion showroom where she was to work. The rails were filled to the brim with the very latest styles for women who could afford quality garments. Irene's face broke into a big smile when she spotted her favourite Horrocks dresses with beautiful patterns and wide skirts. She admired the elegant and exquisite ballgowns made in stunning silks and satins. The latest eye-catching gowns were displayed on mannequins around the showroom. Busts on the counters featured the latest style in blouses, and a plinth in the middle of the showroom was adorned with a figure dressed in one of their most desirable costumes in the hope of attracting the eye of their wealthy customers.

The showroom was long and narrow with an archway going from the gown showroom to another room where suits and coats were sold. George Heyworth's wife Elizabeth sat at a desk close to the archway, attending to paperwork and watching people come up the stairs. George, Herbert's father, had opened their first store in Cambridge in 1914 before moving to their present location in 1928, and grey-haired Mrs Heyworth saw everyone who came in and made it her business to know what was happening.

She would prick up her ears to eavesdrop on conversations between the shop girls and customers. If a woman left without making a purchase, she'd ask the assistant, 'What did she want? Why couldn't we help?' If the reason was that an item was out of stock, Mrs Heyworth made a note so it could be replenished.

Irene worked alongside Mrs Jamison, a ladies fashion buyer in her forties. She always dressed very smartly and was regarded as a very efficient member of staff.

One day Mrs Jamison called in sick. But later that afternoon she was seen by a friend of Herbert Heyworth's at Newmarket Races, dressed up to the nines and having a flutter on the horses. He recognised her and noticed that she was thoroughly enjoying herself, egging on her favourite horse to win.

Mr Heyworth's friend was suspicious about her being at Newmarket on a weekday, so he told Herbert – who was furious. As far as he was concerned, there was only one course of action to take, and Mrs Jamison was sacked instantly.

'Don't bother coming in any more. Your cards will be sent to you,' he said when he called her, in a spitting rage. 'Nobody is going to lie to us and get away with it.'

The news made the shop girls reel. Irene was sorry that Mrs Jamison had been dismissed, but thought her actions were foolish. Sloping off for the day by pretending to be ill was certainly nothing she'd do herself, as she held Herbert Heyworth in too high a regard and loved her job too much to risk losing it for an afternoon jolly!

One of the other girls in the department thought Mrs Jamison had got her comeuppance. Shirley Cook, a young junior in the fashion showroom, didn't warm to Mrs Jamison, and found her aloof. Shirley had almost landed herself in trouble on her first day. The fifteen-year-old, who'd borrowed her elder sister's black skirt and top as she didn't possess any suitable work clothes of her own, had cheekily decided to put her feet up at the end of the day.

She sat down behind the counter, bold as brass, then put her feet up and started reading a newspaper that was laying around. One of the other shop girls saw her and couldn't believe her eyes!

'You mustn't do that. Put the paper down quickly before some-one sees you and you get into trouble!' The urgent warning came from Maureen Turkentine, who also worked in the fashion show-room and was three years older than Shirley. Maureen knew that Shirley would be in big trouble if she was seen by Miss Dolman, head of the department. Shirley leapt up immediately.

Regarded by Shirley as a bit of a tyrant, Miss Dolman was a fashion buyer, a straight-laced woman who wore her long grey hair plaited in braids tied around her head. The other buyer in the department was the more youthful Phyllis Moss, in her thirties, who was also a director of Heyworth's.

Miss Moss couldn't have been more different from Miss Dolman. She was gentle and reserved and had lovely, gracious ways with the customers. She was an attractive woman, very neat, and lived with three or four sisters. Irene had heard that she had been engaged to Herbert Heyworth at one time.

Irene was fond of Miss Moss and admired her perfect manners and grooming. She also became fond of Betty Dean, her namesake, who was second lead sales assistant after Miss Moss. Aged about twenty, Betty oozed glamour and was a head-turner. She wore bright lipstick, lots of make-up, a tight skirt and high heels. She had a confidence and cheek that appealed to Mr Heyworth as well; everyone liked Betty Dean.

Perhaps surprisingly, Betty got on particularly well with Miss Dolman, and could often be seen confiding in her, sharing secrets about her love life and having a giggle, even though the two women were like chalk and cheese.

But what Irene admired most about Betty was that she was a fantastic saleswoman, one of the best in Heyworth's. She would sprint to a cubicle to wrap up her sales, with tissue paper folded around the garment before it was placed in a carrier bag. She would easily sell half-a-dozen coats in an afternoon.

The fashion showroom attracted the wives of many distinguished academics from Cambridge University, including Lady Todd, who came in regularly to buy their fabulous Hebe and Windsmoor suits. She wore her hair drawn back into a bun, and had twinkling eyes and a lovely kind way about her, which put the younger shop girls at ease. You would never guess that she was the wife of one of the country's most distinguished organic chemists, who was in great demand to sit on government advisory councils, as she was a very down-to-earth woman with no airs and graces.

Irene enjoyed hearing about the escapades of the young shop girls in her department. One year, four of them, including Shirley, Eileen Pryor, whose sister Jean worked in the corsetry department, and Joyce Benstead, booked a week's holiday in Bournemouth. They were all sixteen and this was their first holiday away on their own. Much of their time was spent sunbathing on the beach, as well as dancing at night and whooping it up at the funfair.

It was a baking hot summer and very soon they began to suffer for their time spent trying to catch a suntan. Joyce, a redhead with a fair skin, suffered the most and was in terrible agony. When the girls returned to their hotel, they stuffed cotton wool into their bras to ease the pain and protect their tender skin against the weight of outer clothes pressing on to their chests.

Irene was happy with her work and enjoyed the friendship of the girls in the fashion showroom. But an unexpected development meant that she had to resign.

'You'll never guess what – I'm pregnant!' she told Peter.

His face lit up. 'That's wonderful – it's the best news ever!' he exclaimed.

Irene had only been at Heyworth's for two months and the pregnancy had not been planned. But they felt it was nature's work, and they were thrilled. Irene knew Peter would make a wonderful father. She was sorry to hand in her notice so soon but Mr Heyworth was very understanding. He wished her well and said he was sorry to see her leave so quickly.

When the day came that October for Irene to leave Heyworth's, she was presented with an array of gifts, a first sign of Herbert's generosity towards her even though she had only worked at the store for a short time. He invited her to select a maternity suit from the shop and two outfits for her baby, one in pure silk. She was left speechless by his generosity. That was not all, as the shop girls also presented Irene with a Lloyd Loom wicker bedroom chair and matching linen basket.

She began looking forward to planning for her baby but, within days, the phone rang. Irene immediately recognised the voice on the other end: it was Herbert Heyworth.

'Can you please come in and see me, Miss Fiander?' he asked. 'I'd like to ask you something and would appreciate it if you could come in soon.'

Irene was surprised to hear from him. She pondered why he should want to see her again so soon after leaving.

'Of course Mr Heyworth, I'll call in tomorrow,' she said, feeling puzzled.

When she met Mr Heyworth, the reason soon became clear.

'Miss Fiander, I wondered if you could please come back for a while. We're short-staffed and I'd be very grateful if you could help with pricing tickets.'

Irene was not expecting to hear this, but she was pleased to be asked back and had no hesitation in accepting. Irene's new duties were intended to be a sitting-down job so she would not have to exert herself too much. But she aroused great concern from Mrs Heyworth, who spotted Irene carrying boxes up the stairs.

'Miss Fiander,' she said sharply, 'don't you dare carry any boxes again. I nearly lost my Herbert because the cord was around his neck!'

Irene was shocked to hear this and didn't carry any more boxes during her pregnancy. She continued cycling to work and was easily spotted in her voluminous bright red coat, her large bump clearly visible. She told Peter, 'I feel I look like a number-one bus!'

She left Heyworth's after Christmas 1948 and Patricia was born late in May 1949. Irene settled into motherhood, away from the thrill and excitement she felt at work and the glamour of being surrounded by beautiful clothes.

Two months after Patricia was born, Herbert Heyworth called Peter at work, asking him, 'Can you ask Irene to come in and see me? And ask if she can bring the baby in, too. I'd like to see them both.'

When Peter passed on the message to his wife, she thought Mr Heyworth simply wanted to see the baby and ask about how she was getting on. She called in at Heyworth's the following day, not expecting to hear the words that followed: 'I'd like you to come back. We now have a vacancy for a buyer in the accessories department, and the job is yours if you'd like it.'

Irene couldn't believe what she was hearing. 'But how will I manage with the baby?' she asked.

'Don't worry about that. I'll pay for your housekeeper on top of your wages. Now that Miss Hayward has retired as our buyer, I thought you'd be interested,' he added.

Irene was stunned. Although this was the job Mr Heyworth had referred to when she first met him, she had forgotten all about it now she had a baby daughter, and she had certainly not considered returning to work so soon. But Irene didn't need much time to make up her mind. She was excited to be offered a job that she knew she'd enjoy.

'I shall need to talk about it with Peter, but thank you, Mr Heyworth, I would like to accept, as long as Peter agrees.'

'Of course, Miss Fiander, I understand. I look forward to hearing from you very soon.'

Mr Heyworth bent over and glanced into the pram, admiring Irene's daughter Patricia's cherubic features and her large, wide eyes.

'She's a lovely baby,' he told Irene, smiling at her as she left.

Irene had sensed a thrill walking back into the store and realised how much she missed the camaraderie. Having been offered her dream job, she now couldn't wait to return.

'What do you think Peter? Should I go back?' Irene asked her husband later that night.

Peter wasn't too sure at first, but Irene convinced him that it would work. They realised that Peter's wages at the bank were not enough and agreed that it made financial sense for her to return to work so they could save for a place of their own. As they didn't have a separate bedroom for Patricia at Peter's mother's house, they realised they would need to find somewhere larger to live soon.

Peter's mother doted on the baby and was only too happy to look after her while Irene returned to Heyworth's. She had a housekeeper called Maude, and Mr Heyworth's generous offer to pay her wages meant that Irene's mother-in-law could spend the days looking after her without worrying about the household chores. It seemed the perfect plan.

A month later she returned to Heyworth's as a buyer. Any doubts Irene may have had about leaving her three-month-old baby at home soon vanished once she stepped inside the store. Irene felt she was back where she belonged. She revelled at being a buyer again, responsible for buying accessories, including gloves and scarves, while Patricia thrived under the care of her besotted grandmother. When she checked her weekly pay packet, she noticed that Mr Heyworth had topped it up with extra cash to cover Maude's pay, just as he had promised. Irene felt she had to pinch herself – it was almost too good to be true!

Irene knew how important accessories were for women, regarding them as an essential fashion item. Buying a new scarf, belt or gloves was the best way to freshen up an outfit and give it a new look. All smartly-dressed women wore a pair of gloves to complement their outfit, particularly if it matched their hat and handbag. They were made from chamois leather, cotton or lace – with white, cream and yellow being the most popular summer colours – or suede with fur trimming in the winter. Elegant, over-the-elbow satin gloves were popular for evening wear, in the style that Hollywood starlets wore them.

Irene also bought hosiery, and the newly introduced nylon stockings were one of the most sought-after and desirable items she had to source. They were still in short supply after the war, and she simply couldn't get enough to meet demand. A few years before there had been reports of riots in America in the mid-1940s, when forty thousand women in Pittsburgh queued up for thirteen thousand pairs of stockings.

Nylon stockings were hugely popular because they were more durable than those made from silk, and were shrink-proof and moth-proof. They also fitted the leg perfectly and didn't sag around the ankle. Heyworth's struggled to keep up with demand, restricting customers to only two pairs each, which was why Herbert decided to join Irene in persuading suppliers to let them have as many pairs as possible.

He and Irene scoured the country to place orders for nylons, with Herbert driving her to warehouses or manufacturers in his latest racy sports car. He wanted to meet the suppliers to drive a hard bargain for the best price.

One of his cars was a stylish two-seater Armstrong Siddeley with a powerful engine and soft-top. It had plush leather seating – and Herbert Heyworth liked driving fast. As they sped around bends, Irene hung on to the side of the car for dear life, once even rolling on to him. When she protested about his driving, he told her she was not a good passenger.

'Well I don't think you're a good driver,' she retorted.

'The trouble is, it goes down on one knee when I round a bend. Just hang on tight,' he replied.

Riding in Herbert Heyworth's luxury car was always a thrill, and sometimes his chauffeur, Nick, drove her if Herbert couldn't take her and there was no direct rail link to a manufacturer outside London.

One day Herbert drove Irene to Kayser Bondor in Baldock, one of the country's largest suppliers of stockings, as well as corsetry, and a major supplier to Heyworth's. Originally called the Full-Fashioned Hosiery Company, it was on a distinctive Art Deco site that was requisitioned during the war to make parachutes, taking on its new name when the war was over. Staff moved back into the premises in 1947, and the production of stockings boomed again.

Irene was overawed by its elegant 1930s façade. She then spotted a swimming pool at the front of the building.

'Why is that there? Do they really have their own pool?'

'Yes, it's for the staff,' replied her boss.

'I've never seen anything like it before,' Irene replied, thinking how lucky people were to work there.

Herbert Heyworth also drove Irene to Ballito's stocking factory in St Albans, as well as others in Leicester and Derbyshire. They decided to make a trip of it and stay overnight in Nottingham after calling in at Bear Brand, another leading hosiery manufacturer.

They stayed at the Black Boy Hotel, built in a gothic Bavarian style with timbering and turrets by Nottingham's most flamboyant architect, Watson Fothergill. A uniformed doorman greeted Herbert and Irene when they arrived, and although the hotel bar was for men only, they both dined together at night. The hotel had an old-fashioned air about it, which Irene found charming.

The following day they set off for Matlock in Derbyshire to place an order with their stocking supplier, Tor. Irene was glad to have her boss with her, as he liked to be closely involved in sealing the best deal with manufacturers. Due to the dire shortage of nylon stockings, suppliers had the upper hand. Herbert and Irene couldn't simply state what they wanted and place an order: Tor told them how many pairs they were prepared to sell and could dictate their own terms.

The supplier told Herbert, 'You can have twenty dozen.'

This was not enough for Herbert. 'Come on, Fred, you can do better than that – we're good customers here.'

The manufacturer checked his figures and scratched his head. 'Okay then. I can stretch to another five dozen.'

'Done!' said Herbert triumphantly. The two men shook hands to seal their deal.

Irene smiled as she watched the transaction and admired how Herbert always succeeded in getting the best possible deal – by hook or by crook – despite the shortages.

Pure nylon stockings sold at £2 11s a pair. They were Heyworth's highest-priced stocking, and flew off the shelf. In one week Heyworth's took nearly £2,000 in sales from nylon stockings alone. At the time it was a staggering sum!

Heyworth's also sold silk and rayon stockings, but only the fully fashioned stockings with perfectly stitched seams running along the back, which were shaped to fit the leg perfectly, and not the cheaper unfashioned stockings or 'mocks', as they were called, which were inferior quality, with a poor fit.

Irene enjoyed her buying trips with her boss. He was generous towards her, making her feel a valued member of staff, and always remembered to ask after Patricia, while Irene regarded him as a father figure. Also, the arrangement was working well at home. It was going so well that Irene never had the chance to finish bathing her daughter because her mother-in-law or sister-in-law would quickly step in and wrap the towel around Patricia, and take her away. But she always managed to read her a bedtime story; that was their special time of the day, when Irene opened up a book of fairy tales to enchant her with.

As an experienced buyer, Irene was used to working within her budget and managing the girls in her department, Beryl Flack, Sue Bradford and Rita Barrett.

All the buyers were given their budgets at the beginning of the year and couldn't go above it. Each time Irene went buying, she was careful not to overspend, fearing she would be in dead trouble if she did, but she never faced Herbert's wrath on this account.

Irene taught new juniors how to speak to customers correctly, helped by Miss Flack. When young Rita started, Irene took her under her wing, saying, 'When a customer walks in, you must say "good morning" to them in a nice voice and ask if you can help them. You must smile at them – you should smile before you even speak. And remember, nothing is too much trouble. You can learn by watching us and seeing what goes on every day.'

Although the Heyworth's shop girls were highly regarded for their polite and courteous service, customers would very occasionally complain. Irene was outraged when one awkward woman complained to Elizabeth Heyworth, saying, 'I want a pair of black gloves, not ordinary black, but soot black.'

Irene couldn't believe this, thinking, 'What on earth is soot black? How can anyone differentiate soot black from any other black? It's ludicrous!'

On another occasion, an irate customer moaned about not being shown enough gloves from their vast selection.

'But we have so many trays of gloves, it's not possible or reasonable to expect us to take them all out,' Irene protested when hearing this complaint. 'Some people are simply impossible to please!'

Irene never lost sleep over complaints she felt were unjustified. She knew how polite and diligent her girls were. They were creative too, often scooping the prize for the best display inside the store in the competition Herbert held regularly. Irene's team in the accessories department was hard to beat.

On one occasion they'd spread different-coloured woollen tights around a makeshift fire on a stand, using logs and red transparent paper with a light behind it to resemble warm embers. It was simple but effective, and it clearly caught Herbert's eye.

'Once again, Irene's accessories department wins the prize for the best display,' Herbert boomed, as the rest of the staff applauded.

The competition was motivating, and inspired Irene's staff to think creatively, as well as working as a team. It was sometimes hard to come up with ideas, but it was always worth it in the end when their display won.

'I only came up with the idea – it was Miss Flack who put it all together. She's very artistic,' Irene told Herbert.

'Very well done, Miss Flack,' he said.

Beryl Flack blushed and smiled appreciatively. The shop girls were thrilled with their prize – they were each being treated to a meal at a local restaurant. Irene had a soft spot for twenty-four-year-old Beryl, a bubbly young woman with lovely brunette hair that had natural lighter streaks in it. She had recently married Chas, a Polish prisoner of war. She mimicked his amusing use of English swear words, telling Irene how he had returned home one day and noticed a pigeon had come down the chimney.

'What are you doing with that mess?' Beryl asked him.

'A pigeon came down the chimney. Bloody!' he replied in his thick accent.

'Ah, bless him,' said Irene. 'He's a lovely man.'

Irene was pleased when her friend Betty Lipscombe started working in the millinery department. The age difference between their babies was only three months, and one Thursday, early-closing day, Irene asked Betty, 'Shall we go to the baby clinic together this afternoon after the store closes?'

'Oh yes, that would be good,' agreed Betty, and the two women strolled down the road pushing their prams together on their way to the clinic at Cherry Hinton Hall. It became a regular Thursday afternoon outing.

Irene looked at Betty's young daughter sleeping peacefully with slight envy. Jennifer, who was three months older than Patricia, always slept like an angel, never murmuring a sound, while Patricia tugged restlessly at the straps in her pram, writhing her way to the opposite end.

Irene tried to placate her fidgety daughter, but to no avail, and she continued wailing. Irene then came up with a novel suggestion: 'Do you mind if we swap our babies and I walk with your baby to the clinic and you can have my noisy baby, just so I can have the quiet baby with me for a change?'

'Here you are then,' said Betty, laughing as she walked down with Patricia, still crying, while Jennifer gurgled contentedly with Irene in charge of her.

The two women chatted animatedly away as they walked the ten minutes to Cherry Hinton Hall. Their main topic of conversation was their baby daughters and everyday lives; they never talked about their wartime experiences.

It was always a pleasure walking to Cherry Hinton Hall, as its vast grounds were stunning. The distinctive property had been built as a small 'family mansion' in the Elizabethan style in 1839 and was set in the midst of exotic and beautiful grounds. Both women enjoyed its lush, attractive surroundings – it felt like being in the countryside.

During the war the Hall was used to train the local Home Guard and also provided a home for young evacuees. After the war it was used as a mother-and-baby clinic where Patricia and Jennifer were weighed and given their inoculations, plus rationed formula milk and rosehip syrup.

When they returned home and Irene put Patricia down to sleep after she had finally settled, she hugged her daughter and kissed her. She loved her to pieces, but she knew she would never be content staying at home as a full-time mum, that she needed the stimulation from a working environment, and working in Heyworth's fulfilled that need.

Irene was so pleased she had helped Betty. Irene's home life could not have been more different from Betty's, who lived with a harsh father and had to support herself and her daughter financially. Just as Betty relied on her mother to look after Jennifer while she worked, Irene herself had greatly appreciated the help of her mother-in-law in caring for Patricia.

Then Gladys died suddenly at the age of fifty-seven. It was a terrible shock.

'Poor woman – what a very young age to die. She was so good to Patricia and doted on her. I don't know how I could have managed without her,' she told her boss.

'I would like to offer you our sympathies, Miss Fiander, and to assure you that you can work hours that suit with your new circumstances if it helps you,' Herbert said.

His words were music to Irene's ears. Patricia was four years old and would soon be starting school. Maude had offered to continue helping with Patricia up until then, and, thanks to Herbert Heyworth's kind offer, she would be able to return home in good time in the afternoon.

'Thank you Mr Heyworth, I very much appreciate that,' replied Irene gratefully. She knew how fortunate she was to have a boss who was sympathetic and prepared to work around her difficulties.

Maude was in her late forties, and rather drab-looking. She rarely smiled and her hair was tied back in a tight bun. She wore thick stockings and skirts and heavy lace-up shoes. Neither was she very bright, but Patricia was used to her, and the arrangement was only for a few months. When she started school, Maude left and Irene worked around her daughter's school hours, arriving at Heyworth's at 9.30 a.m., and leaving at 3 p.m. in good time to collect Patricia.

Among Irene's customers was Marjorie Heyworth, her boss's wife, who was always elegantly dressed. Mrs Heyworth would arrive in expensive-looking fur coats or wearing the latest ladies' styles in suits and dresses. Sometimes she bought long satin gloves for evening wear, as well as the beautiful silk scarves Irene bought for the store. She had some of her clothes specially made for her too, as well as her hats, and would ask Irene to look out for special accessories for her in a particular colour to match a new outfit.

She would hand Irene a small piece of ribbon from a newly made hat by Mrs Pugh, the store's milliner, and ask, 'Please look out for a beautiful pair of gloves to match this colour.'

Irene always delivered what was required, delighted to please her boss's wife, who thanked her appreciatively for finding just what she needed.

Irene had a new order to source for Marjorie Heyworth in London and needed to figure out a way to visit their suppliers to place her orders while Patricia was at home during school holidays. Herbert Heyworth suggested a solution.

'Why don't you take Patricia to London with you? I'll pay for her rail ticket. I don't mind if she goes with you on your buying trip,' he said.

'Yes, why not? I'll see how it goes,' said Irene.

Patricia joined her mother on the Fenman train from Cambridge to Liverpool Street Station. The journey was a great adventure for the five-year-old girl. Cambridge railway station, with its enormously long platform, was always frantically busy. Many of the people standing on the platform were military personnel, peacetime conscripts on National Service dressed in smart uniforms. As the engine steamed into the station at 8.31 a.m., having left Hunstanton on the North Norfolk coast at 6.45 a.m. for its journey through the flat Fenland landscape, Patricia eagerly boarded the train. She paced along the corridor looking for two seats in one of the many compartments, which were rapidly filling up. Irene followed and opened a carriage door, where Patricia flopped on the seat, her mother next to her.

With all the passengers on board, the stationmaster, dressed smartly in a dark suit and bowler hat, waved a flag to the engine driver, blew his whistle, and the packed train hissed out of the station on its journey to Liverpool Street Station, arriving at 10.03 a.m.

Irene was visiting showrooms that day to buy new silk scarves, gloves, umbrellas and handkerchiefs, and any other stylish accessories that caught her eye. The suppliers' eyes lit up when they spotted Patricia and they spoiled her rotten. It was like Christmas Day for the young girl, who returned home laden with free goodies, like handkerchiefs with the initial P embroidered in the corner and children's pop-bead necklaces and bracelets.

'Oh, she's so lovely. Do bring her again,' the suppliers enthused, as a beaming Patricia looked up at them,

Irene smiled back, 'Of course I will. I don't think I'll be able to keep her away!'

After Irene had finished her business, she treated Patricia to lunch at the Quality Inn in Argyll Street, near the London Palladium. It was a highlight of the day for Patricia, who requested her favourite – Aunt Mary's apple pie. Patricia's eyes sparkled when the dish arrived and she couldn't wait to tuck into it, probably because Irene never made it at home.

These trips to London became a regular fixture, but on one occasion Irene suffered her worst nightmare when she momentarily lost her daughter. One minute they were standing together on the platform at Oxford Circus underground, and the next minute, Irene had stepped inside a carriage and the doors closed behind her. To her horror, Irene looked outside the carriage window and saw Patricia still standing on the platform – alone, frozen to the spot and terrified.

As the train sped off, Irene looked back at Patricia's frightened face until it vanished out of sight as the train sped ahead. She was panic-stricken and a sick, churning feeling welled up inside her. All sorts of terrible thoughts went through her head about what could happen to Patricia; she was terrified in case she wandered off, lost and alone in the big city.

Irene leaped off the train at the very next stop and frantically dashed in search of the stationmaster. She was breathless when she reached him.

'Please, please can you help me? I've left my daughter at the previous station. She's only five and she's on her own there. Can you please ring through and see if she is still there?' she asked him, desperation in her voice.

Irene's heart was thumping as the stationmaster called through to Oxford Circus, and she stood by anxiously waiting for his reply. She didn't know what she would do next otherwise – whether to ring Peter or the police.

Mercifully, her fears were allayed. 'It's all right, madam. One of the passengers on the platform noticed what happened and he's looking after your daughter. He'll bring her here on the next train.'

Irene immediately felt relieved and thanked the stationmaster. But she wouldn't feel reassured until she saw Patricia again with her own eyes. She paced around the platform, her eyes eagerly scanning the track for the next train's arrival. It seemed to take ages. When it drew up and the carriage doors opened, a tearful Patricia was led out of the carriage by the attentive man who'd travelled with her.

The young girl ran sobbing straight into her mother's arms, crying her heart out. Irene clutched her tightly, then looked up and profusely thanked the man.

'I'm pleased to have helped after seeing what had happened – think nothing of it,' he said, before leaving to catch the next train.

Being parted for those few moments had been the most horrible and frightening experience for Irene, who was weeping tears of joy. Her sense of relief was overwhelming.

To compensate for what had happened, Patricia was given even more special treats that day than usual. Irene told the suppliers about their ordeal and they inundated the young girl with children's jewellery. Patricia never forgot the big scare she had that day, too, reminding her mother about it for years to come.

Heyworth's

FAMOUS SALE – NOW ON – GENUINE REDUCTIONS IN ALL DEPARTMENTS

The word Heyworth's in the advert on the front page of the *Cambridge Daily News* was printed in its familiar swirly script, while the rest of the promotional text was written in upper-case bold lettering to catch the eye of bargain-hunters.

Pictures of animated women wearing hats and coats and carrying baskets were grouped around the box of text.

The sale was one of the highlights of the year for the store, and Herbert Heyworth, who couldn't bear the thought of crowds rushing in, insisted on admitting customers in an orderly fashion and giving them an assigned shop girl to serve them one at a time. It was the way his father had managed their sales, and he planned to continue doing the same. It meant there were never any fights or disorderly behaviour, with customers pouncing on the same garment and refusing to give in to the other.

The sale was held twice a year, in January and July, and attracted hundreds of women. In 1950, half-a-dozen bargain-hunters waited all night. The first woman waited fifteen hours to buy a brown suit reduced from 79s 6d (about £120 in 2014) to 20 shillings (£30 in 2014). It was the slashed-down prices of Heyworth's fur coats that caught many women's eyes, with prices marked down from £37 (£1,100 in 2014) to £10 (£300 in 2014).

Another year a man was the first to arrive at 3.45 a.m. to buy his wife a red whipcord coat reduced from £10 10s to 29s 11d. He was joined at 4 a.m. by a commercial traveller who wanted to buy his wife a grey gabardine suit marked down from £21 10s to 59s 11d.

One or two people had even walked three or four miles to join the queue and, by 9 a.m., tickets had been given out to 370 people waiting to secure half-price bargains, which they would hand in to the shop girl when allowed through the doors.

The customer was given a ticket while in the queue which described what they wanted to buy and where it could be found in the store. The description was written by the manager Jim Clarke, or anyone else helping to manage the outside throng, with the queue snaking around the corner down Market Passage.

Once the customer was in the store and had been assigned a shop girl, the same girl stayed with the customer until they'd got everything they wanted. They could be sent to any department, not just their own. The strict code of politeness and personal service was as important then as any other time, regardless of the large number of customers still waiting outside to be served. Sometimes it would be as late as 3 p.m. before the queue had reduced to a manageable size and Herbert Heyworth agreed that the last shoppers could be admitted all together in one batch.

It was always exhausting for the shop girls on the first day of the sale as they raced around different departments, but it was a huge money-spinner for Heyworth's, and it was always a joy to see the windows filled with their next range of stock.

Irene counted her blessings, feeling that she had the best of both worlds, and couldn't have worked for a more considerate boss. Then one morning the phone rang in her department. She was ordered to go straight to Mr Heyworth's office.

'Miss Fiander, could you come and see me straight away – and I mean now!'

She shuddered at his hostile tone and quickly obeyed his wish. When she walked into his office, he had a look of thunder on his face. What could she have done wrong?

BETTY

1949

'Forward number one, please!'

The order was made in a clear voice by Miss Richards, the straight-laced head of Heyworth's millinery department. The first shop girl moved briskly to serve her waiting customer and Miss Richards nodded approvingly; there was never any hanging around once Miss Richards barked her instructions.

Betty was number three sales assistant. Although she was twenty-five years old and had worked in a shop before, she still had to start at the bottom of the pecking order to learn her new trade. She learned by watching those ranked above her, and she picked it up quickly. Her starting salary was £2 10s a week, with two weeks' holiday.

While she didn't have to sweep the floors and dust shelves, she was shown how to brush their fabulous collection of hats, which all women wore in 1949. When a woman bought a new coat or suit, she bought a new hat to match, usually felt for the winter and straw in the summer months.

Betty, dressed smartly in a black skirt, white blouse and black high-heeled shoes, had a trim figure and shoulder-length wavy hair swept back off her face. Her eyes scanned the ground floor; a wall of mirrors ran along one side of the millinery department, and in front of it was a long wooden counter fitted with deep drawers, deeper than coffins, where the hats were neatly stored. They were placed on top of each other, two or three deep, with tissue paper placed carefully between each layer.

The latest styles were perched on top of the counter or on plinths: neat, trilby-style hats fashioned after the men's version, and others with small turned-up brims, some decorated with feathers.

Heyworth's even boasted the petite and charming Mrs Pugh, its own milliner, whose work was in great demand. She made hats to order for well-to-do women who wanted something special to match a new outfit, or wanted a unique style. Her tiny attic workroom was a hive of industry and had colourful rolls of felt and trays of decorations. No other shop in Cambridge offered this service, and the selection of Heyworth's hats was unrivalled in the town.

Betty took a soft brush in her hand and, one by one, picked up the hats on display. They each had to be brushed at the end of the day and placed away in the drawers for the night so they did not attract any dust. The following morning, Betty took them out again, gave them another brush to freshen them up, and placed them on display.

After two months she was promoted to number two assistant and could start selling. If two customers arrived at the same time, Miss Richards called out, 'Forward number one and number two, please.'

Betty, with a welcoming smile, would approach the customer saying, 'Good morning, how may I help you?' They would then be shown to a seat by the counter and wouldn't pick up hats and handle goods unless they were given a hat to try on by an assistant. After a purchase was made, the shop girl took the money to the cash desk, as the customers were not expected to walk backwards and forwards.

Miss Richards was in her fifties, and had previously worked for a London store but now she lived in a bedsit in Cambridge. She was not very modern, but was always smart and tidy, wearing knitted or jacquard suits in dark colours. Miss Richards was not a good-looking woman, with plain features, sallow skin and dark hair. Her toes were knobbly, probably because of arthritis, and because of this she wore unattractive, heavy lace-up shoes. She always wore a hat, sometimes keeping it on for work.

But Betty warmed to Miss Richards, with her quaint, old-fashioned ways, even though she always spoke her mind if any of the girls needed pulling up about something.

All the shop girls left at 6 p.m. sharp on a Saturday and Mr Heyworth would speak to the buyers to ask them what kind of week they had had. On one occasion, after he had checked Miss Richards' books and seen that business had been brisk, he asked her to go to London on Monday to order more hats.

The following Monday morning, Betty arrived at work to find a note on Miss Richards' desk saying, 'Gorn to London'. The girls laughed at her unusual spelling; her written English was never very good, but she knew everything there was to know about hats, and Betty thought she was the salt of the earth.

Miss Richards rarely talked about her private life, but Betty knew she had never been able to find her Mr Right, and now seemed to have no interest in men.

'I could never marry a man unless I could kiss his feet,' she told Betty, by way of explanation.

Betty sympathised, knowing that Miss Richards had been young during the First World War, when so many men got killed that there were few for decent single women to fall in love with. She had heard that Miss Richards had had affections for a young man in the past, but didn't know what happened to him, whether he had perhaps died in the Great War.

One day, when Miss Richards was walking down the stairs carrying an armful of boxes from the stock room, she missed her step and tripped over, knocking the handle off the phone, which was fixed to the wall. It was an old-fashioned telephone with a handle that you had to turn to make it ring through to the office or other parts of the store. There was an almighty crash as she fell down the stairs, her legs flying in the air and her skirt around her waist – giving everyone a good view of her bloomers!

The phone was immediately picked up at the other end by Miss Money in the workroom, who thought someone was trying to ring her. She could be heard repeating loudly, 'Hellooooo, helloooooo!' into the receiver.

The shop girls dashed to the aid of Miss Richards, who picked herself up and pulled her skirt down quickly. She was uninjured, though shaken by her embarrassing fall. Once she could see Miss Richards was all right, Betty allowed herself a smile at the memory of the old-fashioned bloomers her boss had been wearing. Very few women then still wore bloomers – there was a reason they were called 'passion killers'! Betty had been given some as part of her kit with the ATS, but she'd never worn them; they were far too old-fashioned and a teenage girl would never dream of being seen dead in them.

That was not the only occasion when Miss Richards had a red face. A new junior, Maureen Turkentine, joined Betty in millinery just before Miss Richards retired. She had been transferred there from the fashion showroom at her request.

'I just didn't like working up there. I much prefer it here,' she told Betty.

Betty and Maureen soon became friends, despite their eight-year age difference. They laughed as, once again, Miss Richards gave the shop girls a full view of her bloomers which, without any warning, fell down to her ankles.

Maureen's eyes almost popped out in disbelief when she saw this and the shop girls tried hard to conceal their giggles from their straight-laced boss.

'Did you see that?' asked Maureen, who couldn't believe what she had seen. 'Poor Miss Richards. The elastic must have gone from her knickers.' Miss Richards, cool as a cucumber, bent down to pick them up and walked away without a backward glance.

One of the shop's regular customers was the spitting image of the actress Margaret Rutherford in the film *Blithe Spirit*. Harriet was a real character. She rode around town on a bicycle and always wore a navy blue broad-brimmed hat, the kind that nurses used to wear, and would dress it up with a feather to give it a lift, or a nice big bow. Sometimes she added flowers for a fresh look.

Harriet was a lovely woman, well educated, and usually a pleasure to serve, with her old-fashioned ways, but she counted her pennies.

'I'd like a new ribbon for my hat,' she told Betty. 'How much will it cost?' This was an economical way of giving a hat a new lease of life instead of buying a new one. Betty asked the milliner, Mrs Pugh, and they calculated the cost of the ribbon and labour.

'That will be four shillings and sixpence,' Betty told Harriet.

'Oh, I'm not paying that,' she said indignantly, flouncing out of the store.

Another time panic set in when word got around that another well-known character had set foot inside the store in search of a new hat. Annie was a relic from the Victorian era and wore long, grubby black dresses or skirts with old-fashioned boots that laced up with studs all the way up her legs. She also liked wearing broad-brimmed hats over her dirty hair. Miss Richards was most particular about how her hats should be handled, and she made it clear that she did not want her beautiful hats touched and tried on by this eccentric woman.

If one or two of Annie's favourite style of hats were on display when she was spotted through the window by one of the shop girls, action was taken quickly.

'Quick, go and get the hats out of the window – Annie's here!'

The hats were swiftly removed and the shop girls made out they had nothing suitable for her.

Miss Richards regarded the hats as precious merchandise, and the shop girls were shown how to hold them carefully and pass them to customers. Miss Richards felt that if a hat had been tried on several times, it would be no better than second-hand goods, and believed women didn't want to buy a hat if it had been tried on by lots of others before them.

It was the fashion for women to wear their hats tilted forward over their foreheads, and Miss Richards was concerned that they would be soiled by make-up, particularly on the band that lined the rim inside the front. This could easily happen, and the shop girls used methylated spirits to clean the hat if it had been marked in this way. If this didn't work, the hat was put in the sale.

The analogy Miss Richards used to drum home this important message to her shop girls was to say, 'It's like buying a swimming costume: it's personal, and no one will want to buy it if it's been worn by others first; the same rule applies to our hats.'

She would have turned blue if she had returned unexpectedly to her department during her lunch break. The shop girls could not resist trying on the hats in front of the mirror and admiring themselves, though Betty never felt hats suited her.

Thursday afternoons were special for Betty; it was early-closing day, so she walked to the baby clinic at Cherry Hinton Hall with Irene and their two baby daughters. The formula milk there was cheaper than Cow & Gate, and they had the choice of a free bottle of orange juice or rosehip syrup.

Betty always behaved professionally and courteously with customers, but sometimes she found her patience tested to the limits. One Thursday a demanding customer kept her in late, just as she was preparing to leave. The shop shut at 1 p.m. that day, but when a feisty woman arrived at five minutes before closing, Betty's heart sank.

'Oh no,' mumbled Betty, 'just as I need to get off quickly.'

This was no ordinary customer. It was the wife of the Mayor of Cambridge, and she was flustered.

'For goodness sake find me a hat!' she demanded, looking around the department. 'I had forgotten about an appointment in my diary this afternoon for a ladies' function I have to attend, a tea party where I will be giving a talk, and I must have a new hat.'

The woman was adamant. Betty had no choice but to serve her politely, bringing out a selection of different hats from the drawers for her to try on, hiding any resentment she was feeling.

'I hope she finds a suitable one soon,' Betty muttered under her breath, watching the clock.

The Mayor's wife finally succeeded in finding the perfect hat.

Betty heaved a sigh of relief and wished her a good afternoon. The woman would have known that Heyworth's was due to shut its doors very shortly, but she didn't mention this, and neither did she apologise for the inconvenience she was causing. But it would never have occurred to Betty to say, 'Sorry madam, but we are closing now. Can you come back tomorrow?' The customer always came first.

A year after Betty started at Heyworth's, Miss Richards retired.

'Mrs Lipscombe, you work very well here and I would like you to be our millinery buyer and head of department,' Mr Heyworth told her. Betty didn't need to be asked twice and immediately accepted. She was thrilled with the offer and delighted to have climbed the career ladder so quickly.

While Betty's mother doted on her young granddaughter, her father remained as cold-hearted as ever and there was no praise from him following her rapid promotion.

Betty dedicated every free minute to being with Jennifer. She never went out with other girls in the evenings, on trips to the cinema or dancing, but spent every evening and weekend at home. She didn't even join the staff outings to the seaside, which were always so much fun. She felt she had had her dancing days while serving in the ATS.

She never felt she was missing out on life, as everything she did was to provide for her daughter and give her the best she could. Working hard and looking after her daughter were her only interests in life, but she enjoyed hearing about the fun others were having. She accepted that that was the way her life was.

As well as becoming the millinery buyer, Betty was in charge of the shop girls in her department. One of the juniors under her wing was Margaret Bebee, who joined Heyworth's two years before Betty, aged fourteen.

Betty was eleven years older than Margaret, who was very pleased to have a much younger boss in place of the old-fashioned Miss Richards, whom she felt was far too bossy, always sending her on errands up and down the stairs.

Margaret, a slim, shy girl known as Bee by the shop girls, had initially wanted to join the alterations department, where her friend Jean Morley had just started, but there were no vacancies and she was offered the junior's position in millinery instead. As well as working under Miss Richards and Betty, she also assisted Mrs Pugh.

Unusually, Margaret's eyes were different colours – one was blue and the other brown. She had been born with two blue eyes, but as she grew up, one of them changed colour. Strangely, a girl down the road from the village where she lived, Shepreth, also had similar differently coloured eyes.

'As long as I can see, it doesn't bother me,' Margaret told Betty.

Betty never forgot Margaret's story about her dramatic first day at work back in January 1947, as it was so extraordinary. The ground that day was blanketed with thick snow, and the weather was treacherous – the coldest winter on record, with snowdrifts 20 feet high in some areas. It snowed every day for weeks.

Margaret's mum waved her off. She was well wrapped up in a thick coat for her first day. Her mother looked at the deep snow, saying 'My goodness, you're going to have a nice journey!'

It never occurred to Margaret to stay at home. She set off with other workers from her village to catch the bus, trudging through knee-deep snow. She knew she'd have to make every effort to get to Heyworth's if she wanted to make a good impression as a new junior. The bus usually drove along the main road from Royston to Cambridge and passed through Shepreth. But because the weather was so atrocious during the winter of 1947, the country lanes were sometimes impassable, and commuters had to walk to the main road to catch the bus.

Some days the weather was so treacherous that the bus could not even make it as far as Foxton. Margaret and her friends, who worked in other Cambridge stores, stood at the top of the main road and waited in vain for the bus to arrive, frozen to their core.

'Right, the bus must have frozen up – let's go,' said Margaret, deciding they must somehow make their own way into work, and worried she would be in trouble if she didn't turn up.

They looked down the snowy road, scanning for a vehicle to hitch a lift from. Suddenly they spotted a lorry and waved frantically at the driver to stop. He pulled over and opened his cab window.

'The bus didn't make it this morning and we need a lift to work,' pleaded Margaret.

'Hop in,' he said, and the girls jumped into the back of his open truck, driving along the deserted roads and being dropped off at Cambridge.

'Thank you so much,' they chorused, as they jumped out of the truck and went their separate ways to work, relieved to have finally arrived.

Betty nodded as she listened to Margaret's story. She knew that all the shop girls went to great lengths to arrive at work, whatever the weather, as excuses for not turning up would be looked at dimly. Betty had also struggled with her bicycle through snow, sometimes taking the bus if the roads were too treacherous for two wheels.

Margaret's heroic journey to work also impressed Mr Heyworth, and he commented on the great efforts made by the 'country girls' to travel in.

If there was a thick fog, he told the shop girls, 'Come on, I think we should let the country girls go home early today,' giving them time to catch an earlier bus and arrive home safely.

Margaret never worried about the snow and, however deep it was, it never made her miss a day's work, however frozen she felt, her fingers white and numb. She smiled when she heard Mr Heyworth say, 'How is it that the country girls get in early, and the ones in town don't?' Her bus home didn't leave until 7 p.m., so it was a long wait for Margaret at the end of the day. She would buy fish and chips with her friends to pass the time and satisfy her hunger pangs.

Margaret thought the 'town girls' had it easy getting to work each day, so they didn't bother so much about getting in to work on time, using the weather as an excuse, but Mr Heyworth soon clamped down on that.

When the sales were held, Margaret stared in disbelief at the length of the queue outside.

'How long is it going to take to serve all of them?' she wondered. Customers were only let into the store when they were assigned a shop girl who would serve them their bargain purchase and see them to the door before another customer could be allowed in. If the weather was bad, the customers would still wait outside in the rain for several hours, often until the middle of the afternoon, before the doors were opened and everyone still queuing was allowed in, when it was felt that the store would not be swamped.

'I've lost my assistant,' one confused shopper told George Heyworth, Herbert's father, who had run the store before him and was keeping on eye on things. The woman, who had queued for several hours to buy a coat she'd seen in the window and set her heart on, looked around the heaving shop floor, but couldn't find the assistant who had been serving her.

'Well, you'll have to go outside and come in again when the rush is over,' he told her firmly.

Margaret listened in disbelief. It seemed very uncharacteristic for George Heyworth to speak to a customer this way.

'That's not fair; I've waited my turn. It's so busy here – I can't help it if I've lost her,' she protested.

'I'm sorry, but you will have to go outside and queue up again,' he insisted.

The disappointed woman had no choice, unable to make her bargain purchase without an assistant to serve her.

When the sale was drawing to a close, George Heyworth slashed prices further and announced loudly, 'Come on, girls – everything in this window must be reduced to five pounds.' With bargains galore on offer, customers were only too happy to queue up patiently and take home a longed-for item that would normally have been out of their reach.

As buyer, Betty replenished the stock each season. She scoured the best millinery showrooms in London to provide the most fashionable headwear for Heyworth's.

During school holidays Betty sometimes took Jennifer with her on her buying trips. Jennifer, who was seven years old, was the centre of attention at the millinery showrooms, where the staff made a big fuss of her, spoiling her with treats and buying her ice cream.

The most popular styles in the early 1950s were small, brimless, close-fitting hats in different pretty colours, some of them decorated with little jay's feathers or ribbons, plain cloches and snoods, which had fabric draping over the crown of the head on to the shoulders.

Betty's buying list included Queen Mary toque hats, the elaborate and decorative styles favoured by the wife of King George V, with large plumages at the top. They were made in satin and velvet, as well as felt, and were sought after by Heyworth's most distinguished customers.

When the Newmarket Race season was in full flow, Betty had one special customer who always loved to wear toques. Her husband was a horse trainer, and she always wore lavender. Sometimes she bought ready-made toques from the store, and other times she had them specially made. She came into Heyworth's one day and placed an order for a toque to be made in mauve velvet for an important race meeting.

'I would like it to be covered with mauve pansies,' she told Mrs Pugh.

'Yes, of course, we can make that for you,' said Mrs Pugh.

The velvet fabric was placed over a wooden block the shape of the crown of the head to prepare the base of the hat. The fabric was cut to size and then decorated all over with exquisite hand-made pansies cut from different shades of mauve velvet and stiffened with starch.

'It's certainly fit for a queen,' said Betty, standing back to admire the stunning floral hat.

One of Betty's favourite designers was Mitzi Lorenz, a prominent London milliner whose showroom was behind Cavendish Square. The Viennese-born designer was renowned for her ornate hats, with fabric stylishly twisted around the crown or sticking up like a wing from the side. Mitzi's hats were eye-catching and synonymous with quality and good taste. Her innovative styles included turbans and baker-boy hats, as well as pillboxes and straw hats covered in stunning silk flowers or petals; the mauve pansy hat was very similar to Mitzi's popular style worn by the celebrities of the day. They were stunning and much admired creative works of art.

Betty could also place orders for new hats at the centuries-old timber-framed Lion Hotel, which could be found just off the marketplace in Cambridge, surrounded by medieval alleyways and stable yards. It was an old-fashioned hotel and had a Victorian air about it.

Here Betty would meet representatives from millinery suppliers, who rented a room at the back. The hotel was like a rabbit warren and the first time Betty visited, she ended up walking up and around several passageways, diving under the low ceilings, until she found the reps she had arranged to meet. They had travelled in vans with great big boxes to display their hats.

Easter was their busiest time. Different reps would arrive each week and lay out their wares. Every woman wore a hat at Easter and Betty was naturally keen to ensure they had ample supplies. One occasion a rep came to Heyworth's to show Betty the latest stock, driving there in his van. As she walked into the room at the Lion Hotel, she could see scores of hats laid out on tables. Some of the cheaper ones she could take away with her on the day, but she had to place an order for more expensive hats, which would be delivered later.

Betty didn't feel she needed to bargain with the rep for a better deal. She accepted the price they offered if she felt it was reasonable, though sometimes the rep would come down a little if Betty hesitated.

Like other buyers, Betty was given an annual budget to stick to. Herbert Heyworth never queried how much the buyers spent unless they went a bit mad, but Betty never strayed beyond her limit. As she kept a close watch on her budget and her figures were spot-on, she didn't see the need to haggle. As everything was fine in the millinery department, Mr Heyworth just left Betty to it.

Mr Heyworth always kept a close watch on their expenditure and was not happy with the way one buyer was spending her expenses, telling her stiffly, 'We will have less of the taxis and more the buses, if you don't mind.'

Although he was generous, he didn't want to be taken for a ride.

'Where are you going for your holidays this year, Margaret?' Betty asked her assistant.

'Jean and I are going away together. I can't wait. We're going to Margate.'

Jean Fuller was a cashier who sat at a cash desk close to the millinery department. She was nineteen years old, and sat perched on a high chair inside a cubicle. The shop girls paid their customers' purchases to her, and those with accounts called in to settle what they owed.

When it was quiet and Jean got bored, she brought out her knitting. She could knit a jumper in three weeks, but was always careful to be discreet about this.

The two young women struck up a friendship and headed for the coastal resort in Kent, staying in a hotel owned by friends of Margaret's family. Although the hotel didn't meet their expectations because they were put up in a prefab, where they felt scared being apart from the main building, they still laughed the whole week.

'I thought you knew,' said the hotel owner when they complained.

'Oh no,' they said. 'We thought we were staying in the hotel.'

Betty's Saturday nights were spent at home with her daughter and parents, but the other young shop girls were keen to have fun and find romance. Jean was very petite, with a tiny 22-inch waist. Her light brown hair was permed into a short wavy style. She loved dancing and went to classes every Tuesday and Friday night, where she was taught the foxtrot, quickstep, waltz and jive.

Jean owned five satin dresses that fell just below the knee. They were in different colours and each Saturday night she wore a different coloured dress. At the end of the five weeks, she started again, from turquoise to pink, green, yellow and, finally, her black-and-white striped dress.

After work one Saturday, she rushed home and slipped into her turquoise dress for a special night out dancing at the Rex, a large ballroom and one of Cambridge's top dancing venues.

It was billed as a free night's dancing for two hundred men and women serving in the forces – the army, navy and RAF, as well as American GIs. Jean was really looking forward to it, the chance to swing along to a live band playing the latest songs for her to practise her dance steps.

As she walked into the packed ballroom with her girlfriend, June Butler, the music playing loudly, Jean began tapping her feet along to the beat. Couples were jiving in the corner so they did not jostle into others on the dance floor during their wildly energetic moves.

Jean and June wasted no time and started dancing straight away. Jean was enjoying herself so much that she barely noticed the handsome man in the RAF uniform who came up to her, asking, 'May I have this dance?'

His friend had partnered June and Jean readily agreed, feeling attracted to the tall man with dark wavy hair and a lovely smile.

'My name's John, and I can see you like dancing,' he told her. 'I love dancing too and have been taking lessons. Isn't this a great night!'

They both found their dancing lessons had paid off, as they had perfect rhythm and stayed on the dance floor all night. Suddenly there was a loud commotion and angry raised voices.

'Oh my goodness, what's happening?' asked Jean, looking at the crowds that had gathered around a group there.

'It's those Americans again – they're starting more trouble,' John told her.

Jean gasped as she saw two GIs with bleeding scratch marks on their cheeks. They had both been fighting over local girls who wanted nothing to do with them and had resisted their advances by scratching their faces with their long fingernails.

'Their faces look terrible,' she said, 'but they got what they deserved.'

'Come on, let's get out. Can I walk you home?'

John took Jean by the arm and as they walked into the night, Jean asked her new dance partner, 'How are you going to get back to your base at Duxford? You won't make the last bus at ten-thirty.'

'I'm not worried about that, I'll walk back,' he told her, without a second thought about how long it would take him to walk the 11 miles to his RAF base.

Jean couldn't wait to tell Margaret about her dramatic night at work during their coffee break the following Monday. Margaret, living out in the country, didn't spend so much time dancing in Cambridge at weekends.

'You should have seen the fight last night, it was terrible,' Jean said.

'Well, I'm glad I wasn't there,' replied Margaret.

'But I did get to meet a really nice man called John and he's taking me to the cinema on Thursday,' smiled Jean. 'I'm really looking forward to it.'

Margaret had started dating Alex, a trainee architect who travelled on the same bus as her into Cambridge each morning, as he lived in the next village. He sat on the bus staring at her, until one day one of Margaret's friends said to him encouragingly, 'Go on, why don't you ask her out?'

'He sounds a lovely person,' said Betty approvingly, when Margaret shared news of their romances.

The millinery buyer never felt she was missing out on fun by staying in every night; Betty's life was being Jennifer's mother. Being ten years or so older than the younger shop girls, she felt protective and caring towards them and was always interested in their personal lives. But they knew nothing about Betty's private life, and she never discussed it.

'I'm going to Royal Ascot and I'd like a new hat for each day,' the distinguished-looking woman told Betty. It's not every day you get to serve a member of the royal family.

'Certainly, madam, how can I help you?'

The Marchioness of Cambridge always sought Betty's expertise to provide her with her headwear for her important public engagements, like Ascot, where she would be sitting in the Royal Box.

Ascot was held over five consecutive days, so Lady Cambridge, who lived in Little Abington, near Cambridge, having given up her apartment in Kensington Palace, needed five hats to match her different outfits.

It made Betty proud to think that Heyworth's hats would be admired in royal circles in the presence of King George VI and Queen Elizabeth, along with their daughters, the princesses Elizabeth and Margaret.

Lady Cambridge was married to true blue blood, which belonged to the so-called Old Royal Family, a term used for those who were direct descendants of King George III from the House of Hanover, or married to his descendants, but not descendants of Queen Victoria.

As Miss Dorothy Hastings, the granddaughter of the Earl of Huntingdon, she married George, the eldest son of Prince Adolphus of Teck, a direct descendant of King George III and the Kings of Württemburg.

Lady Cambridge was passionately interested in racing and was a racehorse owner. Betty knew how much she looked forward to Royal Ascot. In her younger days, she was renowned for the elegant outfits she wore and featured regularly in lists of the best-dressed women.

Although a regular customer at Heyworth's, Lady Cambridge was thrifty too, telling Betty, 'I get my dresses from Marks & Spencer, but it's important to always have good accessories – nice gloves, shoes, handbags and a good hat – to stand out, and nobody will guess.'

Betty smiled and thought what good sense she spoke.

Lady Cambridge had chosen some beautiful floral dresses to wear for Royal Ascot. She cut some fabric from the generous hems and handed it over to Betty. Betty took the fabric with her to the millinery showrooms in London, placing orders for her special customer.

Betty knew the kind of hats that Lady Cambridge liked to wear. As it was summer, the hat would usually be made from straw with soft tulle netting or flowers added, and a small upturned brim.

'Thank you, they are perfect, Mrs Lipscombe,' she told Betty when she returned for her purchases. 'I knew I could rely on you.'

'It's my pleasure. I'm so pleased you like them,' replied Betty, thrilled that her royal orders were to the liking of Lady Cambridge, and knowing they would most probably soon be admired by senior members of the royal family.

'She's a real lady,' Betty thought. 'She has no pretentious airs and graces.'

Heyworth's served many women with airs and graces. Yet here, Betty thought, was a real, titled lady who was always gracious, polite, a delight to serve and never showed off her royal connections. Lady Cambridge really was a down-to-earth woman, and actively supported the Girl Guide movement, the Red Cross and the Royal Cambridge Home for Soldiers' Widows.

It was Friday afternoon, and Margaret's eyes looked up at the sweeping staircase that led to the fashion showroom. Herbert Heyworth was standing there on a platform, casting his eye over his departments, hands on hips, fixing his stare on the shop girls.

Most of the junior shop girls had no direct contact with Mr Heyworth, including Margaret. She was a bit nervous of him, as she felt he could sometimes be abrupt. He wasn't as polite as his father, George, who had seemed more kindly when he had run the store, handing it over to his son on his retirement.

As she looked up at Mr Heyworth, Margaret tried to avoid his direct gaze. She had heard how a shop girl could be fired by Mr Heyworth for no reason, and would never know why. If the red light was on outside his office on a Friday afternoon, that was a fair indication that someone had been called up and was being given her cards. While Mr Heyworth could be charming to senior staff, he had a very strict and authoritative stance with those who were lower ranking, and was feared by some of the shop girls.

One Friday evening Mr Heyworth's gaze fell on Margaret – exactly what she had dreaded.

'Can you step into my office Miss Bebee?' he asked her.

Margaret froze on the spot. 'Right, that's it – I shall be out,' she told her friends.

Her heart was thumping as she walked up the staircase, wondering what she could possibly have done wrong. The red light went on as she entered Mr Heyworth's office. Margaret expected to hear the worst and resigned herself to being sacked without any cause or justification.

Herbert Heyworth looked at Margaret's worried face and asked her, 'Why are you looking so nervous? I'm not going to eat you!'

He was in a jovial mood, but Margaret said nothing in reply, waiting to hear her fate.

'You've been in millinery long enough and you're just the height we like for fashions,' he told her.

Margaret felt a great sense of relief.

'What do you mean?' she asked, unable to grasp why she was moving departments.

Mr Heyworth felt that taller girls looked better in the fashion showroom. 'One of the girls has left in fashions and we like our shop girls to be tall, so you fit the bill.'

'Well, yes, all right,' she replied, stumbling over her words.

It was not at all what she was expecting to be told, but she was thrilled to have kept her job, and walked out of his office with a big smile on her face. But it meant that Betty lost one of her shop girls to the fashion showroom.

One afternoon when Betty returned from lunch, she was summoned to Mr Heyworth's office. Mr Clarke, the office manager, told her she had to make her way there straight away. Even Betty was a little nervous of her boss.

'Oh no, what have I done now?' thought Betty, worried that she was in trouble.

As she nervously entered his office, Mr Heyworth's face was red. He was very angry, and Betty had no idea what had upset him so much. He slammed some cards on his desk and said, 'These are Mrs Green's cards. I want you to sack her.'

Betty gasped in surprise, and asked, 'Why – whatever for?'

Herbert Heyworth stared at Betty; she had rarely seen him so cross. 'She was leaning against some fixtures and I don't pay people to lean against fixtures, so she can go.'

Betty picked up the woman's cards and walked out of the office.

She felt dreadful having to break such devastating news to Mrs Green, who was in her thirties.

She felt sorry for her, knowing she had a broken marriage behind her, was living with another man and had recently suffered a miscarriage. Poor Mrs Green arrived for work looking pale and drained, but Betty never found fault with her work.

It was her misfortune to have been seen slouching by Mr Heyworth when he walked through the millinery department, instead of standing straight and alert, which he insisted upon. Herbert Heyworth felt very strongly that his staff should be busy at all times, and that he didn't pay their wages for them to stand around idle. Even if you had a brush in your hand and looked as if you were busy, that was better than standing there doing nothing.

'Poor Mrs Green,' thought Betty, who knew how strong Mr Heyworth's views were about this, 'she was probably exhausted after losing her latest baby.'

Betty had never fired anyone before and dreaded the task she had to perform.

'Oh dear, how can I tell her this terrible news?' she thought anxiously.

Betty felt helpless. She knew she had no choice other than to obey Mr Heyworth's orders, and felt Mrs Green didn't deserve to lose her job over such a minor issue. But she was aware that if Mr Heyworth had taken a dislike to somebody or thought they were wasting their time at work, he would not tolerate having them around.

'I'm sorry Mrs Green, but Mr Heyworth has told me that you have to leave,' she told the disbelieving woman, trying to break the news as gently as possible.

Mrs Green was stunned. 'Why? Whatever are you talking about?'

'He walked through the millinery department after lunch and

said he saw you leaning against some fixtures and he didn't like that. I'm sorry,' Betty told her, feeling absolutely awful.

Mrs Green's shock turned to tears. 'I can't believe it. There must be something else. Did you want to get rid of me?'

'No, it was nothing to do with me, I promise you,' insisted Betty, upset that Mrs Green could believe for a moment that she had stitched her up. 'You know what Mr Heyworth is like.'

Mrs Green took the cards from Betty's hands and walked out without looking back.

Betty felt miserable. 'What a terrible day, I hope I never ever have to do that again.'

ROSEMARY

1958

'Cross my palm with silver and I'll tell you everything.'

Rosemary took a shiny shilling out of her purse and handed it over to Molly, a friendly-looking gypsy woman who had spoken to her in Heyworth's. The young shop girl sat opposite the brightly dressed woman in her tiny caravan, a crystal ball on the table between them. Molly was in her mid-thirties and had tied a silk scarf over her bright, frizzy, ginger hair; her wrist was heavily weighted with thick gold bangles and large jewelled rings adorned her stubby fingers.

Although the fortune-teller's appearance was bright and gaudy, she was clean and her caravan was spotless. Rosemary looked around the tiny room where vases filled with plastic flowers brightened up the sideboard and sat alongside a display of china donkeys, dogs and cats.

It was Midsummer Fair week in Cambridge, which attracted thousands of visitors from miles around. Some of the gypsy women spent generously at Heyworth's, buying elaborate dresses for their daughters, and Rosemary wondered where they got all the money from, because it took weeks for her to save up for anything. This particular fortune-teller had just bought a dress for her little girl to wear around the fairground and she spoke to Rosemary as she left the store. 'Why don't you come to Midsummer Fair? I'll tell your fortune if you like.'

Rosemary's eyes lit up. At sixteen, she was curious to know what she would be told about her future. Other shop girls had crossed the fortune-teller's palm with silver, so she plucked up courage and decided to go there with her friends.

As they walked around Midsummer Common after work one evening, Rosemary spotted a row of caravans where fortune-tellers advertised their trade. Rosemary was keen to find the gypsy who had spoken to her at the store, and instantly recognised Molly. She rubbed her silver shilling into the gypsy woman's palm, and Molly stared deeply into the crystal ball.

The fortune-teller held Rosemary's hand and brought it closer to her face. Rosemary held her breath in anticipation of hearing what the future would hold for her while the gypsy slowly ran her finger along the lines of the shop girl's upturned hand.

Molly spoke in a soft voice. 'You will fall in love with someone and he will be in a job where he gets promoted. The person you meet will have to move,' she told Rosemary.

Rosemary felt her heart flutter. She had been hoping to hear that she would meet someone special, and was thrilled to be told this would happen.

None of the shop girls shared details of their readings, keeping what they were told close to their chests.

'I wonder when it will happen? How long will I have to wait for the fortune-teller's prediction to come true?' Rosemary asked herself, excited at the prospect of one day meeting her Mr Right.

The gypsy woman had warned her not to repeat what she had been told, and although Rosemary kept it secret from her fellow shop girls, she couldn't resist blurting it out to her mother when she returned home.

Sophia scoffed, 'What a surprise! I expect he's going to be tall, dark and handsome too, like they all are!'

'Well, you never know – who's to say she isn't telling the truth?' Rosemary replied defensively.

She was thinking about this as she cycled to Royston Heath with a small group of shop girls, including her friend Kathleen Goodrum, who worked in the knitwear department. Kathleen, who was two years older than Rosemary, came from a well-to-do family and had gone to a posh school in Cambridge, the Perse School for Girls. Her parents wanted her to settle into a professional career, but Kathleen liked being a shop girl; she didn't want to work in an office.

Although she was more reserved than Rosemary, the two girls became good friends, despite their different backgrounds. Kathleen was an only child and enjoyed having fun with the others, as her parents were quite strict.

Rosemary felt it was a welcome change of scenery to cycle to Royston Heath on a Thursday afternoon when the store closed early. Then the group of girls rushed home on their bikes to change out of their work clothes and pack some sandwiches and drinks before setting off on their 17-mile ride.

'Come with us, Kathleen, it's good exercise,' Rosemary said.

Kathleen needed little persuasion. But some of the other shop girls didn't fancy it. 'You must be mad, Rosemary! We're not biking all that way!' Rosemary found it exhilarating. The girls pedalled energetically, taking an hour and a quarter to reach the Chalk Downs across the Cambridgeshire border in Hertfordshire. While the flatness of the Cambridgeshire countryside was a joy for cyclists, the Downs made them almost feel like they were in a foreign land, as they were not used to hilly terrain.

The girls lay their bikes down on the grass and flopped down breathlessly beside them. They unpacked their food, devouring their sandwiches and throwing back their heads to swallow much-needed drinks. Rabbits scurried around, bobbing up and down on the grassy bank. It was a perfect summer's day and Rosemary gazed up at the cloudless sky, casting her mind back wistfully to the prediction made by the fortune-teller.

'You look a million miles away. A penny for your thoughts,' said Kathleen.

'Oh, it's nothing,' said Rosemary, suddenly awakened from her daydreaming. She smiled furtively, revealing nothing about her secret, just as the fortune-teller had advised.

'Have you heard some of the girls are going on holiday to Butlins? Are you going? I'm putting my name down,' she asked Kathleen, to change to subject.

'Yes, I love it there,' replied Kathleen. 'Beryl Burton from the underwear department is arranging it. She's collecting the money each week from us to pay for it.'

'I'm really looking forward to it as well. It will be my first time away on holiday without my family,' Rosemary said.

The girls lay back on the grass and closed their eyes, soaking up the sun, and without a care in the world. The last thing on Rosemary's mind was her work or Herbert Heyworth, who barely spoke to her, but was a boss she respected; they were just enjoying the chance to rest their aching feet which felt the worse for wear after standing on them all day. It felt heavenly to lay back and absorb the tranquillity and vast open space, England at its best.

They planned a detour on their ride back. Instead of cycling straight back to Cambridge, they would stop off at the home of their friend Catherine, who worked in the accessories department, in the picturesque village of Barrington. The village, with pretty thatched cottages and old-fashioned English gardens around the long village green, was halfway between Royston and Cambridge and made the ideal place to stop and break up their journey.

'Oh, it's lovely stopping off here to have a rest and drink,' said Rosemary appreciatively, when they arrived at Catherine's house. The fresh lemonade and cakes were instantly devoured.

'Don't get too comfy. We need to get back to Cambridge before it gets late,' Kathleen warned.

Sophia was waiting for Rosemary at the gate, pleased to see her daughter return safely from her long ride. 'Goodness me,' she exclaimed. 'I don't know where you get your energy from!'

'It was fun! I'm famished now, though,' Rosemary replied. 'But don't worry, we're not doing it every week, just now and again. Besides, the fresh air and exercise is good for you.'

'Oooh, it's not long now,' said Rosemary excitedly, counting the days to her holiday at Butlins in Skegness.

She was sure it was going to be the best holiday she'd ever had. Her family holidays, when they could afford them, had always been spent in a caravan at Great Yarmouth, on the Norfolk coast. Going to Butlins would be a totally different experience. Lots of teenagers stayed in Butlins without their parents and had the time of their lives. In the austere years following the war, when the Skegness camp became a recruitment and training base for the Royal Navy, Billy Butlin set about bringing back much-needed colour and happiness to people's lives. Its low-cost all-inclusive deal appealed to the shop girls.

Rosemary had heard what great value Butlins was – three meals a day, accommodation in a shared chalet, plus free entertainment, competitions and attractions provided throughout the day and evening, when live bands played. Even the fair rides and roller-skating were free. There was always a choice of dancing on offer, from ballroom to rock 'n' roll, as well as entertainment with comedians, singers and dance bands.

Eight of the shop girls booked for a week at the holiday camp and, at sixteen, Rosemary was the youngest. An avid follower of the latest fashions, she bought new clothes especially for her holiday so she could look her best.

'I love this twinset – can I have it on appro until payday?' she asked Kathleen on knitwear.

'It's lovely,' Kathleen said, holding it out to Rosemary. 'It will really suit you.'

Rosemary had a passion for wearing twinsets, a thin-knit short-sleeved sweater that had a matching cardigan. She particularly liked the Wolsey or Pringle brands in pastel shades, which were both renowned for their excellent quality. Every week Rosemary fell in love with a new twinset that had just come in to the store. She bought seven or eight sets in quick succession.

Rosemary wore tight-fitting skirts with her twinsets, a favourite being her silver-grey skirt with pleats around the bottom. She also loved her wide black felt skirt, which she wore with a tight-fitting top to show off her shape, a cardigan, short white socks and black plimsolls.

'What are you doing with my sugar?' her mother asked her one day, seeing Rosemary in her kitchen pouring sugar into a bowl of water.

'I'm going to make a sugar petticoat for my black felt skirt. All the girls do it,' she replied with a grin. 'You have to dip it in a bowl of warm water and sugar and let it soak. Then when you hang it up to dry, the petticoat will stiffen.'

'Goodness me. I've seen everything now,' exclaimed Sophia, marvelling at the transformation of Rosemary's plain petticoat. It was a good money-saving way of owning a petticoat like this, an essential item for flared skirts and dresses to make them stand out.

Rosemary felt wonderful wearing her voluminous black skirt, which was all the rage for lovers of jive and rock 'n' roll. She loved the feel of the skirt swirling around full circle as she spun around on the dance floor, showing a flash of her sugar-stiffened petticoat.

Rosemary bought few dresses, but liked those with wide skirts similar to the brightly decorated Horrocks style, and she'd sling one of her favourite cardigans over her shoulder.

She packed her new clothes ready for her trip to the Lincolnshire holiday camp. The shop girls boarded a bus heading for Skegness, and talked excitedly on their journey there about their plans for the week.

When they arrived at the camp, Rosemary's eyes widened as she spotted the famous Redcoats. They were perfectly dressed and smiled broadly, welcoming the girls when they booked in at reception. 'I'm going to like it here, I know we're all going to have a wonderful time,' Rosemary said excitedly to Kathleen, as she threw her case on the bed to unpack.

They had three chalets next to each other. Rosemary shared a twin room with Kathleen and although their chalet had a bath, there was never enough hot water to fill it, so they had to stand and have a strip-wash each day.

The day started with a loud early-morning call broadcast around the camp, intended to rouse the hard of hearing – and party lovers who'd had a late night and were hoping for a lie-in.

'Good morning, campers. Rise and shine! Today we are going to …' and the day's list of activities was announced over the speaker.

'How about going swimming, or on the boating lake? Or we could watch the knobbly knee contest. There might be some nice young men taking part,' Rosemary suggested.

The girls went along expecting to see some young, attractive fellows taking part in the contest. Instead, they were disappointed to find a parade of old men who rolled up their trousers to show off their bony legs, heartily joining in the laughs from the crowd.

The shop girls looked forward to all their meals, and always sat at table eleven, which they naturally called 'legs eleven' after the bingo call. For breakfast there was a choice of cornflakes or porridge or a boiled egg and toast, there were no big fry-ups. Lunch was a snack, such as beans on toast or a sandwich, and then there a tasty hot dinner was provided each evening, something like roast chicken. The puddings were a big hit and included spotted dick and treacle pudding with custard.

Each night the shop girls dressed up for dinner. It had been ingrained in them at work that they must look their smartest, and they believed this counted at all times, including their holiday. They all sat together at a long refectory table covered with a printed cloth. Sitting alongside them were scores of other smartly dressed teenagers, all smiling and giggling, relaxing away from the constraints and stresses of work and family.

While the dance halls in Cambridge closed mostly at 10 p.m., Butlins provided music, dancing and live entertainment until 11 p.m. Rosemary and her friends revelled in their newfound freedom.

'Oh, it's lovely here,' said Rosemary, feeling grown up to be holidaying with a group of girlfriends. 'There's so much to do! I can't wait to go dancing again tonight. I love the bands and the Redcoats. Have you seen the good-looking one called Des O'Connor? He has a wonderful voice.'

Des O'Connor was one of the Redcoats and all the shop girls had been knocked out by his looks, singing voice and the jokes he told when they'd seen him perform the night before.

The following evening they took part in a quiz at the end of dinner. Far from languishing at the bottom of the score table, which Rosemary had dreaded, they found that they had the joint top score. They were simple questions: one of them was about how many eggs you put in a Yorkshire pudding, and Rosemary knew the answer.

'You put one egg to four tablespoons of plain flour, a pinch of salt and a little drop of milk and water, and mix it all up to make a batter,' she replied confidently.

A tie-breaker question was held to decide on the winning team. Quick as a flash Marlene Ward, the brains of the group, answered the question correctly. Rosemary was gobsmacked!

'The winners are table eleven!' it was announced. Everyone in the room looked at them.

'I don't believe it. I've never won anything like this before,' said

Rosemary, amazed at their success. 'This will be something to tell the other girls at work.'

They were presented with a bottle of champagne as their prize. The waiter poured it into wide-rimmed Babycham glasses and handed them to the girls. As they smiled for a photograph, Rosemary triumphantly held up the bottle of champagne as the camera's flash went off.

'Hey, you can't hold that, you're only sixteen – you're under age for drinking alcohol,' the girls teased her.

Suddenly worried that she was doing something illegal, she handed the bottle back. 'All right, here it is.'

'We're only joking!' they reassured her. 'Come on, let's have a drink and celebrate our win.'

Rosemary tentatively sipped the sparkling drink, but she hated the sharp taste and spat it out. She left the rest of her glass untouched.

When they returned to Cambridge, Rosemary was bursting to tell her mother that she'd had the time of her life.

'Oh Mum, it was wonderful. It's such good fun and I can't wait to go again,' she burst out.

And, sure enough, the following year Rosemary returned to the same Butlins camp with three shop girls, Kathleen Goodrum, Beryl Burton and Marlene Ward.

'Why don't you go in for the Miss Butlins competition?' Kathleen asked.

'Don't be daft, I won't stand a chance,' Rosemary replied. She was quite shy, despite her bubbly appearance, and was nervous about parading in front of everyone in a bathing suit.

'Go on! We dare you,' they insisted.

'Oh, why not? I suppose I've got nothing to lose,' she agreed reluctantly after her friends finally twisted her arm.

Dressed in a navy blue swimming costume and high heels, Rosemary stepped on to the stage set up round the swimming pool.

Four judges sat on the front row, watching closely as each girl paraded in front of them. Rosemary eyed up the competition, noticing how stunning some of the girls looked. They had endless slim legs and perfect figures, and with their immaculate hair and make-up, they could easily have stepped out of a fashion magazine.

The audience loved the beauty parade and cheered wildly. The compère asked each girl to give their name, age and describe their work. Several of the beautiful girls told him they were models and strutted off confidently, smiling at the judges.

'No wonder they're so stunning. I don't stand a chance against these modelly types,' Rosemary told herself, resigned to lose but going ahead as she was a good sport and thought it would be fun. 'I'm up here now and I'll give it my best shot.'

When it came to her turn, the compère asked her, 'How long have you been modelling?'

'Modelling?' she giggled, flattered that he considered she looked good enough to be one. 'Oh, I'm not a model,' she replied. 'I work in Heyworth's, a ladies' fashion shop in Cambridge,' smiling sweetly at the compère all the while.

Everyone cheered and Rosemary smiled at the audience as she strutted off the stage. She was very much the fresh-faced girl-next-door with a natural air and cheeky smile, which appealed to the judges and everyone there.

When it came time to announce the result, Rosemary was sure she'd come last. But to her shock she ended up as the runner-up – she couldn't have been more surprised as she stood on a podium with a sash draped around her shoulder, standing next to the winner – a beautiful model with lovely blonde hair.

'Oh my goodness, I don't believe it!' she said as her friends in the audience cheered, delighted at her success.

'I just never expected it, not with all those models there,' she said in disbelief afterwards.

'Congratulations, you were fantastic,' they told her. 'Wait till we tell everyone at work!'

It wasn't long before Rosemary had another trip to the seaside to look forward to: the annual Heyworth outing to the Essex resort of Southend-on-Sea.

'I know it's going to be a good day. Everyone says how generous Herbert Heyworth is to his staff on their outings, that nothing is too much trouble,' Rosemary told her mother.

Herbert provided two coaches and paid for them all to have a meal at a restaurant. The annual outing was one of the highlights of the year for staff.

On 28 September 1958, Rosemary and the entire staff of Heyworth's piled on to the two waiting coaches outside Cambridge Senate House in King's Parade, the pick-up point for their day out to Southend, 70 miles away.

It was gloriously mild and many of the shop girls wore light twinsets with smart straight skirts and thick belts. They were in ebullient mood as the coaches drove off. Rosemary sat next to Kathleen and they chatted animatedly about their plans for the day. They couldn't wait to breathe the fresh sea air deep into their lungs and walk along the seafront together.

They walked happily along the promenade and past the donkey rides and the boating lake at Pier Hill, stopping to buy pink candy-floss. It was something Rosemary always looked forward to when she arrived at the fair or seaside, watching the big drum spin around while the delicious cobweb-like sugary treat gravitated towards the turning stick as if it was a magnet. 'It's lovely here,' said Rosemary to Kathleen, Maureen Childs from knitwear and her old school friend Judy Parker, from hosiery.

Rosemary took a deep breath and inhaled the smell of the sea. She loved the seaside. They walked past the Punch and Judy shows along the seafront, the stalls selling mushy peas and others selling cockles and whelks, although these weren't a favourite of the shop girls, and they steered clear of them.

'Let's walk down the pier pavilion,' Rosemary said, 'and then it will be time for lunch.' The domed pavilion at the end of the pier was the key landmark in Southend. It had two cafés, a theatre and wall of mirrors. The girls laughed as they posed, their images contorted to look tall and skinny, short and fat, thin on top and fat on the bottom, and a whole variety of other unimaginable shapes. They pulled faces and giggled at each other's incongruous, unrecognisable images.

They looked at their watches, noticing it was almost time to meet up for lunch. Rosemary was ready to tuck in, she was famished.

'We're having a great time,' Rosemary told Mr Heyworth, as she tucked in hungrily to her fish and chips, mushy peas and bread and butter, all washed down with tea. It was her favourite seaside food, just the smell of it frying made her feel ravenous.

'What are you going to do in the afternoon?' one of the girls asked her.

'We're going on the fair rides. I love the dodgems,' she replied.

'Are you going on the ghost train too?'

'Oh no,' Rosemary shuddered.

'I'm not going on it either,' Judy Parker chipped in, looking across at Rosemary, her old school chum. Marlene Ward had already been on the ride with one of the other shop girls and came out as white as a sheet.

'It was really dark and a monster thing came out from the wall,' she told them, still shaking from her ordeal. There was no way Rosemary was going on the ghost train after what she had heard. They tried their hand instead at winning on the slot machines, pooling sixpence. It cost a penny a time and they took turns to pull the handle, but they never won anything.

'Don't forget to meet up at the coach at five,' Mr Heyworth

reminded everyone, after they finished their lunch. 'I hope you all have a good time this afternoon.'

Rosemary loved the amusement centre at the far end of the seafront with all the rides. As well her favourite dodgems, there was a water chute. One or two of the shop girls were brave enough to go down and not worry about getting a soaking, but Rosemary decided against it as she was wearing one of her best dresses.

As the girls walked past a stall selling seaside souvenirs, their eyes caught sight of a selection of hats on display. One by one, they each picked up a cowboy hat and placed it jauntily on their heads, grinning at their reflection in the mirror.

'Let's all buy one and walk around in them,' suggested Rosemary, who was having the time of her life. They paid up for the hats and walked happily along the promenade arm in arm singing the popular music-hall song and a seaside favourite, 'Oh, I Do Like to be Beside the Seaside'. They didn't have a care in the world and they laughed as they walked along the seafront.

Walking towards them came a group of boys about their age, also wearing the same cowboy hats. They stopped and spoke to the shop girls, pointing to their hats and laughing at how they had all had the same idea.

'Where are you from, then?' asked one of the boys.

'Cambridge, and you?' replied Rosemary, never shy to speak out.

'We're from Essex – not far away. We're just here for the day,' he replied. The boys were dressed smartly in suits and wore shirts and ties. One of them had an idea, 'Let's have our photo taken together!'

Judy Parker smiled and gave one of the boys her camera. She stood between two of the shop girls, with a boy on the other side of them, while Rosemary knelt down in front next to one of the boys, his arm around her shoulder.

'That was so funny,' said Rosemary after the boys walked off. 'Fancy them wearing the same hats and stopping to speak to us.'

Judy laughed. 'I can't wait to see the photo!'

They returned to their coaches for the journey home and Rosemary walked arm in arm with Judy. She was fond of her former school friend who had much in common with her. 'Isn't it funny how we ended up together at Heyworth's after going to the same school?' she said.

'I'm so pleased we did,' grinned Judy, the gap between her front teeth showing as she smiled. Judy had lovely thick brunette hair and a thick fringe that fell an inch above her eyebrows. Like Rosemary, she had a happy, easy-going nature and it was rare to see her without a smile on her face. They both loved dancing and music and they enjoyed going out into town together on a Saturday night to jive.

She had been sent to Heyworth's for an interview for a junior shop girl's job by the Labour Exchange when she left school at fifteen. Although she had never been in the store before, she knew about it from Mary Ryder, their children's buyer, who was her father's aunt.

Judy was tall and slender and had a model's figure. She stood 5 feet 8 inches tall, and she had endless legs that made people's heads turn. When she was born, the doctor was amazed and told her mother, 'I've never seen a baby with such long legs before!'

When she was eleven years old, Judy became very ill after swallowing a mouthful of river water during a swimming lesson. 'I'm afraid she has rheumatic fever,' the doctor at Addenbrooke's Hospital told her anxious parents, Florence and Arthur.

'Her heart is very weak and she must lie flat on her back so she doesn't strain it. It could take several months for her to recover,' he told them.

Judy's family was devastated that their healthy daughter could have suffered so catastrophically from swallowing the river water that countless children had been safely swimming in for years.

Judy, who had always been high spirited, energetic and

adventurous, spent nine months lying on her back. Her younger sister Val, who she was devoted to, couldn't see her in hospital as children were not allowed on the ward. Christmas Day was the only time Val was able to visit, and she arrived to find Judy lying in bed wearing a Christmas hat, her face instantly lighting up when she saw her sister walk in.

'You should have seen my doctor,' Judy told her younger sister with a giggle. 'He came dressed as a Christmas fairy – and he had hairy legs!'

When she returned home after nine months – missing a year from school – Judy's mother regularly rubbed ointment on her daughter's painful joints and handed out the sixteen aspirin a day she had been prescribed for pain relief.

She gradually regained her strength and started walking again. Judy's mother hoped that her daughter would make a full recovery. But the doctor gave her shattering news, 'I'm afraid she won't survive after the age of twenty-five. Her condition will decline and she'll end up in a wheelchair.'

Florence sobbed when given the terrible diagnosis. The doctor added, 'Don't tell anyone about this – ever. If you do, they'll let it slip out and we don't want Judy to know if she's to have a normal childhood.'

Florence never told a soul, not even her husband, for fear of spoiling Judy's youth. She wanted her daughter to enjoy each day of her life without worrying about the possibility of an early death.

When Judy started work at Heyworth's at fifteen, she was still unaware of this threat to her health. She was just one of the girls as far as everyone was concerned, just the way her mother wanted.

Despite her weak heart, Judy cycled two miles to and from work every day. At work she busied herself making the hosiery displays look attractive, pleased to have the chance to put her artistic skills to good use. One day a new batch of stockings were delivered. They were lime green and unlike anything that Heyworth's had stocked before. Judy, who had a strong artistic streak and loved bright colours, thought they were wonderful, as nobody had seen coloured stockings before. They caused quite a stir.

'I must say they are different to our usual nylons. We need to let people see what they look like on,' the lingerie buyer told Judy. Suddenly having a brainwave, she added, 'I know, why don't you put on a pair and walk around town in them? You can let everyone know they came from here!'

'All right,' said Judy cheerily, glad to have the chance to slip out from behind her counter, especially as a model for the latest style in stockings!

She carefully rolled the very fine bright green Aristoc stockings over her legs and clipped the tops of them to her suspender belt.

'You've got amazing legs,' said the buyer, admiring Judy's long limbs. 'They look great on you.'

Judy strolled off confidently to the marketplace in her stilettos. She watched heads turn and look at her legs in amazement, their eyes fixed on the lime green stockings she was wearing.

'Where did you get those stockings from?' she was asked. And she replied, as planned, 'They're new in at Heyworth's.' Customers headed for the store to snap up the new stockings.

She continued wearing them at work, walking up and down the staircase from the ground floor to the fashion showroom, where her stockings caught the eye of passing customers who asked the same question. 'You can buy them from our counter downstairs. They've just arrived,' Judy replied, smiling at everyone and pointing them in the right direction to purchase their own.

'They look good on you, but I don't think I'll buy a pair,' Rosemary told her school friend. 'I prefer my favourite sheer Blue Haze stockings.'

*

Rosemary had arranged to go out dancing that weekend with another friend from the shop, also called Judy – Judy Mortlock from the underwear department. 'Let's go to the Guildhall – it's cheaper there, especially if you arrive early,' said Rosemary, now twenty.

That Saturday night she slipped into her favourite black circular skirt and a tight-fitting top, throwing a cardigan over her shoulders, and walked briskly into town wearing her favourite stilettos.

She had just finished with a boyfriend a few weeks before and was hoping someone new would soon catch her eye. She wasn't keen on the American GIs who were based around Cambridge and flocked to the dance halls; she found them pushy and overconfident, bragging all the time about what they had and what they did. It grated on Rosemary's nerves.

The Guildhall was a large, prominent building on the market-place where the council was based, as well as a courtroom. It was from its balcony on 8 May 1945 that the end of the war in Europe was proclaimed.

The girls entered through a side door and climbed up a winding staircase to a large hall where the dance was in full flow when they arrived. A local band was playing rock 'n' roll cover songs and every-one seemed to be having a good time.

Rosemary scanned the dance hall and spotted a tall man stand-ing in the doorway. He returned her gaze and walked towards her. He wore a smart suit, shirt and tie and was very handsome. He was the best-looking man there, with smiling eyes, and matinée-star looks.

'Would you like to dance?' he asked Rosemary.

'All right, yes, I will,' she replied shyly, her heart fluttering.

It was a slow dance, Billy Fury's 'Halfway to Paradise', and as he held Rosemary in his arms, she sensed an instant attraction. It felt wonderful being held so close to his chest and she didn't want the song to end.

'I'm Bernard Smith,' he said, smiling at her. Rosemary smiled back. She was thrilled to have met such a good-looking man. They ended up dancing together all night. She looked across the dance hall and saw Judy dancing with Bernard's friend, Robin Ladd. Although Judy Mortlock was still going out with Bill who she had met at the Rex, the two shop girls loved going out jiving together whenever they could. Rosemary had overheard Bernard telling someone he had just bought a new car, which impressed her greatly, as she didn't know many people who owned their own vehicle.

As the evening came to an end, she told Judy, 'Mine's got a car. It'll save us a taxi if he asks to take us home.'

'Keep him talking,' said Judy.

Sure enough, when it was time to leave, Bernard asked Rosemary, 'Would you mind if I take you home?'

Rosemary's eyes lit up and she instantly agreed. She followed him outside, greatly looking forward to a ride home in his car. She looked around the street and asked him, 'Where have you parked your car, then?'

'Oh, I didn't bring it with me. It's at home.'

Rosemary was crestfallen. It was an hour's walk to her house and her feet already ached after dancing all night in her high-heeled shoes. She had painful blisters too, and couldn't wait to kick her shoes off.

'It's such a lovely evening for a walk,' Bernard said.

Rosemary had no choice. She hobbled home, her feet hurting like mad. When they finally arrived at her house, she breathed a huge sigh of relief, kicking off her shoes.

Bernard asked, 'Can I see you tomorrow evening?'

'Yes, I'd like that,' Rosemary agreed.

It began raining, so Rosemary lent him her father's coat – and his bicycle so Bernard could get home quickly. The coat was two sizes too big for her father – it was one he had picked up at work and brought home by mistake – but it fitted Bernard perfectly.

'He's going to have a shock when he sees how small my father is,' thought Rosemary.

When Bernard collected her the following day, a Sunday afternoon, her three protective brothers peered through the net curtains to see what her date looked like. Rosemary had told them how good-looking he was and that he owned a car, and their curiosity was aroused. They watched their sister walk off with him, and Rosemary and Bernard walked to Parker's Piece, a large square of common land in the centre of Cambridge, to watch a cricket match.

After the match Bernard took Rosemary to the Regal cinema and they cuddled up together as they watched the film. Rosemary had the time of her life, impressed by his attentiveness and perfect manners.

At the end of the evening Bernard told Rosemary he had to leave for Wisbech, a Cambridgeshire town 50 miles away, where he was stationed with the constabulary, as his leave had come to an end.

'If I miss you, I'll write you a letter,' he said. 'But if not, it's been nice knowing you.'

They didn't have a phone, and Rosemary knew she had no choice but to wait. She gazed into Bernard's piercing blue eyes, her heart racing, as she said goodbye.

After he left she thought about him a lot. 'He's only said that because he doesn't want to see me again,' she told herself despairingly. Her family quizzed her about Bernard as they could see how keen she was on him.

'What does this young man do for a living?' her father asked.

'I think he's in the RAF – he works at some sort of constabulary,' Rosemary replied, as lots of boys who went to the Guildhall served with the RAF.

'It's not the RAF; that's a police station,' her father told her.

Rosemary was astonished. 'Oh no, no, no, he can't be a police-man!' But then she thought some more, 'He's nice though. I really like him, even though he is a policeman. I hope he misses me.'

A thought suddenly flashed through her mind. The words that Molly the gypsy had told her: 'You will fall in love with someone and he'll be in a job where he gets promoted.'

Rosemary's heart thumped. 'I wonder if Bernard is the one. Will he miss me and write to me?'

EVE

1948

'The new buyer is Mrs Ryder,' Herbert Heyworth announced. Eve felt a huge sense of relief. Now aged eighteen, Eve had risen in the ranks of shop girls and was the number-two sales assistant after the buyer. The news was welcomed by Eve and the other girls. Mrs Ryder was easy to get on with – Eve had seen her bring her son Barry in wearing his school uniform on her days off; she worked part-time.

Eve knew Mary Ryder loved her work and didn't want to be a full-time mother. She had a calm, friendly and professional manner, which had won the respect of the younger girls in the department. She had also started as a junior shop girl after the end of the war, when she was in her thirties, and had worked her way up to the top position in the department.

'I much prefer being at work rather than stuck in the house all day, especially now that my Barry is eleven,' she told Eve.

Unlike Miss Stubbings, Mrs Ryder greatly respected Herbert, and found him easy to get on with. She was a perfectionist who, despite her usual calm manner, became flustered if anything was out of place.

'That doesn't live there! Put it back where it belongs,' she would tell the shop girls if her sharp eye spotted anything amiss.

Although she was known as Mary, Mrs Ryder's first name was really Gladys, which she tried to conceal from everyone. If she was ever called by her real name, she retorted sharply, 'No, no no, don't call me Gladys. I want you to call me Mary. I can't stand being called Gladys!'

Her husband Sidney worked for a firm of builders. In many ways, they were opposites. While he was desperate to save every penny he could, his wife enjoyed spending it freely. She enjoyed life and lived for the moment, while Sidney carefully budgeted every penny. He was still haunted by the Depression of the 1930s and the fear of being without money and losing his job.

'You just never know what's round the corner. We need to save every penny we can,' he insisted.

'But we can enjoy life at the same time. Money is also for spending,' his wife replied cheerily.

Their fortune increased suddenly and considerably after winning £100 on the Littlewoods pools. The couple felt richer than they could have hoped for in all their wildest dreams, and Sidney decided how it should be spent.

'We can't waste this money. Let's put it down for a deposit on a house. It's our only chance of getting our own home,' he suggested.

They purchased a two-bedroomed terraced house for £500, using their £100 windfall as a deposit, taking a mortgage out for the difference. Sidney vowed: 'This is the first and only time I plan to borrow money.'

Eve enjoyed her work and was popular with the other shop girls. She became friends with a new shop girl called Mary Gillson, known as Gilly. She was twenty-one and vivacious, and Eve warmed to her friendly ways immediately.

Gilly had previously worked at Laurie & McConnell's, another Cambridge store, but moved to Heyworth's because of its generous salary.

'I was there for seven years and the pay was so bad that my husband told me to leave, as he felt I was only earning peanuts,' Gilly told Eve. 'My pay almost doubled when I came here. I can't believe the difference.'

Eve understood this only too well. 'You did the right thing. Herbert Heyworth may have his funny ways, but he's certainly generous.'

Laurie & McConnell's was founded in 1883 in Fitzroy Street, around the corner from Heyworth's original premises in Burleigh Street. Shoppers could enjoy afternoon tea on its roof garden while Cambridge Town Band were among the bands who played to them, but it was more of a family department store and didn't attract the same posh clientele as Heyworth's.

'This is a totally different class of shop to Laurie & McConnell's,' Gilly told Eve.

Gilly had met her husband Robert at a local dance and was drawn to his good looks. Dressed in his smart RAF uniform, Robert spotted Gilly sitting on the edge of the dance floor along with all the other girls dressed in their best frocks, tapping their feet while the band played. Robert was not a pilot – he helped with ancillary jobs. One of his most important post-war missions included loading up planes with urgently needed provisions during the Berlin airlift. Gilly enjoyed listening to Robert describe how the planes were loaded with food and supplies at bases outside Cambridge, before they flew to Berlin as part of an international mercy mission after the city was occupied by the Soviets.

Around this time, Herbert felt it was time to modernise the store. There had been no changes since it opened in Sidney Street in 1928 and now, twenty years later, Herbert felt it was time to open up the departments and make the stock more accessible to clients.

'He's been to Switzerland and come back with all these ideas. Everything looks different and I like it much better,' Eve told Les. 'We don't have any of those glass-topped cabinets and drawers any more with all the stock inside. The customers can reach everything themselves now, as it's on rails and shelves.'

The gleaming white baby clothes, which were now displayed openly, needed protection to keep them clean and pristine. Each night they had to be covered with tissue paper placed over the hangers to stop them getting grubby.

In quiet moments the shop girls busied themselves replacing any tatty tissue paper by folding new paper in half, cutting a hole in the middle of it and then placing it gently over the baby garment. It was a daily ritual removing the paper each morning and putting it back each night – after lifting off the dust sheets that covered each rail. Every garment was precious and needed to be in perfect condition for their customers.

As well as fitting out the babies of Cambridge's wealthiest families in the finest clothes, Heyworth's also attracted women from the other end of the social spectrum – gypsies from the annual Midsummer Fair.

The previous children's buyer, Miss Stubbings, had noticed how scores of gypsy women who came to Cambridge in June during the fair week bought the most expensive dresses for their young daughters. They favoured brightly coloured satin party dresses adorned with frills, bows and big petticoats for their daughters to wear around the fairground. Mrs Ryder continued the tradition, welcoming travellers in the same way she would have done had they been titled.

Mr Heyworth welcomed them too, seeing how much they spent.

Eve heard how one gypsy woman had gone into their corsetry department and had taken her top off to be measured. When the shop girl walked into the changing room, her jaw dropped. In front her was the biggest diamond brooch she had ever seen pinned to the traveller woman's bra.

'Oh, you're looking at my jewel, are you? I always keep that close to me,' the woman told the stunned assistant.

Eve enjoyed serving the gypsy women, knowing they spent generously. They had no airs and graces like some of their posh customers, and she found them amusing. She could always tell when they were in the store, even if she couldn't see them, as they were garrulous and chatted noisily, and usually had a couple of boisterous children in tow.

As Eve walked over to assist two gypsy women, she noticed they wore thick gold rings on each finger and bangles jangled on their wrists. They had long dark hair and wore bright clothes. It was impossible not to think how different they were from her usual customers.

'May I help you? Is there anything you'd like me to show you?' Eve asked them.

'Yes, for sure you can help us,' one of the women replied; a little girl of about four, who had ringlets in her hair, was hanging tightly on to her mother's skirt.

'I want to buy one of your dresses for my kiddie here. It has to be the best dress you have in the store. I like the one in the window with the pink frills and bows and the big sash. I love all the lace, it's just what my little'un likes to wear. What can you show me?'

Eve led the woman straight to the rails where the elaborate party dresses were hanging. They were for girls aged up to around six or seven and were in all colours of the rainbow. The woman picked up a pink dress with a huge net petticoat underneath its organza skirt; it was one of their priciest, but the woman didn't flinch at the price label.

Most of these party dresses were too expensive for Heyworth's usual customers, but the gypsy women never baulked at the cost, readily spending £6 to £8 without batting an eyelid.

'That feels like good quality to me. My little'un will love that,' said the gypsy woman, feeling the rich fabric between her fingers.

Turning to the child, she asked loudly, 'What do you think of this pretty dress, then? Shall I buy it for you?'

The little girl repeatedly nodded her head, saying, 'Yes, I want it, I want it!'

'Well, we'll have it then. It's perfect. Pink is her favourite colour, too.'

Other gypsy women flocked in to Heyworth's during June's Midsummer Fair too, their purses bursting, all of them vying to buy the prettiest, frilliest and most expensive party dresses. They wanted to show they could afford the best, just like Heyworth's most upmarket clientele.

Heyworth's was also well known for its finest white cotton romper suits and dresses. Each year Mrs Ryder flew to Madeira to place her order. The embroidery thread and cotton on the island was renowned for its softness and superior quality, and they were leading specialists in making the most exquisite baby garments decorated with dainty broderie anglaise.

The day of Heyworth's long-awaited annual summer outing was fast approaching and Eve was looking forward to their trip to the seaside.

'You'll never guess where we're going this year,' she told Les, knowing he was clueless.

'Go on then, tell me. How am I supposed to know?' he answered.

'We're going to Clacton!'

'Well I never! How about that. I certainly hope you have better weather this time,' he replied, smiling.

Eve had bought a new summer dress from Heyworth's specially for the outing. It was her first ever Horrocks dress, and pricier than her other cotton frocks, but she'd instantly fallen in love with it, and managed to buy it at a reduced price with her staff discount. The dress had a turquoise, tan and white striped pattern and a deep white collar, and Eve loved the combination of these colours. Wearing her white strappy sandals, she walked to King's Parade where the coach was picking the shop girls up. Before they left, the staff posed for a photograph. They all looked happy, anticipating the carefree fun day ahead of them.

'Thank goodness it's sunny,' said Eve, as she looked above at the bright, cloudless sky, remembering how the heavens had opened during her honeymoon.

There was a whoop of delight from the girls as the coach drove off. The previous year Eve hadn't been able to go on the summer outing, as she'd fallen off her bike and broken her arm. Her aunt had made her a navy and white seersucker dress especially for the trip. She was very disappointed to miss out, and had been looking forward to wearing her new dress.

This year Herbert Heyworth and his wife, Marjorie, were on the coach too. 'Now don't forget, before you dash off, we're meeting for a fish-and-chip lunch at one,' Herbert called out, telling them where they should meet. 'I hope you all have a wonderful day.'

The glorious sunshine and bright blue sky made Clacton seem far more appealing to Eve that day than it had been on her honeymoon. This time she could buy candyfloss and walk on the beach, and there were plenty of stalls and sideshows to amuse herself on, as well as a funfair to visit. There were no 'closed' signs up this time, and Eve and the shop girls were keen to see as much as they could.

Eve walked jauntily along the promenade with the girls from her department, looking out at the sea on one side, and eyeing up the colourful attractions the other side.

Their stomachs soon told them it was lunchtime and they headed to the fish-and-chip restaurant for lunch, which was in one of the prime locations on the seafront. The shop girls were famished, and their mouths watered when they caught a whiff of the food as the waiter brought it to their table. 'It smells delicious!' said Eve, longing to tuck in.

The batter was thick and crispy and the succulent white flesh of the cod was the tastiest Eve had ever eaten. She sprinkled salt and vinegar on the chunky chips and quickly devoured them.

After lunch, Eve couldn't wait to slip into her swimming costume. She used a nearby toilet to make the quick change, before running into the sea. She dipped her toes in the chilly water, and looked back at the other girls, egging them on to come and join her. It was a perfect day – almost – and would have been even better if Les was with her too.

Although there was a part of Les's life he couldn't talk about, there was a side of him that she alone had seen – he was very romantic. In one tender love poem, he poured out his love for Eve:

> A pair of eyes like emeralds,
> Wreathed with golden hair,
> Her figure like a Venus,
> She walks with graceful air.
> When I behold her smiling
> Or listen to her voice,
> The world is full of sunshine
> And makes my heart rejoice.
> There is no one to equal
> The captor of my heart.
> I'll love her without ceasing
> Until death us shall part.

'I can't always say what I'm thinking, but I can write it down,' he said shyly as he handed over the poem.

Eve was deeply touched by the emotion it conveyed. 'It's beautiful Les, I know how much you love me. I shall always treasure this – I'll keep it for ever.'

Les couldn't talk to family and friends about being a prisoner of war, but he found he could unburden himself at POW reunions. One of the former inmates in Blackpool organised them.

'Can you come along with me, Eve? Do you think you can get a Saturday off?' Les asked.

'There's no point, Les, the answer will be "no". Nobody can get a Saturday off. The only way I'll be able to join you is if I leave Heyworth's.'

Eve didn't see any point in asking, as she was certain her request would be turned down again, just like when she'd asked for a weekend off to be a bridesmaid. She also felt slightly nervous about these reunions, as she didn't know anybody else who would be going and she wasn't confident mixing with people she didn't know.

But she knew how important it was for Les to be there, that it was the only place where he could talk openly and listen to others as they discussed their experiences, how they felt now and how the camp had affected their lives.

'They're like brothers to me because other people outside don't understand what we went through,' Les told Eve.

'I know, Les, and you must go.'

Eve felt that Les had been cheated of being given the Freedom of the City when he returned to Cambridge after the war. She had seen this honour bestowed on the Cambridgeshire Regiment, the troops marching through the packed streets to loud applause.

While there was a rapturous fanfare at Cambridge railway station with a band playing and flag-waving jubilant families screaming out their whoops of joy, there was no similar homecoming for the local boys who had served with the RAF. In contrast, a solitary figure met Les at the railway station alongside his family – his minister from the United Reformed Church, who embraced him when he set foot on the platform.

Les never complained that he had been ignored. He was not the type to make a fuss about it, even though Eve felt he should have enjoyed the same welcome home. 'It doesn't matter to me. It's not worth making a fuss about. I'm home, and that's what counts the most,' Les told her.

Eve and Les started married life living with Eve's mother, along with her younger brother Derek. They were given some privacy and had their own sitting room. But Gertrude Gray didn't like anyone using her kitchen, and insisted on doing all the cooking.

One night there was a ferocious thunderstorm. Eve heard a terrific crash as she was lying in bed asleep. She woke with a start and her mind flashed back to the wartime air raids. Les went out to investigate, and returned soaking wet, saying, 'You won't believe this, the chimney has collapsed!'

The chimney had been struck by lightning and the bricks had fallen in a pile at the bottom of their basement.

Eve gasped as she surveyed the damage in front of her eyes, thankful for Les's protective and reassuring presence. It was worse than the unexpected storm that had terrified her on her way to work, when the kindly Mrs Heyworth had taken her up to her private rooms and helped dry her off.

It was not the only time their house was struck by lightning. During another fierce storm, the lamppost outside their house was struck and electrical currents surged through Eve's mother's wireless, which was on at the time. Fortunately, there was no damage to the house, but the wireless exploded right in front of their disbelieving eyes.

'People tell me not to worry about thunderstorms, but they frighten me, and they always will,' she told Les.

Eve turned up for work one morning and immediately sensed something was wrong. The shop girls were crying and everyone looked sad. The atmosphere was heavy and sombre.

'What's wrong? What's happened?'

'It's Molly Rolfe – she's dead!'

Eve gasped in disbelief. She couldn't believe it. Molly was a junior shop girl in corsetry. She was a sweet-natured, pretty, happy, carefree eighteen-year-old.

'How? What happened?' she asked incredulously.

'She was in an accident coming home from the American base where she had gone dancing.'

Eve's eyes pricked with tears too. Everyone used to tease Molly by saying, 'Here comes Molly in her mocks!' They were referring to the inferior version of fully fashioned silk stockings, which cost three war coupons. Molly, like many other young girls, couldn't afford them and bought cheaper rayon stockings instead.

'Well, mine only cost one-and-a-half coupons,' she would reply with a cheeky grin.

After finishing work on Friday, 20 January 1950, Molly rushed home to change for the dance at the local RAF base, run by American GIs. She loved going there with her friends.

Molly lived with her parents and younger sister in a terraced house in Suez Road, Cambridge, which had originally been built for railway families in the late nineteenth century. Her father James, a butchery manager, liked to keep a firm, parental eye on Molly – some thought he was too strict – and some said he certainly did not approve of her going off with the Yanks, while her mother was more lenient.

A coach picked up girls from the Drummer Street bus stop to take them to the base at RAF Lakenheath, a 29-mile journey.

They were looking forward to feasting on delicious food and dancing to the latest music played by a live band made up of Air Force men. And, of course, they were also excited about enjoying the company of good looking GIs, who knew how to make the English girls laugh.

Eve didn't go to dances at American bases; she was happy being married to Les, and didn't feel the same craving to go out seeking fun and excitement.

The young GIs had a lack of reserve that appealed to many girls in comparison to the British stiff upper lip. The Americans chewed gum, and whistled and yelled when passing giggling girls. Many girls loved their sense of fun and generosity, while others found them a bit rude with their familiar ways.

Tragedy struck when the coach was bringing the girls home from the dance and it crashed just outside Newmarket. The full horror of the accident became clear during an inquest into Molly's death. The hearing was told how the driver had missed a turning near the July Racecourse and crashed head-on into a telegraph pole after he tried to swerve round and turn back. The bus crashed on to its side and its top was completely torn off the chassis.

Molly died instantly from extensive head injuries and eight girls travelling with her were trapped in the wreckage. When rescuers came, they found one of the girls lying on top of Molly's lifeless body.

When news of Molly's death reached Heyworth's, the shop girls felt a huge sense of loss, deep grief and disbelief. They were unable to hold back their tears, and the accident shook them for a very long time.

In February 1952 when the country went into mourning following the death of King George VI, the state procession and funeral was brought into people's front rooms – it was the first time such a major royal event had been televised.

'You must come and watch it on the television at our house,' Mary Ryder told Eve.

Many people could not afford their own television set then, and Eve jumped at the chance.

'Oh, thank you, I'd love to. I'll have to cycle over in my lunch hour,' she replied.

Eve pedalled furiously to the Ryders' house, a ten-minute journey from work, to see what she could of the sombre procession during her hour's break. She listened awestruck to the narration, watching the grieving queen and her two daughters, one of whom was to be crowned Queen Elizabeth II.

Eve and Les had been living with her mother for more than three years when they decided to move house. They wanted more independence and Eve wished to have a kitchen of her own so she could cook for her husband.

Les's parents, William and Florence, offered a solution. They lived on their own and had room to spare.

'Why don't you and Eve move in with us? You can have the upstairs of the house to yourselves and your own privacy there,' William suggested.

As Eve and Les were still on the council-house waiting list, this seemed the perfect solution. The upstairs of the house was made into a self-contained flat. The spare bedroom was converted into a kitchen with a cooker and table and chairs. There was no kitchen sink, and Eve made do by washing the dishes in the bathroom, which the two couples shared. Eve and Les also had their own dining room with a big square table, four chairs and a sideboard.

They were able to use their wedding gifts from Heyworth's: the cutlery set with bone handles that came from an exclusive jewellery shop in Cambridge, and a cream Lloyd Loom wicker chair. A tea set and tray, a wedding gift from Les's former colleagues at the Electricity Board, and other presents from friends and family were unpacked for their first home.

'I know it's not the same as having our own place, but we'll get one soon, especially when we start a family,' Les promised Eve.

'I can't wait for us to have our own house with our own garden. I hope it won't be too long,' she replied.

'I can't wait either. We have to be patient a little bit longer. At least we're lucky to have our own space, even if it is with Mum and Dad.'

Les's mother Florence was a strong-willed woman. She was only eighteen when she had travelled to India to marry William, where he was serving in the army.

'I don't know how you did it, going all that way to a strange country to get married, and to stay and live out there,' Eve said in amazement.

'I never thought anything of it,' Florence told her daughter-in-law, who had never travelled outside England.

Now Eve and Les had their own self-contained flat, there was only one thing missing from their lives to make their family complete.

'I think it's time we started a family. We can't keep waiting till we get a council house,' Les suggested.

Eve agreed. 'But will we have enough room here? How will we manage having to go up and down the stairs all the time with the baby?'

'We'll manage,' said Les optimistically. 'And we may soon have a council house of our own.'

One of the other shop girls, Jean Nightingale, who worked in the hosiery department with Irene Fiander, was trying for a baby at the same time.

As soon as Eve and Jean arrived for work, they would say to each other, 'Are you all right?' meaning, 'Are you pregnant yet?'

Jean became pregnant first, and Eve congratulated her, hoping it wouldn't be long before she was too. The next month, it was her turn, and the two women had their babies a month apart, with Eve's son Martin being born in June 1953.

Eve had handed in her notice, as she was going to stay at home and look after her baby son and Les.

Mr Heyworth presented her with a £1 gift voucher to spend on something for her baby – and Eve had no difficulty deciding what to buy.

'I know what I want. I'm going to buy one of those beautiful smocked romper suits. They cost nineteen shillings,' Eve said. There was no way she could have afforded to buy it, and she had longed to have one for her own baby after selling them to so many well-to-do mothers.

She was taken by surprise when Mr Heyworth asked if she could come back the following week to see him.

'Of course,' she replied, wondering, 'Why on earth does he want me to go back?'

My Heyworth took her breath away by telling her, 'I'd like you to know that if you ever want to come back, there will always be a job here for you.'

Eve was stunned to hear this from a man she thought never had the time of day for her. She replied, 'Thank you, that's very kind.'

The new parents bought a brand new sturdy Marmet pram with big wheels from Eaden Lilley, and Irene Fiander gave Eve her daughter Patricia's cot, stating firmly, 'We won't be needing it any more. You're more than welcome to have it.'

When Eve went back to visit, the shop girls clamoured around her to admire her bonny gurgling baby, who smiled up at them.

'He's beautiful. And he's got your nose and your eyes, Eve,' they told her.

Eve smiled proudly. She missed the shop girls, but being a mother was an important new chapter in her life. There was still no news about their council house. When Les returned home from work at the Gas Board one day, Eve asked him, 'How long do you think we'll have to wait? We've been on the council list for six years now.'

'You're right. It has been a long time. I'll call in and see them and find out what is happening.'

'I'll come with you,' said Eve. She was very disappointed at the long wait, thinking it was an unfair way to treat a former prisoner of war.

The following day they met the housing officer, who said he couldn't re-house them as they already had a home, but suggested that he could help them if Les's parents moved into a smaller house so a bigger family could move into their home. Eve felt awful that Les's parents were being pushed out of their own home to help them, but they agreed to do it. She couldn't understand why it had been necessary, as the new house didn't seem much smaller, and still had three bedrooms; there wasn't much difference in their size.

But the plan worked, and soon afterwards Eve and Les were offered their own home on the new Arbury Estate. It was in a quiet cul-de-sac on the estate, and had a good-sized garden for Martin, who was now eighteen months old, to play in. Eve's friend Shirley Beavis, who worked in the same department at Heyworth's as Eve had, was Martin's godmother, and Shirley's father made a kitchen table for Eve and Les.

'It's lovely, it's everything we ever wanted! I know we'll be happy here,' said Eve. They were both exhilarated.

Les hung some pictures on their bedroom wall, sketches made in the prisoner-of-war camp by fellow inmate Geoffrey Coxhead. These were very precious. Geoffrey had concealed them beneath a loose board under his sleeping mat, and they were a reminder of what life had been like in the POW camp. Eve gazed at the pictures showing the stick-thin men, every bone on their body visible. The beds were slats of board stacked on top of each other.

'It looks unbearable. Those poor men, they suffered so much,' thought Eve, staring at the gaunt, lifeless shapes that looked little more than bags of bones.

Eve kept in touch with some of the shop girls, going to their houses for coffee and meeting up with Jean Nightingale from hosiery every Tuesday on Christ's Pieces for a walk with their babies. These were special friendships that Eve knew she would keep for ever.

'I don't miss work so much, but I do miss the girls,' Eve told Jean during one of their strolls. 'I thought I'd miss it more, as I went to Heyworth's straight from school, but I love being a mum. And I love being home to look after Les, too.'

When Martin was three, Eve and Les then felt it was time to try for another baby so he could have a brother or sister. Eve became pregnant, and it seemed their future happiness was complete. But two months later their dreams were shattered when Eve suffered a miscarriage.

They continued trying and their hopes were raised two years later when Eve became pregnant again, only to lose the baby at three-and-a-half months. After Eve suffered a third miscarriage, when Martin was seven, the couple decided not to try again, and to agree that it was simply not to be. The cause of the miscarriages was thought to be related to her kidney problems.

In 1961, with Martin now nine years old, Eve remembered Herbert's offer that she'd always be welcome if she wanted to return to work. She was a bit lonely during the day and wanted to work again.

'Les, I think I'm ready to go back to work now. Why don't I ask Mr Heyworth if I can work school hours? The extra money will be handy, too.'

She arranged to see Mr Heyworth. Walking back into the store, it was almost as if she had never been away. Eve was welcomed back and told a part-time position would be available for her in her old department, working school hours that fitted in with Martin's needs.

Eve soon familiarised herself with the new stock, and adapted to changes that had been made in her absence. The tissue-paper dust covers had been replaced by plastic, so there was no longer any need for Eve to cut out tissue paper and place it carefully over the baby clothes.

Eve recognised some familiar faces, among them Mary Ryder. She was now working with a Mrs Westcott, a real character. If the shop girls had a laugh about something, she would burst into verse, singing, 'I'm a little teapot, here's my spout, tip me up and pour me out!'

'Whatever does that mean? Why does she keep saying that?' Eve asked Mary Ryder.

'I've no idea. Don't worry about her, it's just a peculiar habit she has. It's very good to have you back.'

'Well, it's great to be back here and to have company in the day, rather than being on my own, especially now Martin is getting older,' Eve said.

Eve noticed that Herbert seemed redder in the face since she had left in 1953 and heard he suffered from gout. She still didn't feel comfortable in his presence and tried her best to keep out of his way.

Eve felt very lucky. She felt she had the best of both worlds by being able to work part-time and enjoy the friendship of other shop girls, and still leave in time to collect Martin from school and cook their dinner. All seemed well, but her floating kidney began to cause problems again. It ached and make her feel sick. One day the pain was excruciating and she returned to the doctor's.

'It's flared up again and really hurts,' Eve told him. She was very upset that the pain was getting worse.

After examining Eve, the doctor said, 'I'm afraid the kidney has perforated and you'll need an operation to have a large chunk of it removed. I'll book you in at the hospital.'

Eve was aghast. She was worried about leaving Martin, but knew she had no choice if she wanted to be cured. She was admitted to Victoria Ward at Addenbrooke's Hospital. There was a table in the middle of the room where matron sat in her starched uniform and white hat. It was a big ward with beds running along both sides of the ward. Very sick patients were placed in beds right in front of matron, so Eve was put there following her operation. She was gradually moved further back once she was able to walk around slowly, though the pain was still immense.

It was a major operation involving removing part of Eve's right kidney and inserting a plastic tube into it. Nurses gently eased the plastic tube a little further out of the kidney each day, cutting the end piece off. The operation left a huge scar, about a foot long, running under her breastbone.

Eve missed her son desperately; it was the first time they had ever been parted. Children were not allowed to visit the hospital and Eve had to make do with news about him from Les.

'Tell him I won't be long now, I'll be home very soon. But first I have to go to a convalescent home in Hunstanton,' she told Les.

Eve was taken to a grand nursing home on the Norfolk coast by ambulance. She felt every bump in the road on the journey and hung on firmly to the side of the vehicle, worried about being thrown about so soon after her operation in case it worsened the injured site. She felt sheer relief when she finally arrived at the convalescent home almost two hours later.

The shop girls had sent her a pretty nightdress and toiletries, and Eve gradually regained her strength after being given the best care and attention. She loved sitting in a shelter on the seafront and watching the waves, the seagulls soaring overhead, and enjoyed the delicious home-made dinners that helped rebuild her strength. She visited a little church around the corner to pray for a speedy recovery so she could be reunited with her family.

But she sorely missed Les and Martin. Les didn't have a car and wasn't able to visit Eve, so he wrote to her regularly at the nursing home, which helped keep up her spirits. Thanks to the kindness of a woman Les worked with at the Gas Board, who offered to drive them to see Eve one weekend in her car, he and Martin finally visited the convalescent home.

Eve was thrilled beyond words at the thought of seeing Martin again. It had been almost a month since she had been admitted to hospital. She imagined him rushing over and throwing himself into her arms for a hug. But when Martin saw his mother, he didn't run to her as she'd anticipated. Instead, he stood frozen to the spot.

Eve realised her long absence from their home had upset him, and nobody had given any thought to how an eleven-year-old boy would feel after being parted from his mother for so long.

The operation was a success and Eve returned to work. Heyworth's no longer used a pecking order for shop girls by then, but their strict code of decorum when serving customers was still scrupulously adhered to.

'Things aren't the same any more. But then I'm not the same fourteen-year-old who went there straight from school during the war years. I'm now a married woman with a son,' she thought wistfully.

She imagined she would stay at Heyworth's for the rest of her working life and never envisaged that it would one day close its doors for ever. She never gave a thought to Herbert Heyworth wanting to give it all up, that he would be unable to carry on due to poor health and retire with no successor.

But she discovered that what had seemed impossible was to happen.

She was summoned with the other shop girls to be told the

devastating news – that Heyworth's was to close down. She felt a lump in her throat, worried about being without a job, and sad at the demise of what was once Cambridge's finest ladies' department store.

She listened as Herbert Heyworth helped allay their fears about future employment.

'I'll do everything I can to find you all jobs,' he promised the shop girls. 'I'm speaking to all the other department stores in town, and I'll make sure you have other jobs to go to.'

Eve felt desolate. 'I've only worked at Heyworth's! Where else can I go and work in a children's department?'

True to his word, Mr Heyworth found Eve a position in the childrenswear department at Laurie & McConnell's. It might not have had the same posh clientele as Heyworth's, but it was a job, and nobody knew more about this department than Eve.

'I just can't believe it's really closing,' Eve told Les, tears in her eyes.

She reminisced about the days when she started at Heyworth's as a fresh-faced fourteen-year-old and how George Heyworth had given her a job with extra pay because he felt sorry for her widowed mother who had seven children to feed.

When the final day approached, 5 November 1965, Eve felt a huge wave of sadness. Heyworth's had been a major part of her life for many years and it was unbelievable to think it was now coming to a sudden end.

She looked at the other shop girls. They were all upset, fighting back the tears and promising to stay in touch with each other after they left.

An emotional Herbert Heyworth spoke to his staff. 'After so many years of trading as Heyworth Fashions, a business started by my father, this is a sad day for me, as much as it is for you. I'd like to thank you all for the support you've given us and to wish you every success with your future jobs. Whichever store you go to, they are very lucky to have you.'

'Perhaps he wasn't so bad after all,' thought Eve, as she walked out of Heyworth's for the last time.

IRENE

1957

'I wonder why Mr Heyworth wants to see me, and why he sounds so cross,' thought Irene as she walked quickly up the sweeping staircase to his office.

'Come in!' he boomed when she knocked on his door.

As she stepped inside his office, Herbert held up a letter in his hand and waved it in front of her. His round face was red and he was in a spitting rage.

'What is the meaning of this?' he asked in the angriest voice she had ever heard.

'I have no idea what you are talking about, Mr Heyworth,' replied Irene, clueless as to why he was waving the letter at her. 'Can you please tell me what has happened to make you so upset? What does the letter say?'

'As you know, we don't allow staff to have personal mail sent to them here, and this letter arrived for you this morning,' he told her. He showed her the envelope. It had the word 'Personal' written clearly on the front. Irene was stunned. She had no idea who could have written a personal letter to her at work.

'It's from Mr Ross and he says he wants to meet up with you,' he continued in a loud voice.

Irene was baffled. 'But why should Mr Ross want to write to me? I only met him for the first time at the trade fair earlier this week.'

'That's what I wanted to know. Why should he say he wants to see you again?' Mr Heyworth asked his astonished buyer.

'Well, I have no idea why he should write saying that, no idea at all,' she replied adamantly, very confused about this herself. 'I'm a married woman with a young daughter. I'm as surprised as you are.'

It never occurred to Irene to be cross with Herbert Heyworth for opening the letter, as she knew staff weren't allowed to have personal letters sent to them at work. As the managing director of a major hosiery company, Mr Ross was an important business associate for Heyworth's, and she was at a loss to understand why he should have written to her that way. Herbert tore the letter up in front of Irene and threw it in the bin.

'I hope that's an end to the matter. Thank you, Miss Fiander. That is all.'

Irene could see that her boss was still upset when she walked out of his office. She had never witnessed such anger from him before, and believed it was based on the fatherly and protective feelings he felt towards her as a valued employee, nothing more than that. She was astounded by Mr Ross's unwarranted advances, and couldn't believe he had misinterpreted anything she said to him during the brief time they spent together. She knew she had not encouraged any advances from him – they had only talked shop together.

Irene had met Mr Ross for the first time only a few days earlier. He had been invited by Mr Heyworth to visit Heyworth's stand at the Cambridge Trades Fair, which was held after the war to promote local business. It was a spectacular event and known as a 'miniature Olympia', with vast numbers of exhibitors' stands stretching a mile. Herbert Heyworth invited all his important business associates to the show, billed as the biggest trade show under canvas in England.

All of Cambridge's major businesses had a stand at the event, including Heyworth's rival stores, Joshua Taylor and Eaden Lilley. It was held in a gigantic marquee on Midsummer Common during the first week of September, with traders paying £3,000–£4,000 for a stall; the value of the total exhibits was estimated at a colossal £1 million.

The highly publicised event attracted thousands of visitors, who paid sixpence admission. The Heyworth shop girls offered the same impeccable, courteous service to customers at the show as they did in their store. They displayed a selection of their upmarket stock, from hats and childrenswear to accessories, stockings and blouses.

A grand civic opening ceremony took place, with a fanfare of trumpets and a host of special dignitaries, some from overseas, to mark the very special occasion. The marquee was decked with stunning floral arrangements. Sitting with the Mayor, Archibald Taylor, his wife, the Mayoress, and the Sergeant-at-Arms, was His Highness, the Oba of the Benin Kingdom in Nigeria. He looked resplendent in his flowing white robes, orange-beaded headdress and sandals. They sat on a dais opposite a colourful flower-banked fountain pool, watched by hundreds of visitors who had flocked to the opening ceremony.

Celebrations continued at the end of the first day of the show, with a spectacular firework display, which many of the shop girls went to, marking the end of a truly extraordinary day for Cambridge businesses – and Heyworth's.

Business was brisk. 'It's going really well, we're very busy,' Irene told her smiling boss.

'I can see that. I've heard that there have been twenty-six thousand visitors here in the first two days alone,' replied Herbert Heyworth in ebullient mood.

Their stock was flying off the stall. Midsummer Common had been a venue for trade for exactly one hundred years since the Mayor of Cambridge opened the first fair there, a point that the present mayor commented on during his opening speech.

Mr Heyworth invited his guests to join him for a celebratory lunch at Great Chesterford Country Club, near Saffron Walden.

Among them was Mr Ross and Irene, as well as directors and representatives from companies they dealt with, and other buyers from Heyworth's. They made up a party of about fifty and Herbert was treating them all.

He provided a coach to drive them there, and Irene sat next to Mr Ross, both on their way to the club and on the return journey back into Cambridge. Herbert Heyworth was warmly greeted at the club by its owner, Richard Tothill, a great friend of his. Herbert and Marjorie had shared many holidays with Richard and his beautiful wife, who had once been a model. The two men had known each other for many years and they shared a love of Spain, both having holiday homes close to each other on the Costa Brava.

Irene also found herself sitting next to Mr Ross during the lunch. He was in his fifties and not particularly attractive. Irene's female intuition told her that Mr Ross was attracted to her, and she felt a little flattered by the attention of a successful businessman. Being an important business associate, she felt it her duty to be good company and make small talk, but polite conversation was all she had in mind; she was a happily married woman and was merely doing her best to be a charming companion and had not been flirtatious in any way.

The atmosphere was relaxed and jovial and the wine flowed as they tucked into their lunch. As far as Irene was concerned, it was nothing more than a business lunch, and she had never intended to give any other impression to Mr Ross, who, she sensed, was married anyway.

Irene wore a wedding ring, so the man could easily see that she was not single, though the subject of whether either of them was married never came up. Then again, he could have been confused about Irene's marital status, as Herbert Heyworth called her by her professional name, 'Miss Fiander', in Mr Ross's presence, which could have inadvertently given the impression that she was single.

Irene didn't know whether her boss said anything to Mr Ross about the letter, but although Heyworth's continued buying stock from his company, Irene never crossed paths with Mr Ross again. Her business transactions were conducted with buyers, so she never had any need to meet managing directors. She put the incident to the back of her mind and Herbert never raised it again.

Irene and Peter decided it was time to move into their own home. They were still living in Peter's mother's house with his sister, Rita, but wanted their own place. When Peter's mother died, she left the house to Rita, who wasn't married, and left Peter sufficient money to buy a piece of land.

They found the perfect site in the north of Cambridge on the edge of a new council estate being developed in an area called Arbury. At the time there was a fifteen-year waiting list for a council house, so the estate was being built to meet this desperate need.

The council had then discovered a loophole in the planning regulations that didn't allow them to build council houses on land fronting Arbury Road, so had to sell these plots of land for private housing. One of them was snapped up by Irene and Peter.

At the time you had to get a licence from the council if you wanted to build your own house, and you could only get this if you had a child who didn't have its own bedroom; Irene and Peter fitted these requirements perfectly.

The architect drew up the plans for a three-bedroom detached house, but it was going to cost £2,150, which exceeded their budget.

'We can't afford that. We can only pay up to £2,000,' Irene told him.

The plans were scaled back, with the size of the rooms being reduced, making the their project cost a more affordable £1,950. The plans were perfect, everything they hoped for, including a 150-foot garden for Patricia. With Patricia now at school and Maude no longer helping out, Irene decided that she ought to stay home to settle in to their new home.

'I think I should give up work, Peter. We're a bit out of town now, and I'd like to get everything sorted here,' she said.

Peter couldn't believe his ears. 'Are you sure? I know how much you love your work.'

'Yes, for now, anyway. I think I ought to. With a new house to look after, there will be more than enough for me to do here,' Irene persisted.

Irene broke the news to Herbert, who accepted her resignation, wishing her every happiness.

'You know you can stay here and work the hours that suit you – you can come back any time,' he told her.

But Irene's mind was made up. 'I do know that, and I appreciate your kindness. It's just that I feel I need to spend time in our new home.'

Mr Heyworth presented Irene with an exquisite glass crystal bowl for her new home as a leaving gift and, as she walked out of the doorway, she had no thoughts about returning to work.

Irene settled in to her life as a housewife, but with Patricia at school, there was little for her to do. Although she enjoyed spending time in her new home, deep down she missed the friendly chatter with her shop girls and the thrill of negotiating business deals on buying trips. Within weeks, Herbert Heyworth rang Peter at his bank.

'Will you ask your wife to call in and see me, please? There's something I need to ask her.'

Irene went the following day. She had no idea why her former boss had asked to see her within two months of her leaving and was not expecting the words she secretly longed to hear. 'The reason I rang Peter and asked you to come in is because I'd like you to come back as our buyer. You can work your own hours to fit in with Patricia – you can work whichever hours suit you best,' he said.

It was music to Irene's ears and her face instantly lit up. Two months as a housewife was enough – she desperately wanted to go back.

'Of course, I'd be delighted to,' replied Irene with a big smile, bursting with happiness, 'But I'd like to discuss it with Peter first.'

Peter never, ever stood in Irene's way, as he understood that she needed to be at work and how bored she felt at home. 'I want you to do what makes you happy,' he told Irene. 'I can see why Mr Heyworth keeps asking you to go back. He's very lucky to have you.'

'Thank you, Peter, you're the best husband in the world. I love you for the way you understand how I feel and why I need to work,' she said appreciatively.

Irene returned as an accessories buyer, continuing to juggle her working life around Patricia's school hours. She had never been happier.

Although Irene and Peter were members of their local Baptist Church, a new church was planned to serve the Arbury community, the Church of Nicholas Ferrar, later to become part of the Church of the Good Shepherd, and Irene was invited to a special ceremony with eight-year-old Patricia for the laying of its foundation stone. Princess Margaret was invited to perform the honours, and later to meet local people at a garden party.

The excitement and anticipation was tremendous. It is not every day that you get to meet royalty, and Irene was thrilled to have this once-in-a-lifetime opportunity.

Patricia was excited too, practising how to curtsy. Irene had bought her a new dress from Heyworth's especially for the royal occasion. She looked proudly at her daughter dressed in her deep royal-blue dress with lovely smocking.

It was a warm sunny day in 1957 when crowds swarmed Arbury Road as the procession of royal cars made its way to the new estate.

Cheering school children enthusiastically waved their Union Jack flags and hundreds of residents leaned out of their windows to catch a glimpse of their royal visitor, waving ecstatically.

As the twenty-seven-year-old princess stepped out of her limousine, Irene gasped. She thought the princess looked beautiful, a vision of radiance in her lovely summer dress with a matching short-sleeved jacket. She wore elegant long white gloves that came above the elbows, and a fitted hat provided the air of formality her outfit required. Irene was thrilled to be there for such a special occasion and to soak up the excitement.

Irene watched excitedly as the service of dedication was carried out by the Bishop of Ely. The princess used a silver trowel and ebony gavel to officially lay the foundation stone. As the excited Arbury families lined up, hoping to be introduced to the princess they so admired, Irene beamed with pride as Princess Margaret stopped to speak to Patricia.

'That's a very pretty dress,' she told the beaming young girl.

Patricia smiled and curtsied. She did it beautifully. Irene curtsied too as the princess passed by; she could scarcely believe that Princess Margaret had singled out her daughter to speak to and couldn't wait to tell Peter and her friends at work.

Standing face-to-face with the princess, Irene could admire her grace, beauty and flawless skin. The princess warmed the hearts of the hundreds who had flocked to see her, stopping to chat and laugh with them, radiating her charm and personality.

When it was time for Princess Margaret to leave, a wasp provided a flurry of unexpected excitement. It was buzzing around inside her limo, delaying her departure for her next official visit in Cambridge, the opening of Langdon House, a home where elderly people could pass their 'twilight years' in comfort.

Irene could barely contain her excitement about her royal encounter when she returned to work, telling Herbert and the shop girls how radiant the princess had looked, how beautifully dressed she was, and how she had made it a day to remember for the rest of their lives.

'It was a wonderful day – and to think Princess Margaret stopped to speak to my Trisha!' she exclaimed, the glow of excitement still with her.

It was not the only royal encounter for Irene and her daughter. The following year the Queen came by train to Histon Railway Station outside Cambridge, where she transferred to a royal car for an engagement in the city. When Irene had heard about the Queen's imminent arrival, she dashed off with Patricia to catch sight of the monarch.

'The Queen looked beautiful. She wore green and her complexion was like peaches and cream,' she told Peter later on. 'It was wonderful to see her in person – she is so beautiful, too, just like her sister. Mind you, Heyworth's could dress our Queen any day!'

The vivid window displays at Heyworth's attracted widespread admiration and never failed to impress. The store had seven windows to dress, and employed a team of skilled display staff to work on it. The window display manager, Mr Dumper, decided on the theme, and worked with two window dressers and a display artist. They went to extraordinary lengths to create fabulous scenes, telling stories to tempt customers in.

Irene always admired the artistry involved in the window displays, the most popular being the 'June in January' display to promote colourful Horrocks dresses at a time when the sky was dull and grey. It was a titillating reminder that spring was just around the corner and lifted the spirits of women who stopped to gawp. It was also a clever way for Heyworth's to promote Horrocks dresses long before their competitors in Cambridge.

Horrocks dresses were sought-after summer frocks made from

practical, quality cotton in innovative bold prints, and sold for £4–£7, which was considered expensive. They were worn by royalty and celebrities, too, who were attracted by their smart, yet fresh and informal appeal. Horrocks was one of the best-respected ready-to-wear fashion labels of the 1940s and 1950s, and their styles appealed greatly to Heyworth's customers.

'I think they look stunning. Nobody in the area creates a better window than Heyworth's. Our displays are absolutely wonderful,' Irene told their new display girl, Pamela Morgan, as they stood admiring the latest display.

Pamela nodded in agreement. As a fifteen-year-old school leaver who loved art, Pamela was attracted to the upmarket ladies store because of its stunning window displays. She loved fashion and sketching, and during her interview had taken her artist's pad with her and proudly flicked through the pages to show off her lovely drawings of women modelling the latest fashions, the kind sold by Heyworth's. Unfortunately, there was no immediate vacancy in the art studio and she accepted the offer of working as a junior in the knitwear department. She was their third sales girl.

At the time Pamela did not realise that the manager interviewing her, Jim Clarke, was her long-lost cousin. He was related to her father's side of the family, and as her father had died when Pamela was a child, they lost contact with his family for many years.

Mr Clarke turned up at Pamela's house after offering her the job, and spoke to her mother. He wanted to make sure that Pamela knew what to wear for work.

'As soon as there is a vacancy in the art studio, Pamela can have it. We have a girl there who's pregnant, and when she leaves in a few weeks, Pamela can have her job,' he promised.

Each morning Pamela cycled to work, gripping the edge of her skirt on her handlebars so it didn't get caught in the spokes of the wheels. Although the knitwear job had not been Pamela's first choice, she felt privileged to have landed a job at Heyworth's. She looked on being a junior shop girl as good experience. Her duties included unpacking boxes of sweaters and cardigans, and placing them in a colour-coordinated layout on shelving behind the counter. Each Monday morning she had to shake out every jumper on the shelves and replace them so they fitted exactly into the square corners of the shelving unit. She used a Heyworth's polythene bag to measure them up against to make sure she'd get a perfect fit.

Account customers and local dignitaries were allowed to have garments delivered to their home 'on approval' to try on. They were wrapped up carefully in tissue paper, put in maroon-and-white striped boxes and delivered. The boxes matched the deep maroon carpet that added a luxurious feel to Heyworth's shop floor. The knitwear department even had American customers, who bought cashmere sweaters, saying they were a lot cheaper in England than in their own country.

Pamela couldn't wait for her transfer to the art studio; she didn't enjoy selling and wanted to use the gift she'd been born with. The day she longed for arrived within a few months and she gladly swapped her black skirt and cardigan and white blouse for a pair of distinctive maroon tartan trousers, the clothing provided for all art studio staff. When the girls went into the windows to change the display, they were given more sombre grey trousers to wear, so as not to draw attention to themselves.

Irene was thrilled for Pamela when her transfer finally came; their departments were close to each other on the ground floor and she knew how desperate Pamela was to use her artistic skills. The studio was on the second floor overlooking Sidney Street. It was a large room and had bare wooden floors and one storage heater, which Pamela had to light each morning – it was always cold in the there.

In the middle of the room there was a very large table with a hole in the middle for the saw to pass through. Pamela positioned herself around the edge of the table, leaning forward through the hole when using the jigsaw to make her elaborate displays.

Irene had been impressed with one of Pamela's first accomplishments – making nesting boxes out of plywood for each of their seven windows for spring. Pamela was trained by Mr Dumper, a short man in his fifties who always wore a three-piece suit and stood with his hands behind his back. He showed her how to make the first nesting box, carefully cutting the strips of wood and making a point at the top of the 18-inch box, and Pamela then made the remaining six. Artificial birds were placed beside them to add the finishing touch.

Pamela stood back and admired her finished work, feeling a great sense of achievement. It had been fiddly at first, but she soon grasped what she needed to do.

Her next assignment proved more challenging.

'We need to make our windows up for the May Balls – and we must have the best display in Cambridge,' Mr Dumper told Pamela. She knew this was one of the most important displays of the year, after the Horrocks dresses for 'June in January', and needed to attract university students to their store to buy their sumptuous ball gowns.

Pamela set about creating a stunning backdrop showing the Cambridge colleges with a simple black and white silhouette effect. It was a huge project requiring great skill and artistry. To achieve the desired effect, Pamela used photographs of the Cambridge colleges and a large lamp to project the images on to the wall, where she'd placed a huge sheet of white paper. This produced an outline of the college building, which Pamela drew around on the white paper. She did this seven times, making an outline of a different college for each of the seven windows. She then coloured her outline in black to give the silhouette impression.

The starkness of the black and white background made the vibrant colours of the ball gowns stand out even more. One final touch was required to add an opulent feel to the windows, and this was achieved with arrangements of large silk flowers, the biggest and best they could buy – unlike any used by their rival stores.

'Oh my goodness, it looks so beautiful,' gasped Pamela, as she stood back to admire her craftsmanship.

Irene was impressed with the knock-out display. 'I don't think there's a better May Ball window in Cambridge,' she told Pamela. 'You've done a fantastic job.'

None of the displays made by Pamela were wasted. They were used again throughout the year for other promotions, and other uses were found for the flowers and nesting boxes in their spring window displays. Even the silhouette backdrop was used again when Heyworth's promoted their little black cocktail dresses.

Mr Dumper had a surprise for the window-display girls one day – new mannequins had arrived. They had limbs that moved and modern faces to replace the dated ones that looked like they belonged back in the 1940s.

'They're simply brilliant,' Pamela enthused. 'Heyworth's clothes will stand out more if they are displayed on modern and youthful-looking mannequins.'

'I agree,' said Irene, before leaving for her coffee break. She was going to Herbert's new café, El Patio's, which had just opened a few yards down the road in Sidney Street. She had heard from others when it opened that the coffee was unlike any other coffee on sale in Cambridge – and she was not disappointed.

'Mmm, that's simply the most delicious coffee I have ever tasted,' said Irene, slowly sipping her drink and enjoying every mouthful.

There was no comparison between this and coffee Irene had tasted before, Camp coffee from a bottle, or Kenco. The El Patio coffee was made using a Gaggia machine, hissing loudly as the milk became frothy, and the pure blend of ground coffee had a delicious taste and aroma. Nowhere else in Cambridge made coffee this way and it became very popular.

'I really enjoyed your coffee Mr Heyworth,' Irene told Herbert when she returned from her lunch break. 'I think El Patio's is going to be very successful.'

El Patio's was a joint venture between Herbert and his best friend Richard Tothill. Irene had met Richard Tothill when she joined her boss for lunch at the Great Chesterford Country Club, the day that she caught Mr Ross's eye. It had a Spanish theme and was the first café of its kind in Cambridge, and also among the first to introduce new foods to the Cambridge palette. Small-sized pizzas were served on oval-shaped Pyrex dishes and the Mediterranean flavours were a welcome change to English taste buds more used to liver and bacon and sausage and mash.

The continental-themed café was a hit with students and shoppers, as well as Irene and other shop girls from Heyworth's, who popped in during their lunch breaks. Its opening had been a closely guarded secret. A large board in the front window had a huge question mark painted on it with the words 'Opening Soon'. It kept everybody guessing for a very long time.

'I love the grapevines in El Patio's,' Irene told Herbert. 'It looks very stylish and continental inside.'

The walls were covered with pictures of bullfights, which Herbert Heyworth and Richard brought back from Spain. One of them in particular caught the eye of a bishop, who could scarcely contain his shock at what he saw. Pointing to the offending picture on the wall, he spluttered, 'That picture is absolutely disgusting. The bull is showing its testicles!'

Herbert Heyworth couldn't believe his ears. He was livid and replied indignantly, 'That's a bull – what's it supposed to do? Sit cross-legged?'

The bishop stormed out – and the picture remained on the wall. Mr Heyworth had no intention of removing it to appease the offended bishop. When she heard about this, Irene couldn't see what the fuss was about.

'I have every confidence that Mr Heyworth knows what he's doing and would never hang up a picture that was in bad taste,' Irene told her husband later, when recounting the tale. 'I'm not surprised that El Patio's is so popular. Times are changing now and young people want somewhere fashionable to go.'

'Miss Fiander, I'd like you to represent Heyworth's at a funeral on behalf of the store. It's for Miss Emerson,' Herbert Heyworth asked Irene.

'Well, of course, I'd be honoured,' she replied.

'Unfortunately, it falls on the same day that I'm taking the buyers to Paris to see a new collection at a fashion show, and so I can't go myself, but I feel it's important that we're represented at her funeral.'

'Of course, I understand, and I shall be there,' she said dutifully.

Irene had also been invited to join Mr Heyworth, his wife Marjorie, senior staff and buyers from Heyworth's and some of his best friends on a privately chartered flight to Paris for the day, but had declined.

'I have no one to look after Patricia for me after school. I need to be home for my daughter,' she told him, turning down what she knew would be a memorable day out. She would have loved to have gone, but since her mother-in-law had died, she had no babysitter she could call on. She anticipated that it would be an exciting day, knowing Herbert's generous nature the way she did.

Miss Emerson had been Heyworth's corsetry buyer, a long-serving, dedicated and loyal member of staff. She was delightful: old-fashioned but businesslike, and fair to the girls in her department.

While Irene dressed in black to represent Herbert Heyworth and the store at Miss Emerson's funeral, the others were dressing in their brightest spring outfits for their trip to the French capital.

'Mind you look your best. Hats must be worn,' Mr Heyworth told the women, mainly buyers.

Herbert Heyworth had chartered a small aeroplane especially for the day, and he was really treating his guests like royalty. It was the late 1950s and, like other fashion stores in the UK, Herbert Heyworth was influenced by the Parisian fashion scene and wanted to know about the latest styles. His Spanish-born PA, Maria Gallego, was among the invited guests, as well as Herbert Robertson, head of a Cambridge motor firm, and his wife Nora.

They flew from Cambridge Airport to Le Bourget airport on the outskirts of the French capital. It was the first time many of those going had flown anywhere and they had certainly never been to Paris.

Irene heard all about their fabulous day when they returned. They described how strange it seemed to be driving on the other side of the road as their taxi sped into the city along tree-lined boulevards.

She heard about the fabulous fashion show they visited, featuring the latest collection of pastel-coloured blouses by French designer Calvin, and would have loved to have been there in the front row with Herbert, knowing how excellent his and Marjorie's taste in fashion was. Calvin's chic, feminine designs had taken Paris by storm, and were eagerly sought after by Herbert, to give him the edge on his rivals.

After the show the group walked animatedly along the elegant Champs-Elysées, taking in the sights.

'This is probably one of the most expensive streets in the world, so I hope you enjoy it. There's nothing else like it,' Mr Heyworth told the others, as they strolled past immaculately coiffured women and saw men sitting in pavement cafés smoking cigarettes and reading the papers. They gazed longingly into the patisserie windows crammed with mouthwatering delicacies and creamy desserts. They gawped at the expensive shops selling jewellery, and giggled at the French artist wearing a striped top and beret standing by a fountain in a pretty square.

The group then piled into taxis for a sight-seeing trip around Paris. Herbert Heyworth wanted to be sure they saw all its famous sights – the Arc de Triomphe, Eiffel Tower, Notre-Dame and the River Seine. It had been an unforgettable day, and they told Irene they'd remember it for the rest of their lives.

'It sounds wonderful. I wish I could have made it, but I really couldn't leave Patricia. It wouldn't have been fair on her,' Irene said wistfully.

Before they flew home, they told Irene how they sampled French cuisine, with Herbert Heyworth practising his smattering of school-boy French to order what the group wanted. He had to try his best, as the waiters couldn't speak English, and the group hoped they would be served their choice from the menu.

'I've ordered snails and frogs' legs. I thought you should try some proper French food,' he jokingly told them.

'I can just imagine that,' laughed Irene.

'It was all right. We got our steak and chips, though they call them *frites* over there!'

Mr Heyworth's generosity included paying for taxis to take his exhausted and exhilarated women home at the end of their long and memorable day.

'It sounds like you all had a wonderful trip. Maybe I can go next time,' she added hopefully.

But there never was another time for Irene.

'I've got some important news,' Peter told Irene. 'It's good news, something I've been hoping for.'

'What is it Peter? Tell me – don't keep me guessing.'

'I've been offered a promotion. I'm going to be made a bank manager.'

'That's wonderful news,' Irene replied, delighted. She knew how much it meant to him. 'Where is it?'

'It's not in Cambridge, I'm afraid. It's in Stevenage. It means we will have to move away.'

Irene took in the news and replied unhesitatingly, 'Well, never mind that, of course we must go. You've always supported me over the years, and now I must support you.'

For the third time, Irene broke the news to her boss that she would be leaving the store. And again, he expressed disappointment and regret at losing her.

'I'm very pleased for you and Peter, but, we'll be very sorry to lose you. Please pass on my congratulations to Peter,' he told Irene.

Cambridge had been Irene's home for fifteen years since she first married Peter. She felt sad to be leaving the house in Arbury, which held many special memories, but she had no doubt that they were making the right decision.

As Herbert Heyworth presented Irene with a farewell gift, she was once again overcome with emotion by his thoughtfulness and generosity.

'Thank you, this is perfect,' she said, accepting a £30 gift voucher for records. 'You couldn't have chosen anything better. I shall miss you all very much. Peter and I will look forward to buying our favourite records and we'll think of you all when we play them!'

They both enjoyed classical music, with Strauss's waltzes being their favourite. Now she was leaving work, she hoped she would have time to listen to them.

Irene looked around at the sea of faces before her, including some shop girls she had worked with since her first day at Heyworth's in 1948. She knew she would miss them, that working at Heyworth's had been a huge chunk of her life, and she'd always remember it with fondness.

Irene and Peter settled into their flat in Stevenage with Patricia, who was now fourteen. Irene missed her job, which had been such an important part of her life, and began thinking about looking for another job in a shop, knowing that she would soon be bored, staying at home all day.

A month later Peter returned from work one day with some unexpected news for Irene.

'Mr Heyworth called me at the bank today. He asked me to ask you if you would go back for the sale and help out.'

Irene was elated when she heard this. She hadn't been able to leave Herbert a personal number, as the flat didn't have a phone. This would make it the third time Herbert had called her to return to work after she'd handed in her notice! As before, without any hesitation, her mind was made up.

'I could manage that. It's only forty-eight miles away and I know how busy their July sales are. I expect he'll need me to start again almost straight away. I'll call him and sort out the details,' said Irene, thrilled.

Mr Heyworth was equally delighted with Irene's acceptance. 'I'll make up the cost of your petrol money, don't worry about that,' he told her. 'Can you come back next week when the sale starts?'

'Yes, I'll be there,' Irene confirmed, the same devoted and loyal employee. 'The journey shouldn't be too bad as it's summer.'

When she'd left the previous month, Herbert Heyworth had been spending less time in the store, and there were rumours about him having health problems. His round face was becoming redder, he'd put on weight and Irene had noticed his hands had a blue tinge. She felt privileged that he had once again asked her to return, and would do anything to help him, especially as he had been so good to her.

Irene had helped out at many sales now and knew the routine only too well. There was the same long queue of bargain-hunters, some of whom had flocked there hours beforehand to be sure of purchasing their desired item at a rock-bottom price. While some of the store's fixtures and mannequins had been modernised in recent years, Herbert still insisted on providing the most personal and professional service to all. The store was heaving and Irene felt a thrill to be back at work in the job she loved.

When the sale finished, Irene agreed to stay on longer. She didn't mind the forty-five-minute drive to Cambridge in her trusted Austin 1100 car and hoped to miss the worst of the traffic by working 9.30 a.m. to 4 p.m.

'I'll see how it goes, I'd like to carry on working there as long as I can,' she told Peter.

'I think Heyworth's would miss you if you weren't there. You must do what makes you happy,' he replied.

Irene's new arrangement worked well throughout the summer months and she didn't mind the drive. She enjoyed her buying trips to the wholesalers, and managing her shop girls again. But her optimism changed as the winter weather took a grip. What had been a pleasant drive now became a nightmare. As the weather worsened, she began to question whether she wanted to be driving in such terrible conditions. One night the fog was so thick on her drive home that she couldn't see her hand in front of her face.

She slowly inched her way home in her car, forcing herself to stop off in Royston when she felt too scared to drive any further until the fog began to lift. She was freezing cold and unable to let Peter know her whereabouts, and she knew he'd be worried.

She finally arrived home exhausted at 9.30 p.m. and slumped into an armchair. While she was relieved to have arrived home in one piece, Peter had been frantic with worry.

He said firmly, 'Irene, my love, I'm sorry, but I think you must give up your work. You can't carry on driving to Cambridge in weather like this – no matter how much you love your job! I've been out of my mind with worry these last few hours.'

Irene nodded slowly in agreement. She realised what her husband said made sense, and she realised she had had enough. She no longer wanted to drive into Cambridge each day – even if it meant giving up the job she loved more than anything.

'I know what you say makes sense. There will never be anywhere else like Heyworth's for me to work,' she told Peter.

With a heavy heart, she told her boss of her decision. 'I'm sorry, Mr Heyworth, but I can't drive in now the weather has changed. It's too far. I'm sorry, but I feel it's time for me to leave Heyworth's. I'm afraid I won't be coming back.'

Herbert Heyworth had no choice but to accept Irene's resignation. Once again he thanked her profusely.

'I do understand and I'd like to thank you, too, for everything you've done for Heyworth's. You'll be missed by us all.'

Irene, her eyes moistening as she realised there would be no going back, added, 'I shall miss you all too. You've been so kind to me, Mr Heyworth, and I have very much enjoyed working at Heyworth's.'

It was the final time Irene handed in her notice. Mr Heyworth never called her again. Within eighteen months, Heyworth's closed its doors to customers for the last time, due to Herbert Heyworth's declining health.

BETTY

1951

Betty is pictured left holding her prize doll, with George Heyworth and shop girl Mary Turkentine, during the Heyworth staff outing to the Festival of Britain exhibition in London

'You go along and have a good time,' Betty's mother Mabel insisted. 'You deserve it – you work so hard.'

Betty was looking forward to joining the staff outing to visit the Festival of Britain exhibition in London. She was really keen to visit this amazing exhibition, which was being held to mark the one-hundredth anniversary of the Great Exhibition of 1851 and promote the British contribution to science, technology, industrial design, architecture and the arts following the Second World War.

This was the first work outing Betty had been on since joining Heyworth's and she was really looking forward to seeing the exhibits and stalls. She had been hooked on it for many weeks, avidly reading details about its royal opening by King George VI.

He made his opening declaration on the steps of St Paul's Cathedral, cheered by thousands of flag-waving supporters, with ecstatic crowds lining the route the royal party passed. It was truly exhilarating and marvellous to hear on the radio, too; Betty's family had no television to watch it on.

As the day for the outing loomed, Betty picked out a smart cream suit she planned to wear and commissioned Mrs Pugh to make a small cream hat to match. Although Betty didn't like wearing hats, thinking she didn't have the right shape face for them, she always wore a hat for special occasions, and this was one of them.

'You look wonderful. I hope you have a fantastic day,' Betty's mother told her daughter on the day of the long-awaited outing.

Betty planted a kiss on Jennifer's cheek and smiled as she stood up to leave, 'Thank you, Mum. I'll tell you all about it when I get back.'

She counted her blessings that her mother was so kind to them both. She helped make Betty's home life bearable, each day facing a father who never spoke a pleasant word to her and took no interest in his beautiful granddaughter.

Mabel picked up Jennifer and they both smiled and waved as Betty walked down the road to join the shop girls on their special day out, catching their coach in King's Parade. Although Betty made frequent trips to London to visit millinery showrooms, she always returned quickly so she could be home in good time to see Jennifer. This was the first time for years that Betty had enjoyed a day out in London for fun.

Everyone from Heyworth's was going, including all the buyers and management, and they were in exuberant mood. Betty smiled as she spotted George Heyworth in the group. He had a warm smile and twinkling eyes and was pleased to see Betty.

'Hello Mrs Lipscombe, I think we're in for a lovely day,' he said.

'Yes, it looks that way,' she nodded in agreement, looking up at the cloudless sky.

She also spotted Mr Downing, the floor-walker, a very upright and distinguished man. He was a former sergeant major in the army and had retained a military appearance. He had a moustache and was always smartly turned out, keeping a sharp eye on all the displays. He was on good form, too.

'It's going to be such a lovely day,' Betty told nineteen-year-old Maureen Turkentine, one of the younger shop girls in millinery. 'Come on, let's get a seat.'

The Festival of Britain was intended to give Britons a feeling of recovery and progress and raise their spirits after the war. Both Betty and Maureen were in jovial mood as the coach pulled up. 'I can't wait to see the Festival Gardens in Battersea Park – I've heard how fabulous they are,' said Betty excitedly.

Maureen, wearing a pretty floral Horrocks dress and dark jacket, smiled back, 'Oh yes, me too.'

As they entered the gardens, they stood back in amazement. They stared up at the Guinness Festival Clock; it was unlike anything they had ever seen before. Standing 25 feet high, it was said by its makers to be the most complex clock made in England in three hundred years.

It was every bit as spectacular as they had been led to believe. Betty and Maureen watched spellbound as the clock sprang to life every fifteen minutes. A mechanical zoo keeper, together with his menagerie, which they had seen featured in popular advertisements, made regular appearances, keeping them entranced.

'Oh look, there's the toucan balancing the beer on its beak,' pointed out Betty. 'It's fantastic! Jennifer would love to see this.'

The two women loved every minute at the Festival Gardens with its amusement park, miniature railway and amphitheatre, featuring music-hall star Lupino Lane.

Both Betty and Maureen returned to the coach laden with prizes they had won. Betty clutched a doll with a clown-like face for Jennifer, and Maureen was thrilled with her basket laden with fresh fruit, including a pineapple, which was an exotic rarity then. George Heyworth spotted them both with their prizes. 'I can see you've both had a good day. Come here, let's have a photo together.'

He smiled broadly as he placed his arms around their shoulders, standing in the middle of the two happy women. 'It's been a wonderful day. I shall never forget it,' Betty told him happily.

She couldn't wait to tell her mother about her exhilarating day, wishing she could have been there as well, and to see Jennifer's excited face when she gave her the new doll.

'I've really had a great time too,' said Maureen. 'My mother will be really pleased with this fruit.' Betty enjoyed the younger girl's company. She was giggly and fun, not weighed down by the same heavy responsibilities that Betty grappled with each day without complaint.

Maureen had joined Betty in millinery just before Miss Richards retired. 'I just didn't like working up there. I much prefer it here,' she told Betty. Maureen had left school at fourteen and started work in Hutton's in Petty Cury, another fashionable clothes shop in Cambridge. It was not as strict as Heyworth's, where rules had to be strictly followed.

Maureen once aroused Mr Heyworth's wrath when working in fashions. She turned up for work in a fuchsia blouse, which he instantly spotted, telling her firmly, 'White blouses must be worn!' Maureen's face turned crimson and she nodded. She'd worn it because she'd run out of white ones, and thought she'd get away with it, as it was smart.

She felt much happier in millinery and loved being surrounded by beautiful hats. She loved wearing the pretty Horrocks dresses too, with their flared skirts and bright patterns, just like she wore for the Festival. She longed to buy a Hebe suit made in a very classic style with a fitted jacket and a skirt with box pleats, but couldn't afford one.

Maureen was pretty with shoulder-length light brown hair, and had an infectious, youthful zest for life. She looked forward to Thursday afternoons when the store closed early. She'd sometimes take the train or bus with her mother into London, to Lyons Corner House in Tottenham Court Road. The restaurant was always heaving with customers, attracted by the inexpensive meals and huge variety on offer.

Maureen would usually ask the waitress, or 'nippy', as they were known, for a Knickerbocker Glory. She could never resist the towering ice-cream cocktail and Lyons was the only place that she knew served it. Her mother preferred the more traditional tea and cakes. It was a fabulous treat for them to sit in the restaurant and listen to the orchestra, which played almost continuously throughout the day. Sometimes they went shopping too, making the most of their 7s 6d rail fare, returning home at 9 or 10 p.m.

At nineteen, Maureen was still forbidden to visit dance halls, even the popular ones in Cambridge, the Dorothy and the Rex. She'd been having ballroom-dancing classes with Margaret Carter, a window-dresser from Heyworth's, and had learned the jive and foxtrot, the waltz and quickstep, and was keen to dance them for real.

'There's no way you're going to the American camps and their dances,' insisted Maureen's strict parents. Even though she was disappointed, Maureen was a very compliant daughter and never contemplated going there. The Americans held dances in Cambridge, too, in a café in Portugal Place, but she knew this was also out of bounds and never dreamed of upsetting her parents and going against their wishes.

The Americans held no interest for Maureen. She had seen them as a child, when she used to run errands for a neighbour who took in American lodgers. 'Here's a shilling, Maureen, be a duck and fetch us some fish and chips for their supper,' she'd asked the twelve-year-old girl, who ran off to fetch the order.

There were several pubs in Bridge Street where she lived, which attracted GIs. Maureen watched wide-eyed as the high-heeled good-time girls went into the pubs with the GIs, then rolled out drunk at closing time and were thrown into a Black Maria police van, which had screeched up after hearing about disturbances there.

Like the other shop girls, Maureen had been shocked to learn of the death of Molly Rolfe, a junior in corsetry who died in a terrible coach crash in January 1950 on her way home from a dance run by American GIs at RAF Lakenheath. She was only nineteen.

They all knew that Molly loved going to dances organised by Americans. Her friends called her 'Molly with the mocks' after the nylon stockings she wore, the cheaper version of the fully-fashioned styles. The shop girls felt the shock of Molly's tragic death for a very long time afterwards.

Finally, after much persuading, Maureen's parents did finally relent, but told her, 'You must be in by 10 o'clock *on the dot*.'

Maureen told Margaret the good news and the two girls put on their dancing shoes for the longed-for night out. Maureen loved every minute she was there, swaying to the beat on the dance floor. But, however much fun she had, Maureen always kept her parents' curfew, even when the evening's dancing had barely started.

Betty noticed Maureen's extra exuberance when she returned to work the following Monday. 'I've had a wonderful weekend! I went out dancing at the Dorothy. I can't wait to go again,' she told Betty.

Betty smiled wistfully, thinking back to her dancing days before she became a mother. She enjoyed hearing about how much fun the junior shop girls had when they went out, but never felt she was missing out by going home each night to look after her young daughter, the most precious thing in the world to her.

On a few occasions Betty's mother brought Jennifer into the store. Her mother never called in to Heyworth's to buy anything – their clothes were far too expensive. But if she was in town with Jennifer, she'd sometimes put her head in the door to see Betty.

'She's such a sweet little girl,' said Maureen, smiling at Jennifer. Maureen knew nothing about Betty's private life and would never dream of asking. She respected that that was her wish.

Maureen didn't need to look far to find a dancing partner. She had an admirer at her dancing classes called Tony. When he asked her to the pictures, she said, 'Sorry, I'm washing my hair.' She didn't feel instantly attracted to him, but Tony didn't give up. He repeatedly asked Maureen to go out with him, and every time she found an excuse.

'That horrid boy has asked me out again!' she told Margaret.

One day Tony didn't appear at the dance class. 'He's ill,' the dance teacher told her. 'He's got pleurisy.'

Maureen found she missed him being there, and visited him at home when he was recovering. She finally agreed to go out dancing with him when he felt better. 'That's the best medicine I could have asked for,' he said, with a grin from one side of his face to the other.

Every lunchtime he waited for his favourite shop girl outside Heyworth's. He brought her a Penguin bar or Wagon Wheel and they walked together. They saw Betty in town one lunchtime and Maureen proudly introduced her new boyfriend to her boss.

'This is Tony. He works with the Post Office as an engineer in the telecoms department.'

'Well, I never. My uncle works there,' Betty said.

'What's his name?' asked Tony.

Betty told him.

'No! Well, bless me, he's my boss!'

'What a coincidence,' replied Betty, smiling. 'Isn't it a small world?'

Although Maureen's parents approved of Tony, a reliable local boy with a good job, who always returned Maureen home before the end of her curfew, they continued their strict control on their daughter. When Tony took her to the pictures, she still had to be home at 10 p.m. 'So we never get to see the end of a film,' she told Betty.

One day Tony asked Maureen to join him at a friend's wedding.

'I've been asked to be best man for Brian. Do you think you can come with me to the wedding?' he asked her.

'I wish I could, but Heyworth's are really strict about us taking

Saturdays off. It's impossible,' she replied despondently. 'I'm sorry to let you down.'

Maureen had begun to feel increasingly resentful that she could never have a Saturday off. 'It's the last straw. I'm going to look for another job,' she decided.

It was a common complaint with the shop girls, many of whom resented having to work every Saturday, even if they wanted time off for a special occasion. But Betty never questioned this hard and fast rule. She put her job and her responsibilities towards providing for her daughter first.

Betty was sad to hear that Maureen had handed in her notice and was going to work at Montague Burton menswear shop. 'I'm sorry you're leaving – I'll miss you. I hope we stay in touch,' Betty told Maureen. She had grown fond of her.

'Of course we'll stay in touch. I'll miss you, too, but I'm fed up having to work every Saturday,' Maureen replied.

It was Boxing Day and Betty was getting ready to visit Uncle Walter's house in Cambridge. Suddenly there was a crashing sound from upstairs and Betty ran up to her mother's bedroom, where Mabel had gone a few moments before to change for their visit to her brother.

'Mum!' she cried out as she saw her mother's motionless figure on the floor. They had no phone at home to call an ambulance and Betty had to run to a neighbour's house for help. He dashed to the doctor's surgery in Cherry Hinton Road, the doctor came over, and then called an ambulance. But it was too late to save Mabel.

Betty was distraught. Mabel was only sixty, and had been her best friend, as well as the most wonderful mother a girl could have wished for, providing her with love and support during her troubles, and doting on Jennifer, who adored her grandmother.

Mabel's death was a terrible shock, as she had seemed well and never complained of feeling poorly. Nobody expected her to die suddenly from a cerebral haemorrhage.

Betty felt as if her heart would break from the grief that gripped her. She cried and cried until it seemed she had no tears left. But she had to be strong for Jennifer, and it was thanks to her love that Betty felt able to continue.

Her father expressed few emotions at the loss of his wife, keeping any feelings to himself. Mabel had stoically learned in her own way how to get on with him, taking comfort in Betty and Jennifer's love, just as Betty had found solace with her mother.

Not long after her mother died, Betty suffered another heart-wrenching blow. She received a telephone call at Heyworth's telling her, 'This is Addenbrooke's Hospital; we've got your daughter here.'

Betty's heart missed a beat. Frantic with worry, she cycled furiously to the hospital, two miles away from the centre of town. Jennifer had recently started horse-riding lessons and had gone out riding with a group of boys and girls. It seemed there had been an accident. Betty's mind raced, wondering what could have happened and imagining the worst.

Jennifer's arm was badly broken. Her face was green, but she wasn't crying, despite the severity of her injury. The nurse said, 'Your daughter's very adamant – she said she wouldn't let us touch her until her mummy got here.'

Jennifer told her that they were in a field waiting go through a gate when one of the boys, who was showing off, came racing up and couldn't control the horse or stop. He rode straight into Jennifer, who slipped off the saddle.

The anaesthetist joined them, but they had run out of gas. Jennifer had to wait for ages while they found a new gas cylinder to put her to sleep, reset her arm and put on a plaster cast. Betty looked at Jennifer's swollen fingers and the doctor advised her to encourage Jennifer to move her fingers to get the blood circulating.

Being young and healthy, Jennifer made a good recovery, but Betty realised she had no choice but to leave Heyworth's. She knew she was needed at home not only to care for Jennifer, but her father too.

Her eyes welling with tears, Betty told her boss why she needed to leave Heyworth's.

'I am so sorry for your loss, Mrs Lipscombe. May I, on behalf of everyone at Heyworth's, give you our condolences,' Herbert Heyworth said.

The shop girls and management rallied round to offer Betty their sympathy and support. They presented her with a beautiful leather handbag as a parting gift, telling her to make sure she kept in touch. Betty was very moved by their kindness and generosity. 'I will always treasure it and think of everyone here.'

It was a terrible wrench leaving Heyworth's after nine years, having climbed the ladder from junior shop assistant to buyer. As Betty walked out that day, her heart was aching with sadness at leaving behind so many wonderful friends and with fear for what the future held.

Betty still had to provide for herself and Jennifer, so she needed find a new job with better hours. She also had to look after her father, cook his meals, see to his washing and keep the house clean. However harsh and cruel he had been to her in the past, she realised it was her duty to look after him now her mother was dead. She knew that in many ways it would be intolerable for her, but she accepted that it was down to her.

She found a part-time job working school hours in a baker's shop across the town in Mill Road run by Miss Peabody, who was in her sixties. The nearby streets were lined with rows of terraced housing built for railway workers. No members of the royal family came in here to buy their loaf of bread; the customers were ordinary, hardworking people at the lower end of the social spectrum. It could not have been more different from Heyworth's.

Betty did not dwell on self-pity, facing the realities of her situation and her need to work. But she hated her new job, frequently getting stung by wasps, which were attracted to the sweet aroma of the buns on display in the window.

It was an old-fashioned shop, which Miss Peabody's father had run before her. She only ever ordered enough bread and cakes for each day, careful not to have any unsold food left.

Betty stuck it out because the hours suited her. She was able to drop Jennifer off at school and start after 9 a.m., and then leave in time to collect Jennifer when she finished school at 3 p.m. These hours also suited Miss Peabody, as she only wanted to pay for help during her busy periods.

As Betty wrapped up the rolls and cleaned down the shelves, she missed Heyworth's and her friends there. She popped in occasionally to say hello, but certainly couldn't afford to buy anything.

After working at the baker's shop for a year, Betty bumped into a woman she hadn't seen for a long time while walking near her house. Doreen lived around the corner and used to work in Heyworth's, but had since left. She was running a ladies' fashion shop in Petty Cury, the busy shopping area in Cambridge.

'Hello Doreen – what a lovely surprise. I haven't seen you for such a long time. What are you doing now?'

As they chatted, Doreen revealed that she needed an assistant, and wondered if Betty would be interested. Doreen even said she could work school hours. The offer was music to Betty's ears. 'I'd love to come,' she replied gratefully.

The shop was part of a chain owned by a Jewish company, and stocked Horrocks-style dresses without the expensive price tags, and middle-of-the-range-priced fashions. They put on fashion shows once a week for the Women's Institute and other women's groups around Cambridge to attract extra sales. Jennifer was thrilled to dress up for these shows, beaming as she walked down the catwalk in lacy bridesmaids' dresses.

Every Saturday, their busiest trading day, Betty cycled home to give her father his lunch before returning back to work as quickly as she could, with barely time to draw breath. He insisted on eating his meal then, and there was never a word of thanks for Betty. Each evening she cooked a hot dinner, as well as doing all the chores – the washing, ironing and looking after the house.

She'd been working at the shop for two years when the regional manager called in and made Betty an unexpected offer. 'We've got a vacancy for a manageress in our Peterborough shop – would you like to have it?'

Betty thought hard about the offer, particularly about leaving her father alone and moving Jennifer away from her school and friends. Her mind made up, she decided to accept, regarding it as the chance to have a fresh start, to be independent and stand on her own two feet. It was her opportunity to leave Lewis and his unkindness, and to find happiness with her daughter in new surroundings.

When she broke the news to her father, she said, 'Don't worry, we'll come and see you at weekends. Peterborough is only forty miles away, it's not the end of the earth.' She didn't really worry about leaving him behind, believing he was capable of looking after himself.

Betty was half nervous and half excited as she planned her big move. The regional manager suggested that she might be able to rent a flat where their manageress lived, so Betty wrote to the land-lady, Mrs Grubbings. A little bedsit at the back of her house with its own kitchen and bathroom seemed perfect, and Betty was thrilled to receive confirmation that she and Jennifer could move in. Her plans seemed to be going well.

She packed her bags and arrived at the house in the evening, thankful that a work colleague had driven them over. She was exhausted after their long day. Mrs Grubbings answered the door and told Betty, 'I've decided I don't want to let this flat; you'll have to find somewhere else.'

Betty was gobsmacked. 'But I can't find anywhere this time of night! I've got my daughter to think about.'

She felt helpless, and was at her wit's end about what to do next. The landlady gave no explanation, and Betty and Jennifer stood forlornly on the doorstep looking at her pleadingly. Mrs Grubbings finally showed some mercy and said, 'You can stay the one night, and that's all.'

Betty was frantic with worry. She had planned to start her new job the following day, but now couldn't, as she had to find somewhere to live. She arrived at the shop at 9 a.m. and explained her plight to the regional manager, then spent an anxious day viewing flats in Peterborough. None of them were suitable; all the places she saw were grubby and she turned them down.

Betty, stricken with fear about her homeless situation, returned to Mrs Grubbings and explained the problem. 'All the places I've seen today were terrible – there is no way I could live in them with Jennifer. I've done my best to find somewhere else.'

She couldn't hold back her tears any longer. She was scared that she and her daughter had nowhere to stay the night and would be turfed out on to the streets. Betty felt desperately alone and more worried than she had ever felt in her life before.

Mrs Grubbings was tall and thin with glasses, and her face was drawn, with pinched features. She stared at Betty and Jennifer, who were both in tears. 'Well, I'm not sure, I don't know what to make of all this. I really didn't want to let those rooms again.'

'I don't where else we can go,' replied Betty, sobbing.

Finally, the hard-faced landlady relented, 'Well, all right then. Let's see how it goes.'

Betty's sense of relief was immense, but she hated living there. Mrs Grubbings crept up on her when she least expected to see what she was doing. She was always telling Betty, 'You can't do this, and you can't do that.' She was neurotic and made Betty's life miserable. Betty soon found she had swapped one unhappy home for another.

On one occasion the landlady walked into Betty's bedsit, peered into the sink, and told her, 'You're not leaving that stuff in the drain, it's going to cause a blockage.'

She walked in when she liked and constantly complained to Betty – even though she was a tidy home-maker – about the way she kept the bedsit. When Betty returned home from work, Mrs Grubbings was sometimes waiting for her just to complain. 'I had a look in the flat today and this wasn't right and that wasn't right. Can you see to it?'

Despite these difficulties, Betty enjoyed being on her own with Jennifer and didn't miss her father. She went back to Cambridge some weekends on the bus to visit him, and sometimes he came to Peterborough on his moped, until the journey became too much for him.

The new job was not working out either. Betty didn't like it as much as she thought she would and the extra responsibility began getting on top of her. She regretted the move to Peterborough, and, most of all, she missed her mother.

'I wish I'd never come here,' Betty thought desperately. 'What a big mistake I've made.'

After two years, when Jennifer was fourteen, Betty decided she'd had enough. They would move back to Cambridge.

She didn't have the courage to contact Heyworth's to ask about a job, feeling there was no way she could go there on bended knee after she'd walked out of a top job. Instead she wrote to Eaden Lilley, one of their rival stores, asking about work. She told them she was returning to Cambridge and was offered a position as a sales assistant in their millinery department.

As Betty started her new job at Eaden Lilley, a wave of nostalgia swept over her, thinking about Heyworth's just across the passageway. 'That's the past now, but I do wish I was still there,' she thought to herself.

It was difficult working as just an assistant after being a top buyer, but that's all Eaden Lilley could offer. Although Betty was grateful to have found work, her heart was not in the job the same way as it had been at Heyworth's, when she could hold her head up high because of what she had achieved and the respect she earned.

When they moved back to Cambridge, Betty and Jennifer returned to live with Lewis, but there was tension between him and his granddaughter, as she challenged his old-fashioned, authoritarian ways. He moaned constantly.

'Why has she left the back gate open after bringing her bike in? Why can't she close it behind her?' he'd ask Betty as soon as she returned from work. Betty was constantly piggy-in-the-middle, coming between their battles, as he had no understanding or patience with teenage girls in the 1960s, a totally different era from when Betty was that age.

'We can't go on like this, it's not fair on Jennifer,' thought Betty. 'We must find a place of our own.'

They moved into a flat in Cherry Hinton Road, just around the corner from where her father lived. 'It's perfect,' she told him, 'We will be able to see each other still and it's not far from my work or Jennifer's school.'

The flat was a haven of happiness for Betty and Jennifer, even though it was small with only a sitting room, one bedroom and a little kitchenette. They had to go downstairs to the toilet and bathroom.

'Lovely – peace at last!' Betty said.

Betty's sister Joyce wanted nothing to do with their father. But Betty continued looking after him, helping with his washing, heating the water in a boiler for his old washing machine and then wringing it through the mangle. She kept an eye on him to make sure he was okay.

Betty noticed that her father seemed to be mellowing in his old age. He was cooking for himself and seemed to be less grumpy and cantankerous. When he collected his newspaper each morning from the newsagent's next door to Betty's new flat, he waited at her gate for her to appear. He knew what time she left to work on her bicycle and waited to speak to her. They had a little chat, but Betty didn't have time to dawdle, as she was always in a rush to get to work.

'He does care,' thought Betty, 'but he just can't show it.'

Word soon got around that Betty had returned to Cambridge. As she busied herself one morning at Eaden Lilley, she was confronted with a familiar face – Mr Clarke, the office manager and Mr Heyworth's right-hand man.

He smiled at Betty. 'Mr Heyworth heard through the grapevine that you were back in Cambridge. He wants you to come and work for us.'

Betty was flabbergasted. She needed no time to make up her mind. 'Of course I want to. I'd love to come back to Heyworth's,' she replied, feeling a sense of joy, and greatly flattered that he should have sent Mr Clarke for her.

Mr Heyworth's face lit up when Betty walked into his office to discuss the position. 'We'd like you to come back and join us. The only thing is, we don't have a vacancy in millinery. Will you work in the fashion showroom? We have a new Eastex concession starting soon and I'd like you to run it.'

'Of course I will. I've been working in fashion, and I won't find it a problem.'

It was more than five years since Betty had left Heyworth's and she'd never expected to return. She knew how much she'd missed working there, the friendships, and Herbert Heyworth's generosity. He'd always been a fair boss to her, though he had his sharp ways with others.

Betty was delighted to see her old friends when she returned: Jean Pryor, the corsetry buyer, and Irene Dean, who had first recommended her to Mr Heyworth in 1949. She was welcomed back with genuine warmth, and was touched by everyone's kindness.

'It's lovely to be back,' she said. 'I really have missed it.'

Betty glanced around and noticed that some modernisation had taken place in her absence, with even more displays on the shop floor, so customers could pick items up as they wished.

Although it was not the same as being a buyer and head of her own department, Betty was happy to be back at Heyworth's; it was like returning to an old friend.

Jennifer also found a shop job. She was very good at art and needlework and her teachers wanted her to take A-level art, but she wanted to go out and earn money, so she left school at fourteen. Betty got chatting to a woman on the bus, who told her that there was a vacancy for a Saturday girl in the shoe shop she worked in, and Jennifer started there.

Betty's life was now settled; she had a cosy flat, her father was mellowing, her daughter had a job, and she was working again at Heyworth's, where she had spent her happiest years and climbed to the top of the ladder.

But it was too good to last. Betty was totally unprepared for the bombshell two years later, when the shop girls were told that Heyworth's was to close, some said due to Herbert Heyworth's declining health.

She felt choked with emotion, worried again about her future security and where she would work. It was another setback, and once again she was in desperate need of a job.

'I promise I will find you all jobs,' Herbert Heyworth told them, trying to lessen the impact of the devastating news.

'I can't believe it's closing, not after all these years,' Betty said, feeling shocked. 'Where will I go next?'

As the 'Closing Down' sale signs were plastered on the shop's windows, Betty smiled as she reminisced back to her first days at Heyworth's, working with Miss Richards, who said she could never marry a man unless she could kiss his feet. Those days were now long gone.

'I shall really miss Heyworth's – there's nowhere else like it,' thought Betty wistfully, as she walked out of their doors for the last time. 'Still, as the saying goes, when one door closes, another door opens. And I've been through a few in my time.'

ROSEMARY

1961

Rosemary picked up the letter and ripped it open excitedly. She didn't recognise the handwriting, but her eyes lit up when she noticed the Wisbech postmark.

'I enjoyed your company. Is it possible that I can please meet with you again? I'm coming home on leave again next week,' wrote Bernard.

Rosemary could not believe her eyes and wrote back straight away, saying, 'Yes, please!' She had no doubts at all. The letter had been written the day after his departure, a sure sign he was keen on her.

Bernard collected her for their next date in his car, a black Morris Minor. Rosemary wore a pretty, Horrocks-style summer frock. In the car down, Bernard handed her a new transistor radio, having found a station that played the latest music for them to listen to while he drove.

'You have to hold it up against the window to pick up the signal,' he told her.

Rosemary did as instructed, holding up the radio against the window. But, to her horror, it dropped out of her hand and landed on the ground – she hadn't realised the window was open!

They rushed outside to pick up the radio from the road. Rosemary thought Bernard would be furious and shout at her, but he never uttered a cross word. He looked at his scratched and battered radio which now had some of its knobs missing and simply said, 'Oh well, don't worry about it.' Miraculously, it still worked.

'So what do you do, Bernard? Are you anything to do with the police?' she asked, thinking about what her father had told her.

'Yes I am,' he replied. 'I'm a police constable. When I'm on leave from Wisbech I like to come back to Cambridge and spend the weekend with my parents.'

'I'd got no idea you meant that kind of constabulary!' Rosemary told him, laughing. She was stunned that she could have fallen for a policeman, thinking Bernard was a constable with the RAF. She couldn't wait to tell her friend Judy Mortlock, the shop girl who was with her the night she met Bernard, that they had been out together.

Judy was still seeing Bill, who she'd met while out dancing in Cambridge, and the two shop girls agreed to make up a foursome.

Bill and Bernard met the girls outside Heyworth's when they finished work on a Saturday. Rosemary usually made an extra effort to look glamorous on a Saturday, especially if she was going out on the town afterwards. She put her hair up in rollers to add some extra bouncy waves and made up her blue eyes. She wanted to look her best, so her make-up only needed a little touching up at the end of the day and she was ready to go out straight after work.

Rosemary spotted Bernard waiting outside and pointed him out to the other shop girls, who had been peeking out of the window. Their jaws dropped when they spotted him. 'He's absolutely gorgeous. Where did you find him?' they quizzed her.

Rosemary's heart skipped a beat as she and Bernard walked arm in arm to the Guildhall. She had changed into a skirt, blouse and high heels and looked forward to jiving the night away.

She learnt more about Bernard, discovering that he was a few months younger than her and had joined the police cadets at sixteen. He was also very sporty and had been a county sprinter, as well as rowing and playing rugby.

Cambridge was a mecca for dancing and attracted lots of chart-topping headline bands, as well as promoting local bands that had a strong fan following. Cambridge attracted hordes of American GIs from the nearby air bases. As well as the Guildhall and the Rex where Rosemary often went, there was also the Corn Exchange, the Victoria Ballroom, the Regal, the Dorothy and the Masonic Hall, all of which hosted live bands and dance nights.

The dance halls were always packed and sometimes the atmosphere became heated and tense, leading to fights. Judy Mortlock and her boyfriend Bill were with Rosemary and Bernard at the Guildhall one night when a fracas broke out between local youths, who began throwing punches. Bernard looked over at them and swiftly produced his police identification card from his wallet, planning to step in and bring the fight to an end.

Bill stopped him. 'Put that away Bernard. You're not on duty tonight.'

Bernard put his card away and they all left. Another night Bill turned red with anger when one of the American GIs made a pass at Judy. She was wearing a dress with a low back and the American put his hand there.

'Here, what do you think you are doing to my girlfriend? Keep your hands to yourself!' he warned, glaring at the GI and brushing his hand away. Incidents like this made Bernard's blood boil. Only a short while before, Rosemary and Bernard were sitting having a drink at the Rex when a young, drunk American came over and asked Rosemary for a dance – right in front of Bernard.

Bernard was having none of it and told him where to go. 'What kind of cheek is that! I'm fed up with them, with their nice clothes and money and their American accents,' he told Bill, who nodded in agreement.

Rosemary liked watching the local bands particularly The Redcaps, as their good-looking singer, Dave Parker, was friends with a good friend of her younger brother Chris; they'd been at school together.

Rosemary took Bernard to meet Dave and watch The Redcaps perform at the Guildhall, telling him how brilliant they were. The band played cover songs from Ricky Nelson, Cliff Richard and Elvis, with Dave swinging his hips like Elvis and strutting across the stage, driving the girls wild, screaming their heads off. He wore a new powder-blue suit with a silk handkerchief in the jacket pocket, made by Ziggy's in Cambridge.

'Hello, Dave. I like your new suit, it's very nice,' Rosemary complimented him. She was used to seeing Dave wearing a white jacket with a black shirt, white tie, black trousers and white shoes. His dark hair was styled the same way that Elvis did his, with a large quiff.

'It's part of my new look. Did you know we've just released a record on Decca called "Stormy Evening"?' he asked her.

'Congratulations! That's wonderful news,' she replied, delighted at his success. The Redcaps had been talent-scouted by Paul Williams, a Cambridge undergraduate who was studying music at Jesus College. He was very impressed with their music and told them they had great potential. He offered to write them a song and launch them to stardom. 'Stormy Evening' was their big chance.

'The only thing is, I had to change my name as there's already a group called The Redcaps. The song has been released under my stage name, Dean Parker, as Decca wanted something that sounded more American than Dave Parker. You should hear it being played on Radio Luxembourg soon.'

'I'll listen out for it,' Rosemary told him, very impressed that her brother's school friend had had a record released that could be heading for the charts.

Hearing that Bernard was in the police force, Dave told him about problems he had witnessed during their gigs. The boys in blue had been called to a nasty fight at the Guildhall and their band continued playing while a boy in the audience viciously kicked youths with his pointed winkle-picker shoes, severely injuring one of them.

The worst fights Dave witnessed took place at the Carlton in Newmarket. There were tensions every time they played there. The dance hall was packed with Americans from local bases and the stable lads turned up, calling them 'Yanks' and egging them on for a fight. On one occasion, Dave turned his back to the crowd to speak to the band and when he turned around again to face the audience, everyone was on the floor scrapping, arms and legs furiously lashing out in all directions.

'It sounds like total mayhem,' said Rosemary, glad she hadn't been there.

The Redcaps were also caught up in the melée after their band played at a charity gig in Cambridge in support of the Earl Haig Poppy Day Fund for the student Rag Week. Dave told Rosemary and Bernard what had happened.

'Several bands had played, including us, and then a beauty competition was held. The girls were walking along the stage and this American guy jumped on stage, slung his jacket over his shoulder and started walking along with the girls.

'One of the husbands got the nark, and, I've never seen anything like it. He ran the whole length of the hall, jumped on the stage on top of this guy and a brawl broke out. There was quite a lot of damage done that night.'

'Oh my goodness, did you get hurt? Was your equipment damaged?' asked Rosemary, shocked.

'Fortunately, we'd already done our bit, but we had to close the curtains as our equipment was still there and things were getting thrown about.'

One Sunday evening in October 1962, Dave's band arrived to play a gig at RAF Alconbury, near Huntingdon. They played at their

NCO club once a month on Sunday evenings and at the Airman's Club on Wednesday. Dave told Rosemary how this particular Sunday evening, it became clear that it was not going to be an ordinary evening. They set up their gear ready to play when the entertainments sergeant suddenly marched in and warned them that they would have to hang around a bit. They waited and waited, making the most of their cheap drinks. They were warned not to leave the premises, and later the alert they were given sounded more ominous. 'We've got an alert on. You definitely cannot leave this building, but the restaurant is open, so please go through there,' they were instructed.

The band members shrugged their shoulders and did as they were told, enjoying a juicy steak, clueless as to what was happening and the reason they could not play. The hours passed as they waited and waited. Rosemary listened riveted as Dave told her what happened next.

By 10 p.m., there was still no sign of anybody coming to listen to their music. Dave and his band were totally baffled. The sergeant told them they were on red alert – the most serious – and that they would definitely *not* be playing that night.

'So why couldn't you leave?' Rosemary asked.

'Well, we found out later that it was the outbreak of the Cuban Crisis. We read about it in the papers when we got home. We finally left at 1 a.m., passing by a massive queue of vehicles waiting to get into RAF Alconbury; they weren't letting anyone in either.'

'What an exciting life you lead,' Rosemary told Dave, very impressed with his latest anecdote.

'And we still got paid well for the night,' he told her, smiling.

'I should think so too, after that ordeal!'

In March 1963 there was great excitement for all music lovers in Cambridge – the Beatles were coming to play at the Regal, where Cliff Richard had played to a full house in 1959.

The Fab Four had just released their debut album, *Please Please Me* and it was top of the charts. Their first single, 'Love Me Do', which Rosemary loved, had been released the previous October. Of course, Rosemary would have loved to see the group, but she couldn't afford a ticket: the cost was equivalent to almost a month's pay.

They were one of six acts performing that night, and their name was printed at the bottom of the poster, where they were billed as 'Britain's Dynamic Beatles', way below 'America's Exciting Chris Montez' who had top billing.

Their arrival in Cambridge caused a sensation. All the shop girls were talking about it, as they read in the local press that more than four thousand fans, mainly screaming girls, besieged the venue before and after the show. The Beatles had to be smuggled out of the Regal using a decoy police van.

Rosemary's romance with Bernard continued to flourish. She had told Mrs Pugh all about him and the milliner was keen to meet her boyfriend.

'When can I meet this lovely young man of yours? Why don't you bring him over for tea on a Thursday afternoon when we close early?' she suggested.

'Thank you, that would be lovely,' replied Rosemary, proud to have the chance to show off her handsome policeman.

When they arrived at Mrs Pugh's house for tea, Rosemary and Bernard were shown into the sitting room and she left to put on the kettle. Suddenly, Rosemary froze on the spot as seven cats had scurried into the room, making the hairs on her arm stand up. She couldn't help but shriek.

Bernard guessed what the problem was. 'You don't like cats, do you?'

'I'm terrified of them,' she admitted.

When Mrs Pugh brought the tea in, she could see Rosemary was flustered.

'I know it's silly, but I'm scared of cats,' said Rosemary, apologetically.

'Please don't worry about it. I'm so sorry,' said Mrs Pugh, shooing them all out of the room.

Mrs Pugh had no children, but she loved her cats. 'Can you think why they make you so nervous?' she asked Rosemary.

'When my mother was pregnant with me, this huge big black and white cat scratched her all down her face. Her first reaction had been to cover her tummy to protect the baby she was carrying,' explained Rosemary.

Bernard put his arm around Rosemary consolingly.

'That's the story I've been told. You won't find me going a million miles near a cat. Even to this day the hairs on my arms stick up if I'm anywhere near them. I can't bear to be in the same room as a cat.'

When they left Mrs Pugh's house, Rosemary told Bernard how the milliner had shocked the shop girls by bringing in a pair of earrings made from artificial eyes. She took them out of their tin and showed them off.

'Ugh, they're disgusting,' said Rosemary when she saw Mrs Pugh holding them up. Mrs Pugh's husband Derek made artificial eyes at Addenbrooke's Hospital and had made her the earrings.

'Those earrings were horrible. They gave everyone the shivers. I can't believe Mrs Pugh really wears them,' she told Bernard.

Jean Moore, who worked in corsetry, thought the earrings made from artificial eyes were in poor taste too. One of Derek Pugh's patients was Ron Stripe, her boyfriend. Ron had been shot in the eye with an air rifle when he was eleven and had to have an artificial eye. It was such a perfect match that nobody could tell unless they looked really closely.

Jean had been a shy fourteen-year-old when she started as a junior in the corsetry department. She had teenage spots on her face too, which made her even more self-conscious. Her duties included helping ladies into the new rubber-lined Playtex girdles. She watching incredulously as some generous-sized customers, huffing and puffing, squeezed into the tight undergarment, pulling it over their bulges. To make this less of an ordeal, she folded the girdle in half and shook a dusting of talcum powder inside before handing it to the customer. This prevented the rubber sticking to the woman's skin and helped it roll up more easily.

It was decided that Jean should be sent on a training course in London. But she was afraid of travelling alone to London, a city she had never visited before. She couldn't sleep at night worrying about it, and decided to confess her fears.

Mr Clarke, the manager, was speechless when Jean told him she didn't want to go; Heyworth's wanted all their shop girls to have the best training and they'd already paid for her to attend. Jean stood in front of her boss, shaking inside, waiting for his response. Finally, after looking at the petrified state of the young girl, he said, 'We're very disappointed, especially since we've made the booking for you and you said you would go, I cannot for the life of me understand what you're worried about.'

Jean was sad to have disappointed her boss, but relieved to shrug off her anxieties about the trip. She told Ron about it when he picked her up from work that weekend. The boyfriends of shop girls often lined up opposite Heyworth's at 6 p.m. on Saturdays and they couldn't resist opening the wooden shutters behind the plate-glass display windows to have a quick peek and see whose boyfriend was waiting outside.

Jean opened the shutters and spotted Ron, looking every inch the modern man of the day with his quiff flopping over his forehead. He wore his favourite teddy-boy jacket, drainpipe trousers and winkle-pickers. Jean had started going out with Ron when she was fifteen, but the romance didn't truly blossom until a year later. Ron was six years older and her mother thought he was too old for her.

They met at primary school after Ron was evacuated to Cambridgeshire with his mother. Even though he went back to London with his mother after the war, he returned to the area when he was sixteen and found work as a boiler engineer at Chivers jam factory in Histon.

When Jean later announced their engagement, she handed in her notice. 'I'm going to have to give up work after I get married and look after my grandparents. We've been trying to find somewhere to live, but haven't found anywhere, and my family suggested we should live with them after the wedding, and I can look after them. They've been really good to me, but I shall miss everyone here.'

Sadly, her wedding day was marred with tragedy. She called in afterwards to see the shop girls and told them how her beloved grandmother had died just two days before the big day.

'My grandfather insisted that the wedding went ahead. He said that's what my grandmother would have wanted. It was a very sad day and my mother didn't come, so she isn't on any of our wedding photos,' she told them.

'Oh, you poor thing, how terrible for you,' Rosemary said sympathetically.

'We buried my grandmother the Wednesday after our wedding. Who could have expected it to turn out the way it did?' added the new bride, who was still visibly upset.

'Don't forget to stay in touch. We're all here for you,' added Rosemary, her arm around Jean to comfort her.

It was Rag Week in Cambridge. Undergraduates in fancy dress stormed through Heyworth's shaking tins and buckets, urging customers to hand over some ready cash for the Earl Haig Poppy Day Fund. Herbert Heyworth never minded; he enjoyed the excitement, shaking out the coins in his pocket into their bucket, very willing to support a fund to benefit ex-servicemen and women.

Cambridge streets might not have been paved with gold, but the students made sure they were lined with copper as the pennies they collected were lined up in the city centre, stretching out to reach a mile.

Rosemary loved their mischievous stunts – pushing beds through the streets in fancy costumes, and even dismantling an Austin 7 van and rebuilding it on the roof of the Senate House in King's Parade – knowing it was all for a good cause. The students also 'kidnapped' local girls and auctioned them off.

'I hope that doesn't happen to me,' she said to Bernard. 'What if nobody wants to buy me!'

But it happened to Judy Parker, Rosemary's school friend from the hosiery department. She was 'snatched' while out with her younger sister Val by two students dressed as Arabs, wearing long white robes and headdress. They had been held up by gunpoint – a toy gun, of course.

'What's happening? Where are you taking us?' Judy asked them as she and her sister were surrounded by the students.

'We're going to auction you off. Come with us,' they told the two girls, who had no choice but to follow.

Judy and Val were led away and arrived at the Guildhall, where they were forced into a room at the back. They spotted a pen where other 'kidnapped' young women were sitting inside on the floor and were told to join them.

There were ten girls in the pen and they were called on to the stage and sold off to the highest bidder. Judy and Val were auctioned off together. They felt vulnerable standing in front of the crowds. They spotted a group of three boys and smiled at them, trying to make eye contact. The boys smiled back and chatted amongst themselves, and then one of them held up his hand to make a bid.

'Who'll give me a pound for these two fine young women?' asked the auctioneer, pointing to the sisters.

The bidding increased, with the hammer going down to seal the deal at half a crown.

Judy and Val laughed, relieved that somebody had wanted to 'buy' them, and looked around for the boys who had paid for them, but they'd run off.

'What a funny thing. I'm not sure I'd want that to happen to me,' said Rosemary, when Judy told her the story.

'It wasn't so bad. I'm glad I had Val with me, though,' laughed Judy.

'Did I tell you about the time that my friend Greg pinched one of the hands off the Guildhall clock?' she asked with a grin. The disappearance of the clock hand made the local newspapers, and all the time Greg had it hanging on the wall over his bed.

'No, never, I had no idea – that's terrible!' Rosemary replied in amazement.

Judy then surprised Rosemary by adding, 'Oh, by the way, I'm leaving Heyworth's.'

'Why? Whatever for?'

'I'd like to get Saturdays off. I want to walk into town and go around the shops with my sister and friends at weekends. I have a new job with the Examinations Syndicate at Cambridge University.'

'I know what you mean, I do understand, but I'll miss you,' said Rosemary, hugging her old friend.

A couple of years later Rosemary reeled after reading an inquest report in the local paper. Her friend Judy, who had always been so full of life, had died suddenly. It was a shock to all who knew her and thought she had been in the best of health.

Judy was only twenty-two. Rosemary was heartbroken as she remembered the happy times they'd spent together, and their Heyworth trip to Southend, when they'd walked happily arm in arm along the seafront wearing cowboy hats.

She learned later that during Judy's last evening alive, she had been getting ready to go out dancing with a new boyfriend and dressed up to the nines as she always did, looking a million dollars. She was cheerful, but felt tired, telling her mother she thought she'd go upstairs and lie down for a while as she didn't feel well.

Her mother noticed Judy's lips were blue and this immediately alarmed her. She worried her daughter could be having a heart attack, knowing that her heart was enlarged and not functioning properly, weakened from the rheumatic fever she'd had as a child. Florence sent her husband out to get a doctor. He cycled furiously to the surgery and the young doctor who came back with him tried in vain to resuscitate their daughter. But sadly it was to no avail. The doctor burst into tears, telling them, 'I can't save her.'

Her family were devastated. They wondered who she'd been due to meet on her last night, as he would have thought he'd been stood up, having no idea why Judy failed to turn up. As the family didn't know his name, they couldn't get in touch to tell him what had happened.

Rosemary heard later how Judy's family looked into her death and questioned the medication and dosage that Judy had been given for her illness by their new family GP, a young doctor, and how suitable it was for her weakened heart, believing it could have contributed to her sudden death, a detail which wasn't mentioned at the inquest. An open verdict was recorded by the coroner.

'It just doesn't make any sense,' said Rosemary, weeping. 'She was so young.'

*

Bernard was still based at Wisbech Police Station, returning home during his leave to see Rosemary, a 50-mile trip. They had been going out together for almost two years when he popped the question, first asking permission from her father, Bill.

'I'd like to ask for your consent to marry Rosemary, who I love and want to spend the rest of my life with,' he said.

'It would be a pleasure. I've got every faith in you. You have my blessing,' Bill agreed, shaking Bernard's hand. Bernard was adored by Bill and well-liked by her three brothers. Bernard knew Rosemary was the apple of her father's eye and that she came from a close-knit family whose approval was of paramount importance.

'I know you'll make her happy and look after her,' Bill added. 'Go on, go and ask her.'

Bernard proposed to Rosemary on her twenty-first birthday, 8 March 1963. He didn't get down on his knees, but he took her hand and asked, 'Rosemary, would you be prepared to marry me?'

'On one condition,' she replied.

'What's that?'

'That you'll be the father of my children.'

'Of course I will,' he said, smiling.

Rosemary's face broke into a huge smile. She had no doubts at all that she wanted to spend the rest of her life with Bernard. Rosemary's response to Bernard's proposal was something they laughed about years later.

'Will you marry me?' Rosemary would jokingly ask him.

'Only if you promise to be the mother of my children.'

The couple started saving for their big day, which wouldn't take place for another two-and-a-half years. They went to H. Samuel the jeweller's opposite Heyworth's and chose a diamond solitaire ring. Rosemary had never been happier, and proudly showed off her ring to her friends at Heyworth's.

Bernard called in at the store to meet Rosemary and bumped into Mr Clarke.

'Congratulations on your engagement,' he said, shaking Bernard's hand. 'You're a very lucky man.'

'I know,' smiled Bernard. 'I'm the luckiest man in the world.'

But their wedding plans changed unexpectedly. Bernard was bursting to tell Rosemary the good news.

'We don't need to wait till next year to get married. We can get married soon!'

Rosemary was stunned. They had only been engaged for six months and were still saving for their bottom drawer. They had saved £96 so far.

'What do you mean? I thought we were saving up and getting married next September?' she asked.

'I know we were. But I've been offered a police flat in Wisbech, so we don't have to save any more – we can move in there.'

'Wisbech?' asked Rosemary. 'So I've got to move to Wisbech?'

'Yes, that's right. We won't need to pay any rent, as it comes with the job.'

'Oh, I hadn't thought about us living in Wisbech.'

'It's too good an offer to turn down, especially if we are going to get a free police flat to live in.'

'Fair enough, let's get married sooner then, there's no reason to wait,' she agreed after thinking about it some more.

The new wedding date left them only five months to plan. They had only been engaged for ten months when it arrived, not the two years they had planned to save up for their bottom drawer. The family pulled together to help them with Sophia making a three-tier wedding cake which they took to the Co-op to marzipan and ice, and her father paying for her wedding dress.

They made it a double celebration and set the date for 15 February 1964, the same day as Sophia and Bill's silver wedding anniversary.

The new wedding date and their planned move to Wisbech meant that Rosemary had to hand in her notice at Heyworth's. It was a terrible wrench, as she'd loved working there and enjoyed the camaraderie with the other shop girls. She felt a lump in her throat when the day came for her to leave Heyworth's, having been there for six years. She was showered with the most thoughtful gifts, which she found deeply touching, having told them that the flat she was moving into was empty and didn't have a stick of furniture or any appliances.

Phyllis Moss, a Heyworth's fashion buyer and one of the directors, gave her a small electric cooker. The shop girls bought a table and two chairs and some pots and pans.

'These are wonderful gifts and will come in really useful. You are all so kind and I shall miss you so much,' Rosemary said, hugging each of them as she said her goodbyes.

When Rosemary walked down the aisle on her wedding day at St John's Church, Cambridge, she wore a fairytale lace dress with a full skirt and an outer layer of lace with ruffled edging. The dress had long lace sleeves and a high neckline, but low enough to show off a single row of pearls. Her short, modern veil fell halfway down her arms. The back of the dress had a long train made from layers of cascading lace. She was attended by three bridesmaids, two of them very tiny, whose headdresses she had made herself – pretty garlands with silk flowers – and she also had a pageboy.

She carried a bouquet of red carnations and white rosebuds, and two horseshoes for luck. One of them was very special and had connections with a champion winning horse at Newmarket. Jimmy, a friend of her grandfather's who'd worked with the jockey who raced the horse to victory, arranged to have a horseshoe made especially for Rosemary and decorated it in red and white ribbons, the colours of the winning jockey. 'This will bring you all the luck you ever need,' he told her.

She walked slowly along the aisle alongside her father. Bernard turned around and drew in a sharp breath, whispering to her as she reached his side, 'You look so beautiful.'

'Thank you,' she replied, her heart bursting with pride and joy.

Several shop girls came to the wedding, including Mrs Pugh. They all wore beautiful hats and wished Rosemary every happiness.

The newlyweds spent two nights away for their honeymoon; it was the only time off Bernard could have from work. Bernard had booked the honeymoon suite with a four-poster bed at the George Hotel in Huntingdon, a beautiful old coaching inn. When they arrived and booked in under their married name, Mr and Mrs Smith, the receptionist looked at them suspiciously, wondering if they really were married, or were just a couple who had come for a 'dirty weekend' away.

'Mr and Mrs Smith?' she asked the newlyweds, looking them up and down, unable to disguise a smirk.

Rosemary felt embarrassed by the receptionist's suspicious glance. She knew what she was thinking. 'Look, we've just got married – here's my wedding ring,' the new bride reassured her.

The next day they drove across country in Bernard's Morris Minor to Hunstanton, a seaside town on the North Norfolk coast, where they planned to spend the next couple of nights at the Angel Hotel. The freezing cold weather had turned to snow. Bernard and Rosemary were frozen and went to the cinema to keep warm, only to find that it had a hole in the ceiling where the howling wind and snow blew in. When they returned to their vast, cold hotel room, they decided they'd had enough and left early for Wisbech the next day to begin their life as newlyweds.

They arrived at their flat at 19 Lynn Road, Wisbech, just around the corner from Wisbech Police Station and unpacked their wedding presents. The flat was part of a large Victorian house that had been converted into two flats, and was huge, with two bedrooms.

They had no furniture, apart from their wedding gifts and some bedroom furniture Rosemary's brother had given them.

When Bernard returned to work, he was on night duty. Although Rosemary loved Bernard and wanted to be his wife, she badly missed her family and the shop girls at Heyworth's. She suddenly felt very alone, a feeling she'd never experienced before. She'd been looking forward to being married and having her own place, but had never left home before and found it hard at first. She also found sleeping at night difficult.

'We're going to have to change bedrooms, I can't sleep with those loud chimes from the church,' Rosemary told her husband. The church opposite their flat repeatedly chimed to the tune of the nursery rhyme, 'Three Blind Mice', and it was driving Rosemary up the wall.

She began looking around for a job in one of the local shops and was offered a sales assistant's job in the millinery department in Keightley's, on the Market Place, one of the best ladies' stores in Wisbech. She was thrilled to have found work in such a lovely store. But her days there were numbered.

'We've got to leave Wisbech. I'm being moved,' Bernard suddenly announced.

'You're being moved? Where to?' she asked, incredulous.

'Ely ...'

'Ely?'

'Yes, that's right, we will be moving soon.'

'But I've only just got a job. I've only been there a week!' Rosemary protested.

'I'm sorry, love, but I've got no choice. We have to move. That's the life of a police officer,' said Bernard, comforting his new bride in his arms.

Rosemary felt terrible having to hand in her notice so soon after starting at Keightley's. They moved into a police house in

Downham Road, Ely. It was vast, one of the biggest houses they had been in. Like the flat, it had nothing in it.

'What are we going to do for furniture?' Rosemary asked, looking around at the empty rooms.

'Don't worry about it. All that will come in good time,' Bernard replied reassuringly.

During a visit to Cambridge, Rosemary decided to call in to Heyworth's to see her old friends. Their faces lit up when they saw her walk through the door and Rosemary's heart gladdened as she looked around at the familiar faces.

'Do you know what? I think I'd like to come back and work here,' she said.

'Well, why don't you ask if you can have your old job back?' they suggested.

'All right, I will, I'll ask Mr Clarke.'

She found the store manager and asked if any jobs were going.

'I'm sure we can find a job for you,' he said, reassuringly.

'What, in the millinery department?' she asked, hopefully.

'Yes, we'd be delighted to have you back.'

'Thank you,' she said, gratefully. 'I never expected to be back again, especially so soon. You never know how things are going to turn out, do you?'

When she started back at her old job the following Monday, it was almost as if she had never left. Mrs Pugh, Betty Lipscombe and Mrs Culpin with her purple-rinsed hair were still there, and Rosemary's position had never been filled; it was like they'd been waiting for her to return.

'It's good to have you back,' they smiled, welcoming the bubbly shop girl back.

She couldn't wait to catch up with everyone's news and arranged to meet up with her friends at El Patio's, the popular themed café round the corner run by Herbert Heyworth and his friend Richard

Tothill. Rosemary ordered from the tapas menu; she had tiny squares of toast with sardines and anchovies.

'This is delicious,' she said, washing it down with coffee. El Patio was renowned for its real Italian coffee: customers could even choose to have a liqueur added, a Tia Maria or brandy, or ask for a Jamaican or Russian coffee.

'It's great to see you again,' said Judy Mortlock. She was still dating Bill. 'We'll have to all go out dancing again.'

'Yes, that would be great. I love being back here. I love the company of the girls,' Rosemary replied.

Back at work, Rosemary was walking past the phone on their landing when it rang. It was close to the millinery department, which had been relocated to the first floor near the fashion showroom so women could walk over and try on a hat with a new suit or coat.

It was a public phone installed for customers to use. Rosemary jumped when she heard the loud ringing, and looked around. There was nobody close by to answer it, so she went over and picked up the receiver.

'Hello?'

'We have a call for Merthyr Tydfil,' the operator told her.

'Merthyr who?' asked Rosemary, who was flummoxed. 'We've got nobody working here by that name,' she told the caller.

'No, it's not a call *for* Merthyr Tydfil, it's a call coming *from* Merthyr Tydfil!'

Rosemary had never heard of the town in Wales and couldn't work out why somebody was asking for a person with such an unusual name!

Funnily enough the caller turned out to be her cousin, who was ringing to ask her to pass on a message to his brother.

'Sorry to trouble you at work, Rosemary, but I've got no other way of letting him know I'm coming home this weekend.'

'Of course, I'll tell him,' replied Rosemary grinning, thrilled that she had received a call from somewhere so exotic.

The shop girls were becoming suspicious. They noticed that Mr Clarke and Mr Heyworth were having lots of meetings, and there was lots of to-ing and fro-ing with visitors.

Suddenly, in the spring of 1965, the reason for the meetings became known. It was announced that Heyworth's would be closing.

'I'm sorry to say that Heyworth's will be shutting in the near future for reasons we do not want to discuss,' Mr Clarke told the shocked staff.

Although this was a very worrying situation for the shop girls who faced losing their jobs, Rosemary soon had her own announcement to make, too. She had been back at Heyworth's for seven months when she told everybody, 'I'm pregnant!'

She knew the shop closure would not make any difference to her, as she was planning to leave anyway. She continued working until she was seven months pregnant, leaving in the spring of 1965 with hand-knitted baby clothes and a shawl as gifts.

When she stepped out of Heyworth's that day in April 1965 to start a new life as a mother, it was the last time she set foot in the store. Her baby son Greg was born on 28 June 1965, and later that year, Heyworth's closed its doors for ever.

It was another four years before Bernard was promoted to detective constable and joined the drug squad in Cambridge.

'I knew the gypsy fortune-teller was right,' said Rosemary with a smile.

EVE

EPILOGUE

Eve is eighty-four and lives in Cambridge. Her husband Les died in the year 2000, after fifty-three years of happy marriage. She has one son, Martin, two granddaughters and one great grand-son.

After leaving Heyworth's, Eve worked in the children's department at Laurie & McConnell's store in Cambridge for twelve years until it also closed. It was not as strict as working at Heyworth's and there was a more free and easy atmosphere. After this Eve moved to Eaden Lilley's and worked in their ladies fashion department for another twelve years.

'I was very happy at Heyworth's; I thoroughly enjoyed it,' reflected Eve. 'I enjoyed all my working life.'

IRENE

EPILOGUE

After Irene left Heyworth's she found part-time work as a shop assistant in a draper's shop called Thurlow's in the old town of Stevenage, Hertfordshire. There was no comparison with Heyworth's; it was a world away from the fabulous Cambridge store with its upmarket clientele and elegant clothes.

Nor did Irene work there as a buyer, as this job was done by the shop's owner and his wife. Irene remained there until 1972, while also dedicating herself to being a good bank-manager's wife, accompanying Peter on official social functions.

Irene was ninety-three in June 2014 and, as well as her beloved daughter Patricia, she has one granddaughter and two great-grandchildren. She was happily married to Peter up until his death, one month short of their fiftieth wedding anniversary. He kept his promise and, following his retirement, took Irene to Burma, the country where he was based during the Second World War and from which he wrote to her so lovingly.

When Irene was asked if she could suggest a taxi driver to bring her from her home in Hertfordshire to Cambridge for lunch to discuss *The Shop Girls*, Irene replied stoutly, 'Oh no, I always take the bus. I like to be independent.'

Some things never change!

BETTY

EPILOGUE

B etty's story does have a happy ending.

After leaving Heyworth's, Betty was introduced to a representative for a dress manufacturer by Miss Moss, one of Heyworth's directors and fashion buyers.

The rep had moved to the area with his wife, who was thinking of opening a new dress shop in Cambridge. Miss Moss recommended Betty as its manager, and over dinner one evening at the University Arms Hotel, she met the couple and later agreed to run the shop for them.

The shop opened in Magdalene Street, but Betty didn't like the clothes they bought, which were cheaper quality than Heyworth's – some of them were even made of Crimplene.

In 1966 Betty met Jim Hume, who became the love of her life. They met at a mutual friend's house, playing cards. Jim was a widower, ten years older than Betty, who had been a Japanese prisoner of war. They married two years later on 3 September – the day Britain declared war on Germany in 1939, a date Betty always remembers.

Betty left her job at the dress shop, and joined Robert Sayle's in Cambridge, part of the John Lewis group, working as a sales assistant in the fashion department for fifteen years, until she retired.

She was blissfully happy with Jim, who died on his seventy-fifth birthday after twenty-one years of marriage. As well as her daughter Jennifer, Betty has two grandsons and one great-granddaughter. She'll be ninety on 15 November 2014.

ROSEMARY

EPILOGUE

Rosemary, centre, on a Heyworth staff outing to Southend

Rosemary lives in Fulbourn, on the outskirts of Cambridge, still very happily married to husband Bernard. They also spend part of the year at their villa in Spain. They celebrated their fiftieth wedding anniversary in February 2014, and have three sons and one daughter, eight grandchildren and one great granddaughter.

After leaving Heyworth's, Rosemary gave up shop work and had a complete career change, taking up catering. She started as a waitress at The Cromwell Restaurant in Ely, where one of the managers noticed she had outstanding cooking skills, and she trained to become a chef; she worked there for six years.

As the fortune-teller predicted, Bernard was promoted in his work, joining the Regional Crime Squad in London, and moving to Harlow.

Reflecting on her time at Heyworth's, Rosemary said, 'It was a pleasure to work there and will always stay in my memory. I will never forget Heyworth's. I still remember the girls there and the good times we had and it was a pleasure to go to work each day. It was a true British shop!'

ACKNOWLEDGEMENTS

Researching and writing *The Shop Girls* has been great fun. It was a privilege to have met so many wonderful ladies who shared their untold stories about working at Heyworth's, an elegant ladies department store in Cambridge which closed its doors 49 years ago.

This book could not have been written without the patience and support of my four lead shop girls, Eve Collis (Gray), Irene Dean (Fiander), Betty Hume (Lipscombe) and Rosemary Smith (Northfield). These lovely ladies did not consider their lives to be extraordinary at all, but the more we talked, the more we laughed, and I couldn't wait to hear more. I regarded them in awe as their captivating stories continued to unfold. They scanned their memories as far back as seventy years, describing their lives during the war years, through to the American GIs and Swinging 60s scene, and allowed me to write their stories to produce a unique social history for this period.

I am very grateful too for the many special memories shared by other Heyworth shop girls, their families, staff and customers, most of which are included in this book, especially Maureen Jolly, Shirley Cook, Margaret King, Mary Abel, Gillian Payton, Sylvia Arnold, Jean Frankland, Jean Stripe, Val Haynes, Judy Mortlock, Betty Smith, Pamela Lucas, Margaret Cole, Helen Balkwill, Joan

Darling, Jane Robson, Maria Carlton (Gallego), Patricia Miller, Barry Ryder and Colin and Christine Moule.

Both Bryan Saddington and Sandy Tothill provided valuable personal insights into the complex life of Herbert Heyworth, an extraordinary man who the shop girls either loved or feared. I appreciated factual clarification provided by Nigel Bass, Herbert's stepson, and his words of encouragement.

I am grateful to my friend Diana Lloyd for telling me about the fun days at El Patio's, the Spanish-themed café in Sidney Street which Herbert ran with his friend Richard Tothill, and for putting me in touch with Sandy Tothill and her step-mother Betty Lloyd who experienced the Heyworth's generous hospitality.

My very competent genealogical researcher, Paula Jeal, discovered the existence of Herbert's secret son, Paul Hales. I am indebted to Paula for her painstaking research and documentation which enabled *The Shop Girls* to be so much more than just a story about shop girls, a poignant human interest story too about the shop's owner.

I can never thank Paul Hales enough for allowing me to include details about his newfound parentage in this book. It must have been a great shock for him to discover that the reason for Paula's research was to gather material for my book, and he readily agreed that his story could be included and helped me piece it together.

My interview notes were meticulously and speedily transcribed by my very capable and cheerful editorial assistant Chloe Taylor. I appreciated this very much and couldn't have managed without you. Without historian Mike Petty kindly writing about my research in the Cambridge News, I would never have come across Rosemary, the youngest of our lead shop girls. Staff at the Cambridgeshire Collection at the Central Library in Cambridge were always on hand when I needed to make historical checks in the local newspapers. And John Simpson, library assistant in the Community History Library at Accrington Library, Lancashire, has been an invaluable source of information about life in the cotton mills in Lancashire more than a century ago.

When I needed a quick answer about life in Cambridge decades ago, I frequently turned to a Facebook site, *Cambridge in the good old days from the 1960s*, and was never disappointed; their members came to my aid straight away providing me with the information I needed within a matter of seconds.

I was thrilled when author Lindy Woodhead replied to my questions regarding links between Mr Selfridge and Cambridge, providing me with additional information, and also for her kind words of encouragement.

Writing a book at the same time as working as a press consultant means that something has to go, and I now look forward to spending more time with my family, my husband Stephen and sons David and James, their girlfriends, Fiona and Chloe, my mother Loula, and my brothers David and Elvan. My time with them has been too brief in recent months. And thank you too Dennis McKenzie for your words of wisdom at the right time.

I am lucky to have a terrific literary agent. I initially worked with Olivia Morris at the Diane Banks Agency whose inspired suggestion for a book on the theme of shop girls has resulted in this publication. She has since left the agency, and I am in the very capable hands of Robyn Drury. Diane Banks has always been there for me too, and I feel very fortunate knowing I am in the best possible hands.

I have worked with the most brilliant and competent editor at Little, Brown, Hannah Boursnell who believed in this book from the very beginning. Her expertise has put together all these fabulous stories to produce *The Shop Girls* into what I hope you feel is a very enjoyable read.